"If I had one word to describe Jim Gray, I would ___ reporters to be honest in the media bu___ questions, even if they're uncomfortab___ about it. And that's why I have always ___ and how he does it."

*K___* ___*ame GOAT*

"I know Jim Gray the man. He stood up for me with tremendous integrity and principle. He suffered the consequences for doing what was right on my behalf and for others for a just cause. Integrity is what matters, and I will never forget his honor and honesty. Jim tells our story in the book, and I appreciate it. I will always hold him in high regard with great respect and admiration."

—*Hank Aaron, MLB Hall of Fame GOAT*

"The first interview Jim ever did was with me. From his first to my last (many years later), we have had a very special relationship. I'm The Greatest and he's The Latest. Jim is the me of his profession. Just don't tell Howard (Cosell)."

—*Muhammad Ali, THE GOAT*

"*Talking to GOATs* captures so beautifully the stories that my husband, Muhammad, shared with Jim. It brought back to life so many great memories and was very moving. I loved it, and I highly recommend this book."

—*Lonnie Ali, Mrs. GOAT*

"Jim interviewed me after my prolific fights. We were a sensational duo. Out of the ring, Jim became my most trusted friend. He's there no matter what and never afraid to give it to me straight, as he does in this book. He's always coming from a place of love and compassion. You know where you stand. Jim talks to GOATs because it takes a GOAT to know a GOAT. I'm so proud he wrote this book to share his legacy and, as you will learn, Jim is the GOAT whisperer."

—*Mike Tyson, Undisputed Heavyweight Champion of the World GOAT*

"*GOATs* has many awesome stories, let me tell you mine. I'll never forget when Jim Gray invited me to sit down with a group of Olympians who he said were the greatest of all time. I was seventeen years old—and before I'd won a single gold medal—and I'm sitting down with Carl Lewis, Sugar Ray Leonard, Mary Lou Retton, and Muhammad Ali. I remember feeling like I didn't belong (and I didn't at the time) and wondered what Jim was thinking including me, until Ali leaned over and whispered in my ear, 'You're going to be the greatest.' That meeting inspired me and strengthened my sense of purpose. Looking back, I can't help but chuckle at Jim's confidence in including me that day, and how matter-of-factly he explained to me why I belonged. A good sports reporter conveys the story of the day; a great one senses stories that will unfold over time and has the conviction to share them with their audience, nonetheless. Jim Gray is one of the greats!"

—*Michael Phelps, Olympian GOAT*

"Jim will ask the questions, and he will calibrate your answers and they better not be silly or off the facts. That's why I nicknamed him 'Scratchy' a long time ago. He keeps that mic in people's faces, as he's always digging and scratching for the story. Jim dug them all out for this book, which I hope you'll enjoy as much as I did."

—*Jack Nicholson, three-time Academy Award–winning GOAT*

"I cherish the moments that I'm alone with a good book, and *Talking to GOATs* certainly qualifies. I love the great interviews that Jim has done throughout his career and the storytelling he captures on these pages. So please pull up a chair and enjoy this fascinating narrative that details his life with so many of the icons, just as I have."

—*Vin Scully, Hall of Fame broadcasting GOAT*

"Jim Gray is as good at his profession as the countless Hall of Famers he has interviewed were at theirs. Every time I did an interview or watched one with Jim, he was well prepared and wasn't afraid to ask tough questions. That's what made them so interesting and informative, leading his audience to remark, 'I didn't know that,' when the segment ended. And when people read Jim's book, I'm sure they will be saying the same thing."

—*Don Shula, Hall of Fame winningest-coach-in-NFL-history GOAT*

"Forty-plus years of exchanging stories, creating memories, and experiencing moments of a lifetime together with Jim Gray—I would call that the very definition of 'friends for life.' Congratulations for successfully sharing your special story with the world. This book is a must-read, and I'm looking forward to our next chapter together."

—*Julius "Dr. J" Erving, NBA/ABA Hall of Fame GOAT*

"I found so much to learn in these chapters. If there is an art to an interview, then believe me, Jim Gray is Michelangelo and *Talking to GOATs* is a masterpiece. Why is he so good? Because he asks tough, hard, fair questions that you have to answer. He could have played for me, because he's tough, and he's a winner. So is this book."

—*Mike Ditka, NFL Hall of Fame player and coaching GOAT*

"Jim Gray's riveting and powerful *Talking to GOATs* is a rare and different masterpiece for the ages. It's a poignant, personal, passionate, and purposeful reveal of what really happened everywhere in the world of sports in the past forty years. As a giant of the profession and the galaxy's most connected human, Jim has delivered a staggering festival of light that is comprehensive in its breadth, depth, currency, and relevancy."

—*Bill Walton, NBA and NCAA Hall of Fame GOAT*

"I got to meet my heroes growing up: Muhammad Ali, Hank Aaron, Joe DiMaggio, and Ted Williams. Then I was able to spend time with the guys in my era that I admired including Michael Jordan, Magic Johnson, Larry Bird, Mike Tyson, Joe Montana, and Tom Brady. We all shared the same dream: wanting to win titles. All of us have been interviewed many times by Jim Gray, as he has shared our stories. Now he shares them with us, and it's a compelling, riveting, and insightful read. I thoroughly enjoyed it."

—*Wayne Gretzky, NHL Hall of Fame GOAT*

"In this fast-moving account, the big moments, big names, and occasional big controversies that have marked Jim Gray's long and eventful career are revisited with insight and a dose of humor. Sports fans will recall many of these moments but may be surprised by the details and stories Jim provides on these pages."

—*Bob Costas, Sports Broadcasting Hall of Fame GOAT*

"Jim Gray, one of the greatest to ever do it. Since I was a little kid, I loved watching him do his thing in interviews with the greats like Ali and Jordan. Just keeping it 100, staying true, and giving us insight. It always made me think, why were all the GOATs so comfortable speaking to Jim Gray? Then, once I became a GOAT, I understood. Once you're a GOAT and you are communicating with a GOAT, it's all gravy, baby. So from the Dogg to the GOAT Jim Gray, you're going to always be a GOAT, and you're going to always be my dog! Read the book, you'll see."

—*Snoop Dogg, musician and rapping GOAT*

# TALKING

## TO GOATs

# TALKING
## TO GOATs

The Moments You Remember and
the Stories You Never Heard

# JIM GRAY

## WITH GREG BISHOP

*wm*

WILLIAM MORROW
*An Imprint of* HarperCollins*Publishers*

A hardcover edition of this book was published in 2020 by William Morrow, an imprint of HarperCollins Publishers.

FIRST WILLIAM MORROW PAPERBACK EDITION PUBLISHED 2021.

Library of Congress Cataloging-in-Publication Data has been applied for.

ISBN 978-0-06-299207-9

21 22 23 24 25   LSC   10 9 8 7 6 5 4 3 2 1

In loving memory of my incredible father, Jerry.

In honor of my wonderful mother, Lorna.

With love and gratitude for the incomparable Frann.

# CONTENTS

# FOREWORD BY TOM BRADY

I doubt many readers know that Jim Gray has a nickname. Well, they do now: it's *Scratchy*. Jack Nicholson was the one who came up with it. When Nicholson wasn't in his courtside seat at the Forum watching the Los Angeles Lakers play, he would come home late, sometimes after filming a movie, and watch the games on replay, with Jim doing all the interviews. One night Jim picked up the phone and heard a familiar voice. *"Way to go, Scratchy. You just keep scratchin' and digging until you get what you want. Keep scratchin' for that story, Old Scratchy."*

Scratching, persevering, pushing—those notions form the core of Jim and have since we first met in 2002 during a pregame interview at Super Bowl XXXVI, when the Patriots were playing the Rams at the Superdome in New Orleans. We ended up winning that game, 20–17.

A few years later, when I moved to Los Angeles after my oldest son, Jack, was born, Jim and I struck up a friendship around our love of golfing and sports. In 2011, we decided to partner together on our own national weekly radio show on Westwood One for the pregame and halftime of *Monday Night Football*. Many hundreds of interviews later, Jim and I still talk on the air every Monday night. Someone once said marriage is a long conversation. My relationship with Jim is the same.

It might seem strange for athletes and sportscasters to become friends, but Jim isn't an ordinary sportscaster. He has no agenda—and never has. He is warm, genuine, caring, and insightful. He remains a man of great loyalty and integrity, with strong principles and convictions. His relationships matter to him, and he works hard to maintain them. It's no surprise that so many of the sports figures Jim started off interviewing later turned into his close friends. I'm proud to be one of them.

Still, being friends with Jim is no guarantee he'll let you off easy in an interview. His M.O. is to dig beneath the surface, though always respectfully. He's not out to make headlines, or create controversies. He won't ever hit you from behind with a question that leaves you stammering. He's after only one thing—authenticity—and he pushes hard to get it.

In fact, a few times over the years, Jim and I have been talking about something on the air, when suddenly he'll start badgering me, drilling down, pressing me to elaborate on something I said. After the show wraps, I've sometimes said, "What the hell were you *doing* out there? I answered your question, and I answered your *follow-up* question, but then you asked me three *more* follow-up questions!" Jim's response? "It is what it is, Tommy. Some questions and answers require follow-ups." Whenever that happens, I totally get where the nickname Scratchy comes from.

Jim has covered pretty much every sport over the years, from football and golf to baseball and basketball and boxing, as well as some of the greatest moments for each. He has worked for ESPN, NBC Sports, CBS Sports, ABC Sports, Fox, and Showtime. He has covered Super Bowls, the Olympics, the Masters, the World Series, the NBA Finals, the NCAA Final Four—you name it. His knowledge of sports, and of leadership, and of how big sports institutions work and don't work, is second to none. He has been at the center of one huge sports story after another. It's not about luck. It's about his instincts, his focus, and his ability to connect an event, or a moment, to what viewers or listeners care about, and what they really want to see or hear.

To my mind, it's not what people do in their twenties that leads to greatness, or a lasting legacy. It's what they *keep* doing, year after year, at a consistently high level. As a sportscaster and sports historian, Jim's career genuinely stands the test of time. He's elevated *all* sports, and on the world's biggest stages, too, by working hard, putting in the time and energy, developing relationships, and telling stories.

Stories? Jim has hundreds, if not thousands, of them—and an insanely good memory, too. It can be hard to play golf with him because I'm too distracted by the anecdote he's telling about *this* guy, or *that* event, and what happened *after* the fight, *during* halftime, or *inside* the locker room. So many of these stories are in this book. Whether he's describing his first and last interviews with Muhammad Ali, or his interactions and friendships with Mike Tyson, Dr. J, Floyd Mayweather Jr., Michael Jordan, Tiger Woods, Kobe Bryant, Charles Barkley, Hank Aaron, and so many others (plus the last nine US presidents), you'll find out the lesson Jim learned early on: that the key to interviewing anyone is to *listen*.

This book is sports history *about* some of the greats *by* one of the greats, who was taking it all in on the sidelines, in the stands or the dugout, by the eighteenth green, courtside, or in the broadcast booth. As for my own long conversation with Jim? It's not over, not even close. See you next Monday, Scratchy, and try to go easy on me.

# PREFACE

Back in 1989, I happened to be strolling the Third Street Promenade in Santa Monica with my friend and fellow broadcaster Bob Costas. We ran into a street performer who might have been homeless and who was rhyming and making jokes. I enjoyed the show, and Bob handed him $5.

The man looked at him. "Yo! Yo! Yo! Bob! Bob! Bob Costa! Come on, Bob! You can do a whole lot better than that!"

Bob handed the man another $20, despite the mispronunciation of his name. The man spit out a few more rhymes, and then he turned suddenly toward me. "And what about you over there? You be on there analyzing some shit!"

We doubled over in laughter, and I handed over another $20. That made $45 total. Big payday. Before we walked away, I said to that man, "If you know who I am, there's no way you're homeless. You're watching way too much television."

The man started laughing. We parted company. "There's the title of your book, my friend," Costas said. "You be on there analyzing some shit."

This is that shit.

# CHAPTER 1

# TYSON

## MUCH MORE THAN THE BITE

On the night before he bit off a chunk of another man's ear, Mike Tyson went to see Don King. More specifically, he went to see Don King about a check. This was June 27, 1997, a Friday, less than twenty-four hours before what's now known as the Bite Fight. That night changed so much, looking back at the events that had transpired, for boxing and its biggest superstar, and even me.

I was in King's small temporary office at the MGM Grand as he scribbled out all those zeros, writing out a check for $30 million, then penning his signature at the bottom. It was a staggering amount of money for one night's work, then or now. But Tyson was worth every penny that King was set to pay him. He was something else: the most exciting, well-known, and thunderous athlete on the planet. On any given Saturday inside a boxing ring, he was liable to hit someone harder than you've ever seen a man hit another person. But he was just as likely to spectacularly combust. King knew all this as he tossed the check in my direction. "You imagine?" he said. "I'm paying him $30 million before he fights the fight!"

King then began howling with laughter and shaking his head. "I know I say it all the time," King boomed. "But goddamn, only in America!"

He wasn't wrong. Tyson was a decidedly American creation, a world-wide phenomenon whose origin story has transformed over the years into something closer to myth: raised in Brownsville, Brooklyn; mo-lested as a child; he ran with convicts and drug dealers, committed crimes, landed in a juvenile detention center; he was saved by boxing and then nearly destroyed by it. At this point in his career, he had only lost twice: to James "Buster" Douglas in an epic 1990 upset and the first time he faced Evander Holyfield, who won their initial bout by techni-cal knockout in 1996. Tyson complained afterward that Holyfield had leaned on and head-butted him, turning the fight into more of a brawl. This mind-set would become important in the rematch, a bout—and a bite—that would come to help define careers. His and mine.

I saw it all, including the night when Don King handed Tyson that $30 million check. "I'll see you tomorrow night," King said. "Now, just don't get into any trouble tonight, my brother. Just keep it calm."

"No problem," he responded, as the three of us went out back by MGM's Grand Garden Arena, where the boxer had parked his brand-new Lamborghini in the loading dock. Back in those days, there were stanchions to protect the vehicles that had to be removed and replaced before and after the cars were parked. Well, Tyson never saw the stan-chion that had been put up behind his car. He backed right into it. He probably did $1,000 worth of damage, maybe less, to a $350,000 car.

He leapt from the car, and with a fastball like Sandy Koufax, he threw the keys as hard as he could to the security guard, who weighed like four hundred pounds. "Take this fucking car, get this fucking car away from me!"

"OK, Mr. Tyson," the man said. "I'll put it in the valet."

Tyson stared back menacingly. "What didn't you fuckin' understand?" he yelled back. "I said get it away from me. Take this car. It's bad luck."

King interjected himself at that point, as he often did when it came to Tyson. "Ay, brother, my man is giving you this car," he said in that cackling Don King voice. "Take it, have a good time, good luck to you."

This security guard could barely fit inside the fancy sports car, and he didn't know what to do, plus he didn't want it to appear like he was stealing the fighter's ride. He squeezed into the driver's seat, and he looked at King, and King looked at Tyson, and the guard looked back and forth between King and Tyson, and he still had no idea what he should do next. He didn't want Tyson to say that he just drove away with the fighter's car. Iron Mike, meanwhile, was screaming that the car was bad luck, and how he wanted to think only positive thoughts in the hours before the rematch. So he gave away the car over a fender bender.

That should give you an idea of the lifestyle he was leading. Just *one-half of that one night*. King and I went to the Palm for dinner with some of his people, and all of a sudden, we could hear this commotion, like a murmur that becomes a roar, and someone came to the table to find King, so he could reel in Tyson, who was a short distance away at the Versace store inside Caesars, shopping.

Tyson and whoever else was with him had racked up something like an $800,000 bill. I remember he bought purple shoes and yellow and orange scarves. The second he took that stuff out of the store, it had no value. He didn't care. He ordered King to take care of it. "Give me back the check," King told him. Tyson handed that $30 million piece of paper back. King would later cut him another check, less the amount Tyson had spent in the store.

The champ indulged in having a good time and everything that went with it, whether that was drinking or women or more women, cars, clothes, jewelry, and watches. You name it. He wasn't living a life of regret. In the span of ninety minutes, I saw him give away a $350,000 car and spend at least $800,000 at Versace. That's $1.15 million in ninety minutes. In 1997!

Tyson has lived his life, on his terms, on a high wire without any net.

I met him years before that, in the mid-1980s, while eating with my father, Jerry, at Matteo's in Los Angeles. I loved Matteo's. The restaurant is still there, on Westwood Boulevard, just off Pico. It used to be an old-school Hollywood hangout, and I thought they served the best cheese ravioli in Los Angeles.

Matty, a real character from Hoboken, New Jersey, was this older gentleman who owned and ran the place for years. He knew everybody. I mean, *everybody*—

On this particular Sunday, my dad and I were sitting near the entrance, not at one of the prime tables, but close enough to the front door where we could see every person who came in. Sinatra and Sammy were there, along with Dean Martin. So were Lucille Ball and Gary Morton, Al Davis, Wilt Chamberlain, Farrah Fawcett, and Sugar Ray Robinson, the greatest fighter who ever lived. Tyson, who was still a teenager at that point, was seated at a table not too far away, in the middle of the action. He was with the incomparable Jimmy Jacobs, a man who collected films of fights *and* comic books, played handball at the sport's highest levels, and came to manage the young menace. Early on, at least.

Jacobs was also there with Bill Cayton, his business partner. King was at a separate table, totally by coincidence, or at least it appeared that way. It's tricky, because at that time, he didn't represent Tyson. At one point, I saw the boxer get up to use the restroom, but on his way there, he noticed this train set that wound around the dining room from the ceiling. He was following the train as it sped around, mesmerized like a kid on Christmas, looked down and there I was. He recognized me from TV, which surprised me. "Mike, how are you?" I said, extending a hand.

He sat down at our table and met my dad that night. King also came over and said hello. And every time I ever saw Tyson in the years since—we're talking decades here—he'd ask about my father. "How's Jerry?" he'd say in that voice, all high-pitched and fast-paced, like he wanted to say everything at once and just might before the night concluded.

Tyson was something like 12–0 at that point. I can't say for sure. He had knocked out everyone his management had put in front of him. He was just beginning his pro career. He had amazing power and potential.

As Mike Tyson climbed boxing's pound-for-pound rankings, ESPN started to send me to some of his fights. I was working freelance for them, transitioning to full time after the Olympics in 1984. We'd always recall that night at Matteo's. As I mentioned, he'd always ask about my dad. It may not have always seemed this way in press conferences, but he always had good manners with me. He'd call me Mr. Gray.

I'd usually go to his fights and try to get an interview afterward. He almost always did them. You could tell this guy was on, and he was raw, and when you started talking to him about boxing, you could tell he knew the history. Much more than me, or anyone else. His current opponents were all but meaningless to him. He couldn't tell you their record, or what victories or belts they held, or if those belts carried any significance. But he knew about specific champions, what they meant, their place in history. The guys he was fighting at that point were just in the way, as he carved his path into boxing lore.

He won his first title on November 22, 1986, toppling Trevor Berbick by second-round TKO at the Hilton Hotel in Las Vegas. King and the rest of the boxer's team would have these crazy, wild parties afterward, the most insane of which took place after Tyson toppled Tony Tucker to become the undisputed heavyweight champion in August of 1987. That meant he held all the belts, and he celebrated like he held them. Wearing this ornate crown, he came into a ballroom, clad in a long, flowing blue cape. He had this scepter he carried in his right hand. It was the craziest thing, and as he walked by the buffet, you couldn't help but notice there was this whole pig, and it felt like something out of the 1700s. That was life around Mike Tyson.

I went up to him after he spoke to the crowd. He was still wearing that outfit. "Isn't this ridiculous?" he said. "I'm just the heavyweight champion of the world, not some king. However, I do want to keep this crown and necklace. Do you think this is a costume, Jim? Don says all the jewels are real." I had no idea if those jewels were, in fact, real. But I do know this: life around Tyson was *surreal*. We laughed and laughed.

They put him on the cover of *KO Magazine* in that getup. That was him, too. When it was time to be serious, we were serious, but when it wasn't, we would laugh. He was sparse with his words outside of press conferences. He was shy, very shy, when you were just talking to him.

People have asked me how I can relate to someone like Tyson. That's easy. I like people, and I'm interested in people. I listen. I ask a lot of questions. It's just my nature; I'm curious. I've always gravitated to people like him, because he can describe the tenets of Chairman Mao in great detail *and* how he impregnated a woman in jail—who wasn't an inmate.

Tyson's career, of course, particularly the feel-good aspect of the narrative, took a sharp turn in 1991, when he was arrested and charged with raping an eighteen-year-old named Desiree Washington in an Indianapolis hotel room. The trial took place in 1992 and lasted for more than two weeks.

I followed it, like everybody else in sports but particularly because I knew and liked Tyson. I saw his chauffeur, Virginia Foster, testify as to Washington's state of shock after the incident. But the boxer proclaimed his innocence, then and now. He testified that the sex between the two of them was consensual and he would later argue, using the lawyer Alan Dershowitz, that the court had excluded three important witnesses and not given the proper instructions to the jury. He lost the initial trial, after ten hours of deliberation, and the Indiana Court of Appeals ruled against him, too, the vote 2–1.

Tyson was only twenty-five years old, just entering his boxing prime when he went to prison. The sentence was for six years, plus four years of probation, although he served slightly over three years. He didn't fight from June 28, 1991, scoring a unanimous decision win over Donovan Ruddock in their rematch, until August 19, 1995, when he won by disqualification over Peter McNeeley. That bout was broadcast on the network I work for, Showtime. So were the remainder of Tyson's fights. I interviewed him for the network countless times right up until the end.

In the interim, he lived at the Indiana Youth Center, from April 1992 until March 1995. That was where he converted to Islam. I received a letter from him, from prison.

Here's the thing about Tyson: he was accountable, and he was responsible for his actions and never blamed his trainers or the referee or the judges or Don King for what happened to him. I asked him at a round table discussion before my Hall of Fame induction why that was. He explained that he was the leader of Team Tyson, and if he did something wrong, or if something went wrong, the one who it affects and the one who did it in nine out of ten instances would be himself. He said that in the tenth instance, when it wasn't him, it still had an impact on him. He had to pay the price, regardless.

All that is interesting as it relates to the letter he sent from prison to my home in Atlanta. It was handwritten, five pages long, and I had not been expecting it. I opened the mail one day, and there it was. The envelope was unsealed, because when you're sending mail out of the penitentiary, prison officials review it. I read the letter with great interest. When Mike got out of jail, he let me do the first interview. It was on *Dateline* and the *Today* show and I brought the letter with me. I wanted to ask Tyson if it was private to me or if I could share it with the public. If he consented, I would read a passage from it on the air.

"Mr. Gray, you can ask me whatever you want," he said. "It's not a problem."

I read from the letter, on the air. On page two, there was a paragraph that said, "Mr. Gray, they will let me go tomorrow, and I will walk out of prison, if I admit to rape. But I didn't rape this woman, and I will never admit to something I didn't do."

Next paragraph: "However, there are four or five other things that I've done throughout the course of my life that are worse than what I'm accused of, so therefore I feel like I'm at the right place at this time."

What were those things? I asked him. What did he mean? What had he done that was worse than rape? He looked at his attorney and then looked back at me, and he said, "Mr. Gray, it's probably best that I don't answer that question on national television because I don't know the statute of limitations." The real shocking part came next. "However," he said, "what I wrote you is true."

In his third fight after prison, he defeated Frank Bruno by TKO, winning the WBC heavyweight crown on March 3, 1996. Six months later, on September 7, he topped Bruce Seldon by technical knockout to secure the WBA belt. Tyson was back and everyone wondered the same thing. When would he fight Holyfield?

Soon, it turns out, and their first meeting took place at MGM's famous Grand Garden Arena in November that same year. Holyfield had retired two years earlier, after losing to Michael Moorer, and many saw him as a fighter who was past his prime.

Their bout, that first one, was dubbed "Finally" in the press. The title seemed appropriate. Tyson was a heavy favorite, at least until the action started. He would lose, and not only would he lose, but Holyfield defeated him by technical knockout, when the referee, Mitch Halpern, stopped the bout in Round 11. In victory, Holyfield became only the second boxer in history to win the heavyweight belt three times. But that wasn't the main story afterward. The main story was how Tyson lost, and his camp believed that Holyfield had been overly aggressive. They felt he had won with a combination of illegal head butts and roughhouse tactics and that he was aided by Halpern, when he had failed to step in.

The shocking loss—and the complaints that followed—set the stage for the rematch. It was scheduled for June 28, 1997. It would take place in the same hotel, the MGM Grand, and the same arena, the Grand Garden. I arrived that week, on Tuesday, a few days before the fight. Our production team met with Holyfield that Friday, as is custom with all fighters before big bouts. He thought it would be easier this time around. Holyfield wasn't intimidated, and he had his own stuff he was dealing with, whether it was the heart condition or the steroid accusations against him or questions as to whether he'd retire or how that last fight had gone. It's not like he was sitting there thinking, *What's going on with Mike Tyson?* Or, more to the point: *Will Mike Tyson bite part of my ear off?*

Tyson didn't come to the fighter meeting. I think he'd had enough. He wasn't going to sit down and tell us what he was going to do in the fight; it was pretty obvious. Plus, so much had happened to him at that point that he didn't want to talk about it. He didn't want to rehash it all and discuss prison, or his divorce to the actress Robin Givens, or the white tigers he owned and kept at his mansion, or the 1990 shocker against Douglas. He certainly didn't want to relive the first Holyfield fight. He'd been doing that for months. Sometimes he'd snap at people, and that volatility stemmed from what was at stake. He was fighting to save his reputation, fighting to win his title back, and fighting to maintain that expensive lifestyle he was so accustomed to. The man had dropped more than $800,000 at Versace that week! Nobody could control him or his finances. He couldn't even control them. So everybody was just kind of hanging on, going through this wild ride that led to this fight, this rematch, this moment that will live forever in sports infamy.

Many thought Holyfield was a fluke. That he couldn't do it again. That he couldn't do it again *especially to Tyson*, and that the first bout was more similar to what happened against Douglas. An aberration. An off night. The boxer not being at his best and not paying attention to his craft. Holyfield was too undersized, a glorified cruiserweight. Few had taken into account that Tyson might not be what he used to be, that we were seeing the fall of this great Roman Empire that started from within. That the rest of his career would be less about boxing and more about theatrics. That this was the beginning of Tyson's third act, after the Rise and the Fall.

All week there was this excitement that built and built. Tyson fights were like Super Bowls. The world stopped to watch, to see what he might do. As he would often tell me, it wasn't just a corporate crowd that came to his fights. It was the superstar athletes, the A-list celebrities, top politicians, pimps and whores and rappers, drug dealers, billionaires, mobsters, Playboy playmates, Michael Jackson, Steve Wynn, and Donald Trump. Every time, it was a collection of people unlike any collection of people that had ever been assembled.

I woke up early on the morning of the fight. I was excited, naturally.

Who wasn't? Heavyweight prize fights of this magnitude happened so rarely, and not only that, but here was the baddest man on the planet trying to reclaim everything he'd lost. They make movies with far less tension than that.

Certainly nobody thought the fight was going to end the way it ended. The chaos . . . the commotion . . . the chunk of ear, falling to the ground.


I did an interview with Tyson before the fight, as is custom on our Showtime broadcasts. We did it inside his locker room. He was focused. He was solemn. He was thoughtful. And he was ready.

Then I took my usual seat, right behind the broadcasters in the first row. They're doing the telecast, and I'm watching, too, working my sources, trying to ascertain what's really happening. My moments happen not only during all these events, but immediately as they come to an end.

Books have been written on the fight itself. It did look to me like they were brawling, and it was clear that Tyson was being head-butted throughout. He was bleeding above his eye, badly, and aggravated to an extreme, and he appeared upset that despite all his complaints from their first matchup, that the referee, Mills Lane, did not dock Holyfield a point but ruled the butt that caused the bleeding accidental. Tyson felt like it was all happening to him again and trailed on all scorecards after two rounds.

Tyson did put together his best—and worst—round in the third. There's no delicate way to put what happened. I saw Tyson lean in close. I saw him sink his teeth into Holyfield's ear. I'm listening to the broadcast through my earpiece, with Steve Albert and the rest of the members of Showtime's telecast describing what happened, instantaneously. They're trying to explain that Tyson had bitten Holyfield, and then spit out a chunk of his ear. I saw him do that. Holyfield was jumping around, pawing at the side of his head. Mills warned Tyson and docked him two points. But after a brief stoppage, Tyson bit Holyfield's other ear. Mills disqualified Tyson for the bites. The arena went bananas. It was pandemonium.

It was also time for me to go to work.

I climbed into the ring. Tyson still wanted to fight at that point, and so they had him pinned in the corner, and medical officials were looking at Holyfield's ear and trying to stop the bleeding. Eventually, Tyson started to move toward Holyfield. No one knew if Tyson was going to hug him, or try to apologize, or see how he was doing. Instead, he started throwing punches. Then the police came in. They were trying to keep the fighters separated, pulling out billy clubs, and Tyson still wanted to go, and I'm standing there, inside the ring, and I'm thinking, *This is not good.* But I wasn't going to get out of there. My job was to be in the ring, to try and get the interview.

I was looking for the ear inside the ring. I was looking at Holyfield, too, to see if I could tell what part of his ear was missing, along with if I could see an indentation there, or bite marks. I could have used that information on the air. But he was moving around so much, and then they put a towel on his head, and I just couldn't see that closely. Still, it was clear that a piece of his earlobe had gone missing.

Meanwhile, everyone is looking at Tyson. I walked into the far corner of the ring, where Mills Lane was standing. I figured that if I stood by the referee, I would not get hit. It's one thing—one strange, deplorable thing—to bite part of an opponent's ear off. But if you hit a referee, you'll never box professionally again. Pretty soon after that, Tyson left the ring. For two or three minutes, chaos ensued. Fans threw beer and everything else at the disgraced boxer as he exited. Some tried to come at him from the stands. I kept wondering the same thing. *How am I going to get this interview?*

Police were protecting Tyson and themselves from the debris, and they finally were able to escort him to the locker room. My producer, David Dinkins Jr., said, "Jim, forget about Holyfield. Go back to the locker room and see if they'll let you in. Use your relationship." So I get back to that space, and there were numerous security guards and policemen, and not only from the MGM but also Tyson's own bodyguards, who were making sure nobody got in.

I was able to speak with Tyson's manager, John Horne. That would be Tyson's soon-to-be-fired manager John Horne. We spoke outside the locker room.

Horne started by declining to comment on the bite. He hadn't seen it, hadn't watched it, all that kind of stuff. Then he went straight for *how* Holyfield had fought *Tyson*. "All I know is Mike got a cut over his eye, three inches long," Horne said. "Evander got a little nip on his head. It don't mean nothing! He (Holyfield) jumped around like a little bitch! That's what he did!"

"I would have liked to see (Lane) let the fight go," Horne continued. "The ear ain't got nothing to do with this fight. It ain't got nothing to do with his arms, his legs, his head, his body, nothing."

I tried to explain to Horne that Tyson had bitten Holyfield a second time. That he was disqualified for *that bite*, for doing it again. At that exact moment, I spied King heading inside the locker room out of the corner of my eye. I finished with Horne just in time to stop King, and we were on camera still, so there wasn't time for him to wiggle away.

King said he was headed inside to speak with Tyson. I said to him, "Don, obviously not the way that anybody expected that this was going to go. Very disappointing to everybody who bought the fight and those in attendance here. Your thoughts on this disqualification?" I had obligated him, right there, on behalf of the viewer.

"Well, I think that the head butts was there," King said. "When he had the head butts, and he had had head butts prior to that, there should have been some point taken away, or something to acknowledge these head butts, because this was said so in private before the fight started. *Watch the head butts.*"

I cut King off right there. "Don, but the fact of the matter is, is the head butts, yes, it is a problem, everybody will acknowledge that Holyfield was in violation with the head butts. The proper reaction, however, is not to bite, correct?"

"Well, I don't . . . the proper reaction is not to bite," King reluctantly admitted. "But I guess when a guy feels that he's pleading with the referee to give him some consideration, and then he don't get the consideration, then he just goes beyond reason. I mean, you must be able to deal with reason and practicality, but you have two athletes in there, highly passionate, very hot, ready to fight and fight they were doing. The fight was just beginning. I don't know why it would be stopped."

I kept pressing. "Well . . . let me stop you right there, before we go on to that. You're saying Mills Lane should not have stopped the fight? On the second bite?" I asked.

"When Holyfield got bitten, Mills Lane said he took a point from us," King said.

"And a second point," I noted. "And then at the end of the round, Mills Lane had said that Tyson had bit him on the other ear, which in this instance I believe would be the left ear. Two bites on the ear."

King shook his head in that hallway. "I didn't see it, so I can't comment on that," he said.

"That's why he disqualified him," I said.

"I'd have to see that before I make any comments on that," King responded. "I don't want to be irrational."

I told King we should move on, asking him what would happen to Tyson moving forward, after the bites. He said he wanted to find out the facts. I asked if he could ever convince Holyfield to take a third fight against Tyson. "I don't know whether I can or not," King said.

"I know you don't make this decision," I said, continuing to press. "But should these fighters be paid for this evening's work? Some sixty-odd million dollars that went out tonight."

"Yes, they should be paid," he said, still clad in a black tuxedo, hair pointed toward the heavens. "They came, they fought. Boxing is unpredictable. You don't know what's going to happen . . . I'm disappointed myself. Because of the outcome, I wanted to see this fight to the finale."

King said he would do his best to make sure that Tyson came out and granted us an interview. He wanted him to explain himself and only Tyson could do that. That's one thing about King. He never wants to be the guy who can't deliver. Lo and behold, I'm not sure how long it was— maybe three minutes, maybe five, maybe ten—and out comes Mike Tyson, still agitated, shifting from side to side. They threw it right to me on the broadcast, and less than ten seconds later I'm interviewing him.

———

I decided the best thing to do was to conduct the interview in chronological order.

"The head butt in the second round, which opened the gash on your eye. Tell us about that, first," I said.

"He butted me in the first round, but then he butted me again in the second round," Tyson said, the words spilling from his mouth without pause, as if unencumbered by punctuation. "And then as soon as he butt me, I watched him, he had looked right at me, and I saw him and he butted me again; he kept going down and coming up. He charged into me. And no one warned him. No one took any points from him.

"What am I to do?" Tyson continued. "This is my career. I can't continue getting butted like that. I got children to raise. And this guy keeps butting me, trying to cut me . . . I gotta retaliate."

I cut in there. "Immediately, you stopped," I said. "You stopped fighting immediately right there and you turned to Mills Lane and you said, what? What did you say to Mills right at that time?"

"I don't remember," Tyson said. "I told him that he butt me. I know I complained about being butted. And complained about the first fight. Listen, Holyfield's not the tough warrior everyone says he is. He got little nicks on his ear. I got one eye! He's not impaired! He got ears! I got one eye! If you take one, I got another one! I'm ready to fight! He didn't want to fight!"

He continued on this way, getting angrier, his posture changing, becoming more demonstrative, his voice rising as he looked around for affirmation. "Mills Lane, though, Mills Lane stopped the fight," I pointed out. "It wasn't Holyfield who stopped the fight."

"He didn't want to fight," Tyson responded. "He didn't want to fight." Horne cut in there, saying, "don't put nothing on Mills."

"Mills said he stopped the fight," I said. "You bit him. Was that a retaliation, for the eye, when you bit him in his ear?"

"Regardless of what I did, he was butting me for two fights," Tyson responded emphatically.

At that point, I asked what everyone wanted to know, what had to be asked, even to a man who had just done what Tyson had done inside that ring. He had to address the bite. Regardless of the head butts, regardless of the referee, he *had to* address the bite. I told him that he needed to. "I did address that!" he said, shouting almost. "I addressed it in the ring!"

"Why did you do that, though, Mike?" I asked. "Is that the proper response?"

"Look at me!" Tyson shouted, repeating that phrase several times. "I gotta go home, my kids are going to be scared of me. Look at me, man." Then he turned around and walked away. When he said look at me, I did. I could see his orbital bone, which was exposed because he had not yet been stitched up. In all my years covering sports, I had never seen something that deep, that raw. It's something you see and never, ever forget. Still, what Tyson had done was crazy, and it was my job as a broadcaster to obtain the most information possible from a volatile and evolving circumstance.

What struck me both in that moment and in the years since was this: even in his worst moment, Tyson had done the interview. To me, it signified that he was a genuine man. That he had just performed one of the most horrific and despicable acts that any of us could remember in sports, and yet he came there, and he answered the questions. He didn't stand behind a press release or hide behind his team. He didn't wait five days. He was facing a lifetime ban, plus losing his whole purse—that huge check I'd seen King hand him—and I respected and appreciated him for talking with me. I can't think of another athlete who, under those circumstances, in such close proximity to what had just transpired, would have done that interview. Only Tyson.

The aftermath of the fight and the bites was intense, for both of us. I went to New York the next day, and then I went on the *Today* show. I did *Larry King Live*. At first, all the folks who interviewed me thought I was nuts. They wanted to know if I worried I was going to get beaten up inside the ring, or what was going through my mind when I interviewed Tyson in that hallway.

I did television and radio spots for something like three straight days. Finally, we got to a point with the NBC and Showtime PR teams where it was just *enough*. We had to start telling people no. I probably had more than two hundred requests, all the big radio stations and all the best television talk shows, and every newspaper. I wouldn't say it was fun, because I felt bad for Tyson, and I didn't want to be *that guy*, who was just there to pile on. I wanted to tell what happened from my vantage point, but I took no joy from the events that had transpired. They weren't good for boxing, and the night wasn't good for Mike, and it was both good and bad for Showtime. Good because of all the attention; bad because it was *the wrong kind* of attention.

Still, I was personally satisfied with my performance and proud of the way my Showtime colleagues handled that broadcast. It was perhaps the single best moment of my career. It's the only interview I've ever done—we're talking tens of thousands here—that I felt I got exactly right.

In 1998, after Operation Desert Storm and before the second war with Iraq, I saw the man who led the first Gulf War, General H. Norman Schwarzkopf, at an event. We had worked together at CBS during the Winter Olympics a few years before. While we were talking he said something I never forgot. He told me in a joking and kidding way that he should kiss a photo of Saddam Hussein every morning. "You ought to do the same with Mike Tyson," the general added. "Without Saddam, I'm just another four-star general. Without Tyson, you're just another sportscaster."

I've known Mike Tyson for over thirty-five years now, and, since the day it happened, everyone asks me about the Bite Fight. Usually, it's one of the first things that people ask me, especially when Tyson comes up. That's because the interview, which won an Emmy, was when our relationship was cemented and became well known, as an infamous moment in sports and boxing history.

Moments like these don't happen without a team of people, trying to put out the best possible broadcast. Nobody does anything in television by themselves. Dinkins cemented his status as a Hall of Fame producer that night. Gene Samuels, our cameraman, got roughed up by Tyson's team as he tried to get out of the ring. They knocked him down with his camera while he was shooting the chaos live on the air. He was assaulted, not by Tyson, but by the horde that surrounded him. If he had set his camera down and gone home, no one would have blamed him. Instead, he stood in there, as a tough, courageous guy, and he came back and did that interview, and it was in focus, and it was brilliant, and he pushed in at just the right time.

If there's nobody there to shoot it, the interview doesn't happen. If the audio guy doesn't have the microphone right, the interview doesn't happen. If the satellite transmission folks decided to go off the air right then, the interview doesn't happen. If King doesn't stop . . . if Tyson doesn't come back out . . . if he's not forthright . . . if I stumble . . . the fact is I was at my best and everyone I work with was at *their* best, too. Viewers just didn't see everything that happened behind the scenes.

I wondered sometimes what my life would be like after that moment. How would subsequent interviews unfold? What would be on that scale? I remember asking that question to Neil Armstrong, the first man to walk the moon. I asked him, "When you've been to the moon, what else really compares?" He said, "I don't really think of it that way, but when you put it the way you did, no, nothing really ever will. You just don't tell anybody about it."

The Tyson interview was like that for me. It's not comparable, in any way, by any stretch, to walking on the moon. But in my life's experience in broadcasting, nothing else for me will ever compare to it. I knew, at that moment, that nothing like that, no matter what I covered, no matter where I went, no matter how many years I did this, would happen to me for the rest of my life. He had that thing around him, an aura, where everybody wanted to see him and everybody wanted to touch him and be around him. The *Mike Tyson Experience*. But this night, the Bite Fight, was something else.

Any time I'm in a public place, or if I'm on talk radio, or at a boxing event, it comes up. I often think I'm grateful that I don't have to forgive myself for screwing that night up, because it would have been really easy to. There are other events I get asked about: the Pete Rose interview, "The Decision," and my relationship with Kobe Bryant. Sometimes, it's the Malice at the Palace, or the 1996 Olympic bombing. Sometimes, it's Brady, Brady, and more Tom Brady. But mostly, over the past quarter-century, people ask about the Bite Fight. And that wasn't my only unforgettable moment with Tyson. Not by a long shot.

Sometimes I wonder if Tyson was the last person in sports who didn't BS anybody. There was a weird paradox with him, because so many people thought he was unhinged, that no one could corral him, and yet in my assessment, he always answered every question. It's hard to put "honest" and "biting someone's ear off" in the same description. But that was Tyson. Both things could indeed be accurate. A lot of times people don't want to hear that kind of truth. They're so used to all the sugarcoating in sports, all the nonsense, all the coach speak, and then when they hear that kind of transparency—like Tyson's transparency—it's jarring. And it can get a little weird.

I once saw him holding a man by his ankles outside the window on the third floor of a hotel. They had had some sort of altercation, probably over money, and Tyson was asking this man, "Bitch, can you fly?" It was more astonishing to me than the ear biting. But he didn't drop the guy. He just made the guy *think* he was going to drop him.

Did I mention that the boxer once told me in a live interview he wanted to eat the children of fellow heavyweight champion Lennox Lewis?

It started innocently enough, after he knocked out Lou Savarese in thirty-eight seconds in a 2000 bout. "Mike, was that your shortest fight ever?" I asked him.

"I bear witness, there is only one God," Tyson responded, a white towel draped over his broad shoulders. "And Muhammad blesses and keeps me upon him as his prophet. I dedicate this fight to my brother, Darryl Baum, who died. I'll be there to see you. I love you with all my heart. All praise be to my children, I love you. God, amen. What?"

I repeated the question. "Is this your shortest fight ever? Any time, amateur, professional, ever?"

He shook his head and continued. "I don't know, man," he said, adding, "Yeah," then segueing right there into something else. "Lennox Lewis, I'm coming for you," he said, his tone turning at this instant, moving toward menacing.

I asked him, "Mike, is it frustrating to train for this like you did and then have it end . . ."

Tyson cut me off. "I didn't train for this fight. I only trained probably two weeks, or three weeks for this fight. I had to bury my best friend. And . . . I dedicated this fight to him." Then, another turn. "I was going to rip his heart out! I'm the best ever! I'm the most brutal and most vicious and most ruthless champion there's ever been. There's no one can stop me."

He continued, voice rising, giving one the best—and most disturbing—quotes in sports history. "Lennox is the conqueror? No. I'm Alexander. He's no Alexander. I'm the best ever! There's never been anybody as ruthless. I'm Sonny Liston! I'm Jack Dempsey! There's no one like me! I'm from their cloth. There's no one that can match me! My style is impetuous! My defense is impregnable! And I'm just ferocious! I want your heart! I want to eat his children! Praise be to Allah!"

Tyson walked away. I was trying to get another question in.

Did I mention he once told me he won a fight with a broken back? It was after he topped Clifford Etienne in 2003. The first fight after he'd gotten that tattoo on his face.

"Mike, were you really sick this week?" I asked him. "What was the problem?"

"I broke my back," he said, with a straight face.

I asked the only natural follow-up question there. "What do you mean by that? You broke . . ."

"My back is broken," he said, again with a straight face.

"A vertebrae? Or what portion?" I asked.

"Spinal."

That's hysterical. Did I also tell you that Tyson threatened to kill me once? Also happened. I had asked him some random question after one of his fights and his response was, "I will kill you, and I will kill Don King, and I will do it right now." It just came out of nowhere. I said, "Why?" Or, "Over what?" He said that King had stolen money from him, taken advantage of him, and so I just let him answer. And after that, when I asked him something else, he answered, then said, "Mr. Gray, I love you," and he kissed me on the cheek.

I've always contended that in those absurd forty-five seconds, it was far more disturbing when he kissed me than when he threatened to kill me.

Tyson retired in June of 2005. He had lost, for the third time in four fights, and to Kevin McBride, a fighter who would retire with ten defeats. "I don't have it anymore," he told me. "I just don't have this in my heart anymore. I don't have the ferocity . . . I'm not an animal." His career was over, and it was sad for me. But Mike had run out of energy and desire. He had been fighting—inside the ring and out—his entire life. He had had enough. We continued to keep in touch.

Flash forward thirteen years. To the summer of 2018. I'm in Canastota, New York, and I'm being inducted into the International Boxing Hall of Fame. The guy who climbed in the ring two decades ago after Tyson bit off part of another man's ear would now join him in boxing's most hallowed halls. He was seated on the stage, next to other Hall of Fame boxers. He was near the podium, and he would help introduce me. He stood up, and we shook hands and hugged. Then Tyson handed me the plaque and a ring and started speaking into the microphone.

"My name is Mike Tyson," he started, "and I'm here to talk on behalf of my good friend Jim Gray."

He said he'd known me for twenty years, although it had actually been thirty-three. Said I'd always been honest, a straight shooter, "even when I (Tyson referring to himself) was wrong."

"Which I was wrong most of the time," he added.

Talk about symmetry. He mentioned my father, right away. "I would have liked to have seen his father been able to come here," Tyson said, and we both started to tear up. "Oh, shit," he said, realizing the emotion in that moment. "It didn't happen, but I know he's looking down, and he's looking at his boy," he said. "He's very proud." I choked back tears myself, right there on that stage, right before I'm supposed to give my Hall of Fame speech. "I'm sorry I'm crying," Tyson continued. "I'm just thinking about his dad." Me, too, Mike. Me, too.

How do you follow that? Well, I told the story of Matteo's. The night we met. How much it meant to me and how much my induction would ultimately have meant to my father. I can't believe we ended up in a place where Tyson, the man who had once threatened to kill me—and kissed me—ended up calling me his most trusted friend. His life has been a roller coaster. He remains a complicated man, forever unpredictable. Who knows what happens next.

# CHAPTER 2

# ALI

## TOUCHED BY THE GREATEST

While in college at the University of Colorado, I interned for Channel 9 in Denver. The station went by the call letters KBTV back then, and it was the local ABC affiliate. The offices were located at 1089 Bannock Street, a thirty-five-minute drive from my dorm room in Boulder, and I performed all the usual unglamorous intern tasks without complaint: ripping important sports stories off the AP wire, watching games, pulling highlights, and making phone calls for the anchors.

This was so long ago that station managers were just starting to convert from film to videotape. Many older editors took buyouts in light of that transition, not wanting to learn a new craft at their advanced ages. But when the people in charge asked if I wanted to become a videotape editor, I understood almost nothing about the job but knew my answer immediately. Yes, of course. I was an eighteen-year-old freshman making fifty dollars a day. That was a lot of money back then. I used the money to make payments on my mustard-yellow Toyota Corolla, and I used a small portion of the leftover cash to purchase beer kegs for my friends in the dorm.

At 7:30 one random Monday morning, I sat down to edit the show "The Broncos with Red Miller." He was the Denver Broncos head coach from 1977 to 1980. The offices were quiet, until the assignment editor, Sue Tews, came barreling into the editing suite.

"You know something about sports, right?" she asked, while trying to catch her breath.

Yes, I told her. I was the sports intern turned videotape editor.

"What are you doing right now?" she asked, still breathless.

I pointed at the screen bank.

"You gotta go right now and interview Muhammad Ali," she said. "He's at the Stapleton International Airport, and he's two hours early."

Apparently, Ali had an interview scheduled with one of the sports anchors. But this was before cell phones, before beepers, before anyone could find anyone else short of catching them at home and near the phone and willing to pick up. The good old days when people connected in person, more or less. But that also meant that Sue had no chance to find the anchor before Ali left the airport, catching an earlier flight without doing the interview. So, instead, she had chosen to send the only person available—me. I wasn't even shaving yet.

Immediately, I ran to the sports office, searching for a tie, or a jacket, anything to help me not look as young as I actually was. I found nothing, so I sprinted to the weatherman's cubicle next. He was this little guy, with the most perfect nickname you've ever heard for a person in that profession. Stormy Rottman. His real name was Leon, but no one called him that after he left the air force and carved out a career on local television. But the jacket didn't fit, so I took off for Stapleton, my stomach swirling, adrenaline coursing through my veins. I would soon conduct my very first interview—with the most famous person, at that time, on earth.

I knew Ali, but I didn't *know* Ali. I used to watch or listen to all his fights with my father. I reveled in his banter with my favorite broadcaster,

Howard Cosell. I didn't have a notepad. I hadn't had time to write down any questions. But I tried to fashion a conversation from what I had seen Cosell ask him for years. I had watched all Ali's fights since I could remember, and I knew his life, inside and out.

I drove myself to the airport, found Ali's gate and walked with him, up a concourse, into a small room. The first words Ali spoke upon our arrival were . . . "You're the interviewer?" he asked as he sat down, incredulous.

"Are you still in school?" he continued, having a little fun at my expense.

I started to ask questions, and he glanced over at his entourage and handlers, maybe a half dozen total, and when no one said anything, like, *hey, this is crazy*, he simply answered the questions that I asked. After a few quick exchanges, he said, "You sound like a local Howard Cosell."

That was the best compliment I had received in my entire life. No exaggeration. That was the thing about Ali, though. He put everyone at ease.

He went on to discuss his global initiatives, his plans to help the poorest people in places like Ethiopia and Afghanistan and Sudan. How he wanted to return to the jungle and have another rumble. He told me about the Muslim religion and what it meant to him, how it defined him.

I learned a great and simple lesson that day, in 1978. That the key to interviewing anyone is to listen. Sounds easy. It's not. I knew Ali would soon fight Leon Spinks in what would become their famous rematch in September of that year. I knew he wanted to stage an exhibition in Denver with Broncos defensive end Lyle Alzado. But exploring those topics was the easy part. I filled the rest of our thirty-two-minute interview with questions based on his previous answers. You'd be surprised how often that *doesn't* happen.

I came back to the station to edit myself out of the interview and Roger Ogden, the news director, came into my edit suite. He wanted to see the Ali tape. He watched it twice. After an hour, he looked at me and said, "I'm putting you and this tape on the air. It's barely adequate."

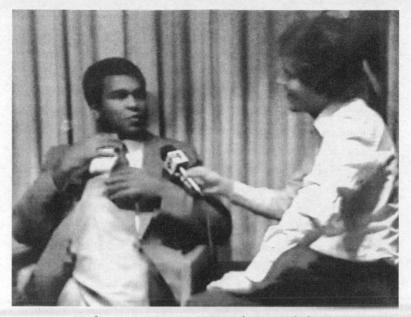

*My first interview was in 1978, and it was with the most*
*famous man on the planet.*

The interview aired that night, marking my first appearance on
9News. It changed my life. The thrill from that day has never faded.

I came to admire Cosell, to rank him atop my early list of icons, the
same way that most people came to know him: by watching his highlights show that aired at halftime of *Monday Night Football*. My hometown team, the Broncos, were rarely very good back then, and because
of their record and how late their games ended on the East Coast, in
most weeks they did not land on Cosell's montage. But every week I
watched anyway, and most times I was disappointed when the broadcast inevitably would flash the same sentence across the screen: "Due to
logistical reasons, we cannot show you Bronco highlights. Please do not
inundate the station."

I started to pay closer attention to all his work outside of *Monday
Night Football*. I loved his interviews with fighters, like Ali. Cosell

became a fixture in our house. My father was amazed that this burgeoning boxer named Cassius Clay had toppled the great Sonny Liston in 1964. I was only four years old, but it made an impression—the fearsome heavyweight lived in Denver and my dad was disappointed the local champ had lost.

Liston's house, oddly enough, was one we visited every year during the holiday season. My parents would drive our family around the city to look at the festive lights, and one stop we'd always make was at Liston's place on Monaco Parkway, out by the same airport where a young me interviewed Ali, because Liston always put together a huge Christmas display. After watching him lose, my father joked that "you could turn the lights out on his career." Confused, I asked if he meant that we wouldn't be able to drive by his holiday decorations anymore. My dad laughed, explaining that "turn out the lights" was an expression. His lights at Christmas would remain on. Whew. What a relief.

My dad was a big boxing fan. Not just of the heavyweights. He would take me to the Golden Glove tournaments to familiarize us with the local fighters who lived in Denver. We knew Ron Lyle, a local convict turned boxer, had made it, like really made it, when Cosell's microphone landed in front of his face. He ended up fighting Ali and losing a very close, tough bout in the eleventh round. I became enamored with Cosell and his approach. I found him funny and smart and he had this voice that was instantly and incredibly recognizable. He was also a fixture at the biggest events, and he interviewed the most famous celebrities in sports. A part of me wondered: *You can make a living doing that?*

A few years into my career, I met Cosell. I had been working at the fights. He took me out to lunch a few times, giving me advice on what to ask, what to look for, how to broadcast. Then he urged me to try my hand at another profession. More than once. "Jimmy, make something of your life," he'd say, in that inimitable Howard Cosell voice. "Please, you're much too smart to be in this industry. These executives who are hired and promoted, please; they're children playing at television. Get out of this. Why would you put yourself through this nonsense? I beg of you." He was being funny, of course, but I could sense some seriousness behind the bluster. He was also encouraging, telling me I had a big future.

As for his relationship with Ali specifically, there was nothing like it, before or since. (Many compared my relationship and on-air interviews with Tyson to their dynamic, and that ranked among the highest compliments I've ever received.) You couldn't miss an interview. You wouldn't go outside when ABC's *Wide World of Sports* was on. The way you perceive and receive a broadcast was so much different, so much more pure. You're not thinking about all the issues—head injuries, money, complicated relationships between leagues and their network partners or promoters—that we think about today. You were simply locked in on the competition and the personalities. I like that guy. I want that guy to win.

*As a young sportscaster, spending time with Howard Cosell left an indelible impression.*

Aside from Cosell, I'd watch Curt Gowdy, a Rocky Mountain hero and national treasure who broadcast the Broncos games on weekends, and I also liked to hear Bob Martin on KOA, the local radio broadcast after games. He was the play-by-play man for the Broncos and Rockets/ Nuggets. I'd sneak my transistor radio to the dinner table, and my dad would let me put the earpiece in. This annoyed my mother. She would say, "Enough with the Broncos already. You saw the game, how much more do you need to know?" But I would listen to those segments and retreat to the back room at our house with my brother's reel-to-reel tape recorder, where I'd goof around, recording my own spots, acting like I was hosting Bronco Talk.

People forget this, but when I was growing up, Ali wasn't this popular, revered, global icon that he became later in his life. The country was divided then, over the war in Vietnam, and depending how any one person felt about the war and our involvement in it, they were likely to see Ali through the same prism: (1) as a champion of civil rights who gave up a chunk of his prime—and prime earning power—to do what he considered right, or (2) as a traitor who shirked his greatest responsibility to his country by not heading to Vietnam to do what he did best—fight.

I was too young to understand the war, or Ali's place outside it. I just understood he couldn't box anymore and that people I knew weren't happy about it.

I was still a kid back then, aware of racial strife in America but much too young to understand all the dynamics and complexities. We had busing for desegregation in my school district and my classes were all diverse. I played organized youth basketball on teams, and against teams, that were integrated.

Mostly, though, the Grays were a typical middle-class family. So many defining American events happened in my childhood: JFK's assassination, the senseless killings of Dr. Martin Luther King Jr. and Robert Kennedy, the Moon Landing. I didn't understand the impact of all that, or why my dad cried when President Kennedy was shot, or why my mom's eyes welled with tears after Dr. King's assassination. I had never seen my mother or father cry before.

We watched *CBS Evening News* every night with Walter Cronkite, plus read the two newspapers in town, the *Rocky Mountain News* and the *Denver Post*, and the *Sports Illustrated* and *Time* magazines that arrived every Thursday in the mail. I came to know enough to see a country that was struggling to find its footing and an athlete that somehow ended up in the middle of all the chaos and division that was swirling at that time. Watergate happened. So did the end of the war. I wanted Ali to fight again. I wanted to see his comeback.

After I did the Ali interview, I thought things would be easy. But they weren't. I was getting great experience, but I wanted to be on the air more. So I started to send out tapes, all across the country, to try to land a full-time reporting job. I still have all the various rejection letters that stations mailed me early into my career. There were many of them. Some of them are form letters, some say the station doesn't have an opening, some suggested I use my hands more, tie my tie better, or get off television altogether. I saved each and every one of them. It motivated me to get better and prove them wrong.

The interview with Ali helped boost me from my perch as a new videotape editor into having the opportunity to do more interviews. But the biggest boost came from Ali himself, as we developed a relationship after that first meeting, and my connection to him helped me to establish credibility. Ali liked me, and he seemed to get a kick out of seeing someone so young covering him. At Top Rank Boxing, promoter Bob Arum took notice. He'd send me to many of the fights he would promote for interviews, and he'd use them for promotional spots and satellite distribution. He did this with several fighters, from Sugar Ray Leonard to Marvin Hagler to Thomas Hearns, and their teams. Arum would fly me in the week before the bouts and give away the content to stations across the country, who then didn't have to spend money to dispatch their own reporters to the fights. The approach was genius— and also how I got into boxing, all because of that first interview with Ali. Don King saw some of those interviews and decided to hire me as well. I believe I'm one of few to have worked for the often-bitter rivals at the same time.

In 1980, before Ali's bout in October with Larry Holmes, while I was going into my senior year in college and working on my broadcast journalism degree, we took a road trip. Ali was in a white convertible Cadillac the size of a submarine. He drove with the top down. We were headed from Atlanta to Columbia, South Carolina, and he stopped for gas right near the state line. As we exited, he noticed a group of children playing basketball on a dirt court. "Watch this, Jim Gray," he said.

Cameras rolled, and the kids continued to hoist jumpers, using a peach basket that had been nailed to a tree. They were all African American and playing shirts versus skins. There must have been at least fifteen players, none of whom took notice when Ali stepped out of the car and, like something from a movie, the ball rolled out of bounds right up to his feet. He picked it up and the kid ran over and recognized him. You ever see those cartoons? The characters whose eyes bulge from their sockets, like they might just come unattached from an animated face? The kid leaned over and took the ball in one hand; I'll never forget it, it was like something out of the movie *E.T.*

"Ali? Are you Muhammad Ali?"

The rest of the children turned around. They knew right away. "It's Ali!" they shouted. "It's Ali!"

They all came running over, and he shot baskets with them for a while, then started with his magic tricks. Fifteen kids became forty people, then ninety, then the crowd swelled beyond what anyone could possibly count. Ali had that kind of instant impact on the world around him. The ground seemed to rumble: kids jumping around, parents carrying their babies, everyone sprinting in circles and delirious. All this took place in a wooded area off the highway, in the middle of nowhere. By the time we departed the field, roughly forty-five minutes later, the car could hardly move due to human roadblocks. Strangers held on to the hood of the car and the trunk, wanting simply to touch him. It was scary. I hoped no one would get injured, or run over. Ali just turned to me and smiled.

"What do you think about that, Jim Gray?"

We stopped at a nearby Waffle House for dinner. Ali put on a hat and sunglasses, insisting that he planned to keep himself disguised. Good luck with that. Four hours later, a line snaked out the door, around the building. We had not left, had not even moved. He signed every autograph, spoke to every waitress, told every story. It was almost like he had forgotten he had somewhere to be.

Ali didn't guard himself the way that athletes do now. He had fun with interviews and the people who approached him. He didn't undergo media training, or ask his publicist to cut off interviews, or dance around uncomfortable topics. Anyone who asked him a question, he answered it, honestly, without trying to spin reporters or curry favor. If he didn't like the interview, he said that, too. I respected that, even though that very honesty, the way his life was so open and so out there, at times exposed his flaws. He was as human as they come, even if he can seem mythical in death.

By the time we took that road trip, you could see Ali nearing the end of his career. He had retired after a rematch with Spinks (he won), only to come back for the Holmes fight. In the ring, he moved more slowly, not by a ton, but it was noticeable. Certainly the years he lost during the war had cost him. As did the fact he had fought fifty-nine times as a pro and more than a hundred times as an amateur and yet he rarely shied away from contact, taking blows while landing them, even when he danced around.

In the Holmes fight, Ali's corner called for a stoppage after the tenth round. That night struck everyone as sad. Few wanted to see Ali lose; no one wanted to watch him get beat up. Holmes punished him, landing heavy, thudding blows to Ali's midsection and face. But Ali had always pulled himself out of everything—out of hatred, deficits, and defeats. Even when he lost, he won, figuring out a way to reinvent himself, stacking victories, avenging failures.

That didn't happen after Holmes. Ali invited me in to see him after that loss. Inside his room, the entourage had thinned and all the hangers-on had disappeared in defeat. His most loyal friends remained. Ali himself was so quiet, the result of the physical and mental beatings that Holmes administered. Ali remained a proud man, and in that moment, his pride had been wounded. He told me he had let the fans down. He said they didn't deserve to see him lose like that, and he wanted the public to remember him as the "greatest of all time."

"This will dull that impression," he continued. "Time is my biggest enemy, not Holmes." Everyone hoped he wouldn't enter the ring again. Instead, Ali fought Trevor Berbick fourteen months later, in December of 1981. The fight took place in the Bahamas. Officials there didn't even have a typical ring bell; incredibly, they used a cow bell instead. Ali lost that fight, too, to a solid but not transcendent opponent, by unanimous decision. Berbick landed so many blows to his liver. Mostly, I remember the mood afterward. It sounded like someone was playing the sad trombone on loop. Ali's career never should have ended that way. He deserved better, deserved to be cared for, cherished and protected.

Ali had also started to develop blood clots in his legs, after a 1976 exhibition against the famous Japanese pro wrestler and mixed martial artist Antonio Inoki, who took the exhibition more seriously than anyone expected, pelting Ali with numerous karate kicks. Years later, it would become difficult for Ali to obtain subsequent boxing licenses. Physicians described his brain as damaged and his speech as slurred. Looking back, they were signs of the Parkinson's disease to come. In addition to not moving as quickly, his speech slowed, and sometimes, he seemed tired, and other times he just looked sad. Most observers missed the accumulation of those signs because Ali retained this tremendous grace and dignity. He didn't feel sorry for himself. He understood that boxers would lose fights, even ones who called themselves the Greatest. He'd always tell me the same thing. "Don't feel sorry for me. No one's had a better life. No one's done more with themselves. Everywhere I go, I'm treated like royalty."

I hoped his career would finally end with Berbick. And it did. I saw Ali a few months before that final bout, in Las Vegas, at one of the greatest matches ever staged inside a ring. Sugar Ray Leonard versus Tommy Hearns, the first one. Ali called me up to his hotel room before the fight. His wife, Veronica Porche, was ironing his shirts. I brought my best friend from college, Tom Dolven, up with me, and she seemed annoyed by our presence. I understood. She must have been sick of sharing her husband with the world.

When we entered the room, Ali was lying on the bed and staring at the ceiling. A smile, *that* smile, spread wide across his face. "Hey, Champ," I said. "How ya doing?"

"Good," is all that he responded.

I introduced him to Tom and after sitting there for maybe forty-five minutes, Ali turned in my friend's direction. He seemed melancholy. "You've been watching me your whole life," he said. "You've been knowing me as well as you've been knowing your own family. And all these great moments, all these things, they're in your head."

"Yes," Tom responded. "They are."

"I made an impression, didn't I?" Ali said.

"Absolutely," Tom responded. "You did."

I can't remember when I found out he had Parkinson's. Maybe when his voice dropped to a whisper. Perhaps when he started to shake. It wasn't just a flat descent. Ali still had a good time, still loved talking, and he still played jokes on people.

One night I went to dinner at La Famiglia in Los Angeles, at Ali's invitation. I brought my dad. This was after the Olympic Games in 1984. When I arrived, the restaurant was empty and mostly quiet. I saw Dean Martin—yes, *that* Dean Martin—sitting in a booth, silent, sipping a cocktail. I did not see Ali. Now, he was always late, because he got held up everywhere, like at that dinner all those years ago. But ten minutes passed, then twenty, then thirty, then ninety. After a long while, with the restaurant set to close soon, I figured he wasn't going to show up.

I went outside to retrieve my car from the valet, and I'm fumbling in my pockets to find the ticket, and the valet is growing impatient, and I still can't find the damn thing. And then I look up—and look closely—and the valet guy is Ali! He was wearing a hat and glasses and a fake mustache. Since he had been obscenely late to dinner, he decided instead to pull a prank. I had already given him $10. "How do you expect someone to make a living off that?" he asked, breaking into that trademark cackle.

I'd see him at fights over the years after that. He never lost his spirit. He'd always sit with me, reminisce. I forget the occasion, but sometime in the early 1990s I climbed into the ring with Ali and his greatest adversary, Joe Frazier, who still carried a grudge from all the insults Ali had lobbed his way before their bouts. Ali struggled to ascend the stairs into the ring. Frazier, in contrast, all but hopped inside.

The ring announcer, Jimmy Lennon Jr., introduced the famous fighters. And Frazier, watching Ali struggle, turned to me, his eyes vacant, steely, and he said, "Who do you think won the fight now?"

The most memorable thing I ever saw Ali do didn't happen in the ring. I had been assigned by my boss, the television legend Dick Ebersol, to cover the Olympic Games for NBC in 1996. On the first day, before the competition started, Ebersol sent me to the opening ceremony. My friends Bob Costas, Dick Enberg, and Katie Couric did the hosting. They wanted me to remain on the infield as all the Olympians walked in for the parade of nations and conduct interviews with prominent athletes and their coaches.

No one knew who was going to light the torch at the culmination of the ceremony. Usually it was someone famous and prominent and tied to both the host country and the world of sports. The person's very presence at that cauldron should lead to a crescendo. I knew that Ebersol had recommended Ali to Billy Payne, the CEO for Atlanta's organizing committee and the former chairman of Augusta National Golf Club. But Ebersol's blessing was far from a slam dunk. In some places, especially in the South, Ali remained a divisive figure, although less so as the years went by. It remained possible that not everyone would fully endorse his candidacy for such an important moment, which was ludicrous, of course. Payne, the *Sports Business Journal* also later reported, wanted the great heavyweight champion Evander Holyfield, the hometown hero, to stand there at the end instead.

I had actually run with the torch. My wife, Frann, oversaw licensing for the Atlanta Olympic Organizing Committee. The torch relay was sponsored by Coca-Cola, a marketing partner for the Olympics. Through her relationship with the beverage company, she recommended me as a torchbearer, and they ultimately chose me to run a leg. With Frann as my escort, we took off early in the morning, like 3:30 or 4:30 A.M. What a special moment that was.

As we drove over for the ceremony, I asked Dick, "Are we going to interview whoever ends up lighting the cauldron?"

"I'm thinking about it," he responded. "But I don't know if we can."

"Huh?" I asked, confused but not for long. "Who is it?"

"I can't tell you," he said. "But what I just said *should* tell you."

It didn't take long to figure out he was talking about Ali. He knew we were close. On the day in question, mere hours before we went on the air, I asked again. His answer changed. "I don't think that he can do it," Dick said. "And I don't want to put him in a situation that would change that moment."

And he still wouldn't tell me who it was.

Later that day, I stood on the infield with a press credential hanging around my neck. The parade of nations started, as all these sprinters, lifters, and swimmers sauntered into the stadium. I interviewed Carl Lewis and Michael Johnson and Janet Evans, but I still hadn't confirmed who would light the torch that night. Even Frann asked me.

"I don't know," I told her.

"Why won't you tell me?" she asked.

My mom and dad, Lorna and Jerry, were with us, and my father ventured a guess. "It's Muhammad Ali, isn't it?" he asked.

They thought I was keeping a secret, but while I had a feeling Dad was right, I honestly didn't know for sure. To my knowledge nobody knew. Not even Costas and Enberg. Only Ebersol and, of course, Payne. I heard that the organizers closed the stadium and that they had snuck in the chosen one for a rehearsal two nights before. I'm guessing Evans, the legendary freestyle swimmer who won four gold medals combined at the previous two Games, also knew, because she had to hand Ali the torch that night for the rehearsal. If, indeed, Ali had been chosen. *Wink, wink.*

As the parade finally wound down, I stood with Frann in our endzone seats and then we saw it. Saw *him.* Ali was standing there; Evans did place her torch atop his; and Ali held on to it, hands trembling. Finally, it did light; the flame did burn; he did raise it to the sky; the stadium did erupt as his arms shook. Since I was on the air, I could hear the broadcast in my ear. "The Greatest," Enberg said on the broadcast. "Oh, my!"

"Once the most dynamic figure in sports," Costas said.

"Still a great, great presence, still exuding nobility and stature," Costas continued. "And the response he evokes is part affection, part excitement, but especially respect. What a moment." Then Costas let the broadcast breathe, let the gravity sink in, a brilliant move. The millions watching this unfold on television could hear the crowd, could feel like, for those few minutes, they were there. Costas didn't remind viewers that Ali had won gold in Rome in 1960, only, according to legend, to throw the medal into the Ohio River because of racial discrimination and being refused service in a restaurant. That moment would come up soon enough.

It was striking and moving and such a great example of American strength. This was maybe the greatest athlete of all time and the most famous athlete on the planet, and on that night, in that stadium, you could see the humanity in him and the fragility of life. He exhibited grace and courage that most people will never know.

For those two minutes, with my parents there, I saw my entire childhood, all the turbulence, so many defining American events. I saw my whole career, too, from the first interview with Ali all the way until then. All the time I got to spend with him. All that joy on people's faces. He was the Greatest, still.

The International Olympic Committee gave Ali another medal during those Games, too, to replace the one he no longer had. He received it during a halftime ceremony of the basketball final featuring the third incarnation of the Dream Team. After some of the best players in NBA history had swarmed Ali at midcourt in celebration, I climbed into an elevator with Juan Antonio Samaranch, president of the International Olympic Committee, Ali, and his best friend, the legendary photographer Howard Bingham.

Ali kept staring at the medal, and you could tell how much it meant to him. He said he would wear it with joy in the accomplishment because his stance had now been vindicated. He stood up against the establishment, and he had been proven right. He felt he could wear the medal and hold pride in his country and what it represented. He also said the replacement version looked better, fancier; an upgrade from his first one.

We could all learn so much from Ali. Start with this: there are some things out there that are bigger than us. Sure, Ali had his selfish moments. But he gave of himself to others for the good of future generations. He gave of himself in that moment with the torch. He gave of himself when he stood by his own principles. No one can dispute that.

After those Olympics, I still saw Ali from time to time. Sometimes, I'd run into him when his daughter Laila fought. He didn't like her boxing. But he would still come, would still pray, and he'd retreat back to the locker rooms after she vanquished another opponent. In those moments, he looked so proud.

As the years went by, I would check in with his strong and supportive wife, Lonnie (they married in 1986), about an idea I couldn't let go of. In the summer of 2004, I wanted to interview all of America's greatest living Olympians together. I reached out to the gymnast Mary Lou Retton, the first American woman to win an all-around gold medal, and Carl Lewis, the most decorated modern-day track-and-field star. I also reached out to a swimming youngster named Michael Phelps, still unknown to the world, who had set his sights on breaking Mark Spitz's record of most gold medals won in a single Olympics—seven, in Munich in 1972.

Ali's presence was not only important but critical. I told Lonnie the interview would be historic and last forever, that it could be viewed in a hundred years by historians and sports buffs. It would show his unparalleled legacy, would give him the credit he so richly deserved. I asked her what it might be like if we had a video of Joe DiMaggio, Babe Ruth, Hank Aaron, Lou Gehrig, and Ted Williams all doing one interview. "Muhammad will be there," Lonnie said.

His *yes* cemented everyone else's participation. And so it happened: Ali, in his last interview, the greatest athlete of all time; Phelps, the next generation who would ultimately become the winner of the most medals in Olympic history, twenty-eight total, twenty-three gold; the incredible Mary Lou Retton, an American idol and the first US woman to win an individual gold medal in gymnastics; Lewis, the owner of nine gold medals; and the fabled Sugar Ray Leonard, another boxing icon who had modeled his career after Ali.

As I worked tirelessly on that project, I thought back to something Bud Greenspan once told me. He was the legendary director, writer, and producer who made the Olympics so vividly come to life. "I don't have children," he said. "So I try to leave my legacy through these great stories and films because if they have my name on it, they will be like my children. That will be my form of immortality." I thought that sounded a bit out there, but over time I came to accept it as truth. We can watch Bud's work with immortals like Jesse Owens, Wilma Rudolph, and the award-winning short documentary *The Last African Runner*. Those stories, those moments, they do matter. Bud was right. The ones I've told are also like my children. They're part of both history and what I have left behind for others to enjoy. I don't want to overstate that. I'm not solving world peace or creating an iPhone or curing a disease. But I love stories, and I can see the value in them.

Like the round table. We did the interview at the Stanford University pool, a few nights before Phelps departed for Greece. The other Olympians, despite their heavy medal collections, all spoke to and about Ali as if in awe. We had torches sent in from Athens and every one of them signed them. One sits in my office, near my desk, and I see that torch—and what that moment represents—every day.

When we were done, Ali stood up and said to Phelps, "I'm the Greatest. You're the Latest. It's up to you now." Then he handed him the torch. "Go win all those medals," he added.

He would never again do another television interview.

We had come full circle. From my first interview, to his last one.

The whole group flew back to Los Angeles together on a private plane. Ali struggled to talk, but when he did speak he had so much to say. At one point, he grew quiet, and he lost himself in drawing, a pastime he enjoyed along with painting. His hands shook a little as he handed me a piece of paper. It was a simple yet beautiful picture of him knocking out Frazier.

My favorite painting I own is one that the artist LeRoy Neiman did of Ali as Cassius Clay, a young boxer getting ready for the Olympics. I told Ali that his drawing was the nicest thing that anybody had ever given me, but that Neiman had nothing to worry about. Ali laughed.

He also discussed living in America as a Muslim—the same topic he broached in my first interview all those years ago—and what it meant to him and why he had embraced that religion. He now worried in particular about the extremists and their terrorism and how some people unfairly perceived all Muslims in that light. He was devastated about 9/11, particularly how those heinous acts had been committed in the name of Allah. He wanted harmony in the world. He had found that in his religion. Even in his later years, though his hands would tremble, he found ways to express himself through art and his mind remained active, as he continued to have an impact on world affairs.

Throughout my childhood, I didn't think too much about the war in Vietnam. I remember my brothers were worried about the draft, and the war continuing as they approached the eligible age. Fortunately, they didn't have to go, but I remember clearly the anxiety they felt. I didn't understand why Ali made the stand he made; I knew only that he couldn't fight. But as our friendship deepened, I came to understand what he *had* fought for. "Why should you go represent a country and oppose people you have no opposition to?" he'd say.

He had to confront more opposition for both him and his family in the streets of America with white people than anyone in Vietnam. He wanted to help people in America, a country that had enough problems. Then they banned him, and he had trouble earning money, and he couldn't get a boxing license. He always had to defend himself. All this meant so much more to me later in his life.

One time he asked me what I thought about all that when I was young. I told him I liked him because he was funny and skilled, but I was too young to understand the politics.

"What did your daddy think of me?" he asked.

"My dad loved boxing," I told him. "I never asked him about the war."

He wanted to know: What did I think of him now? We were sitting at the Beverly Wilshire Hotel. He had been posted outside, doing magic tricks for children, until he retreated back to the lobby for a soda. Scenes from the war raged on nearby televisions. He didn't want another long and protracted fight. He just wanted it all to stop.

"What would you think now about my antiwar stance?" he asked.

"People now look to you for a signal," I responded. "You signaled back then that war was wrong, and it took a long time for your view to be vindicated. But it was. I don't think we have enough information now to know what's going on with the Iraqis. But if we find out something in the upcoming days or months, somebody like yourself needs to stand up and be willing to sacrifice everything."

"I did," he said, his voice low, almost in a whisper.

"How hard was that?"

"Very hard for others," he responded. "But not for me."

My stance on *his* stance had evolved as I got older, along with our relationship. He was right for his religious purposes. He was right for his political purposes. Everybody was wrong, and he was right.

In 2008, before Super Bowl XLII in Arizona, the one where David Tyree caught a football with his helmet and upended the mighty Patriots, I went to see Ali at the house he lived in outside of Phoenix. We spent several hours together, laughing and telling stories. It became harder and harder for him to communicate. He'd mostly whisper.

A year later, Muhammad and Lonnie attended my fiftieth birthday party. The invitation was extended but Lonnie was concerned it would be hard for the champ to travel. He made it, with an assist from my friend Mike Meldman, who picked them up with his plane in Scottsdale and brought them to Vegas. Frann planned the whole affair at the Palms, the casino then owned by the Maloof family. Joe and Gavin Maloof put together an incredible party and even announced my soiree on the marquee out front. *Happy Birthday, Jim Gray.*

Ali still altered the dynamic in every room he entered. That simply was his way. My friends and family were able to enjoy time with the GOAT, and like always, his presence captivated everyone. He stayed the whole night, entranced by the magician we hired just to entertain him. He didn't talk much. He didn't have to. He remained curious, he loved people, and he could still bend worlds with his will. He was Ali.

He lived almost another seven years. It was hard to watch him deteriorate, to see his struggles, but age doesn't spare anyone, even the best boxer who ever lived. The people around him made every effort to ensure he enjoyed the life that he deserved. Lonnie was the greatest champion, maybe even greater than her husband, because she took care of both Ali and his legacy, tending to both as if her own life depended on it. She, or her sister, was always by Ali's side. Sometimes, she'd help him in public, when he would flip a coin before a football game or receive some sort of honor or award. Sometimes, those moments were sad for the public, to see Ali in that condition. But they were good for him. They kept him going all those years.

On June 3, 2016, I had just finished a fighter's meeting at the J.W. Marriott at L.A. LIVE. I jumped into the car, turned on my phone, and the news was everywhere. Ali had passed. He was seventy-four years old.

I had so many messages and voice mails. As I drove toward my house, Fox called and asked about Ali. Did I want to broadcast? Of course. I sped to the studio and went on the air for hours, interviewing everyone from King to Mayweather to Tyson and Steve Wynn. Ali had that kind of impact on so many famous people. I'm glad I got the opportunity that night, because I was able to say what I wanted and pay tribute to the life he had led and the meaning he held for boxing, for America, across the entire world. That and the personal impact he had on me. I wasn't in his inner circle, but I stood close enough.

I went with Frann to Louisville, Kentucky, for the funeral. It was sad but with the feel of a big event. He had a traditional Muslim burial the day before. Thousands lined the streets. I went to the private reception held by Lonnie afterward. It was like looking at the history of America every time you scanned the room. President Clinton was there. So was Billy Crystal. So were Jim Brown, Kareem Abdul-Jabbar, Mike Tyson, and Dick Gregory. We spoke for several minutes with Hamid Karzai, the former president of Afghanistan, who had flown all the way from Kabul to pay his respects. In life, and now in death, no one could have brought a group like this together. This was also vintage Ali.

I talked to Bingham a lot that day. He had provided me with detailed insight into Ali forever, and I was often paired with him on the road, in the background. He was the definition of a true friend: loyal, dedicated, and devoted. His son had died just two months before Ali passed. I couldn't even imagine. Bingham himself would die by the end of the year, proving that he and Ali were inseparable until the end.

The gathering unfolded in ways both beautiful and sad. Lonnie told me what happened, that she hadn't expected him to die—and then he did. She didn't really know right until he passed. She remained calm and exhausted, her anguish palpable. The world had been watching Ali for more than a half century, and now all those eyes focused on her instead. I told her how important Ali had been in my life, impacting my childhood, and my career. He taught me about tenacity, principle, willpower, loyalty, friendship, and how to keep an open mind. He was great with people. I never saw Ali in a hurry. Lonnie said she knew how grateful I was, and most importantly, that Muhammad knew and loved me. It's interesting how words like that can make you cry and smile all at once. There won't be another Ali.

Ali was one of the first athletes to speak his mind and remain true to himself, regardless of the cost. What Ali stood for—and *when* he stood for it—was unique. His actions will stand the test of time.

In the summer of 2019, Lonnie happened to return a phone message I had left her while I was golfing with Brady at the Riviera Country Club. I had to hit my shot, so I passed Tom the phone. This was about five weeks after he had won another Super Bowl, his sixth. They spoke for a few minutes and when Tom passed the phone back to me, Lonnie said thank you, that the call had made her day.

"Really?" I asked. "Why?"

"Because he's one of the very few, if not the only one, who reminds me of Ali, just with the way that he plays and conducts himself," she said.

She had just told Tom that. "Blows me away," he said.

When Ali died, so did a part of me and all of us. But his legend will live on, through his wife and the Muhammad Ali Center, through his words, his accomplishments, and his legacy.

# CHAPTER 3

# MY WORLD WIDE
# WEB

My interest in basketball took root in the 1960s, while growing up in Colorado, when my dad would take me to watch the Denver Rockets/Nuggets. That's when I met Marvin Webster. He was the number one pick in the draft, a lumbering center who was diagnosed with hepatitis in 1975, limiting his rookie season to thirty-eight unremarkable games.

While recovering, the man known as *The Human Eraser* would sit in the stands, and I would talk to him and his wife Maderia before tip-offs. To stay in shape, he'd hoist jumpers at the Court Club downtown, and one day he asked me if I wanted to come to the gym to rebound and throw passes to him. Then he asked Coach Larry Brown if I could come to practices and help him work out afterward. When Brown agreed, I became a ball boy—my up-close introduction to professional sports.

The big man played a big role in the Nuggets run to the Midwest Division title the next season, and yet he was traded soon after.

The move incensed me. The very next season, Webster would play for the NBA title in Seattle, and over Christmas break, my parents let me travel west so I could spend time with him, since they knew him well. Marvin introduced me to his coach, Lenny Wilkens, and my Web of connections and relationships began to expand.

When I compared Webster's loyalty to both me and the teams he played for with the Nuggets' treatment of *him*, I learned a valuable lesson about pro sports: that we expect loyalty from players but not organizations.

Webster played on both teams with Paul Silas, whose wife, Carolyn, once captured that relationship in the best way I've ever heard. Her husband won three NBA titles and played for five teams, and he later coached for eight franchises. They had witnessed all anyone in sports could witness, and she said, "All these people are wonderful to your face, but the next day, they'll trade you, or fire you. The day before, it's 'We want Paul to be here until the day he dies.'" Over the decades, she had gotten used to the whole game. "I understand what it is," she said. "They kiss you on the face. They stab you in the back. I call it kissy-kissy, stabby-stabby."

The Webster trade was exactly her point. I knew that even as a kid. Webster was a player with all the talent in the world and an unwavering commitment, and they just . . . discarded him. I saw up close how badly that hurt him. I was so mad I submitted a letter to the editor for the *Denver Post*. I eviscerated the Nuggets' ownership and coaches for how they had callously treated a good man who had fallen ill. The newspaper must have at least seen a point in my youthful rage, because they printed my entire screed.

I decided right then that I would care less about the teams I long had rooted for and more about the players and my relationships with them. To this day, I refer to Paul Silas as "Grandpa" for all the advice he has given me the past 45 years. Webster died from coronary artery disease in 2009. The obituaries written about his life failed to mention the people whose lives he changed—like me.

In the years that followed, as I began my career in sports broadcasting, Marvin would introduce me to key figures who might help me. They, in turn, introduced me to other players and coaches, and that cycle repeated, over and over, until I managed to gain a foothold in the league.

Those relationships became pivotal to the next stage of my career, which started when I graduated college and wanted to become a full-time reporter. I began to send out résumé tapes—and send out tapes—and send out tapes. As my pile of rejection letters grew, I finally received a job offer, from a regional sports service called PRISM TV in Philadelphia. I drove my Toyota Corolla from Denver to downtown Philly, where the vehicle was promptly . . . towed. PRISM assigned me to the Phillies and 76ers pregame and postgame shows. When there wasn't a game, I did a regional version of *SportsCenter* updates.

The studio, and my office, were in the Spectrum. When I first arrived, I lived close by, at the Holiday Inn in the parking lot of Veterans Stadium. My friendship with Webster played a major role in my smooth transition to Philly. He introduced me to Julius Erving, the silky smooth forward known as Dr. J, at the last American Basketball Association all-star game in 1976. Erving had just won the original Slam Dunk contest, and he came over to wish Webster good luck in his recovery. "Hurry back," he said, "your team, and the league, needs you." Marvin thanked Julius, then added, "This is my friend," as he pointed in my direction.

Dr. J joined those 76ers the following season and starred for them until he retired in 1987. Upon my arrival in Philadelphia, I reintroduced myself, telling him the story about that chance meeting at a random all-star game.

"You came over to wish Marvin Webster well, and . . ."

Erving cut me off. "And you were sitting next to him," he said.

He did remember. After that, Erving seemed to take a liking to me. I'd always arrive early at the arena, and I'd always stay late, putting together a show called *PRISM Extra*. I ran my own camera. I wrote my own scripts. I typed in my own graphics. I ripped my own wire, which in those days meant scanning the Associated Press or United Press International ticker tape to find relevant sports stories. I did my own makeup, checked my audio levels. I ran my own teleprompter, although sometimes aided by a friendly Spectrum security guard I knew (thanks, Leo!). Erving always arrived early to get loose and always stayed late to sign autographs, and because our schedules meshed, and because he saw me doing this all by myself, he seemed impressed with my dedication. We became friends, and he would invite me over to his big, beautiful house, on Creighton Road over in Villanova. I grew close to his wife, Turquoise, and their children, and since I had moved about ten minutes away, he'd also give me a ride to the games.

In Philadelphia, I met Chuck Daly, the longtime coach who became my broadcast partner during the 1981–82 campaign. Daly had been fired by the Cleveland Cavaliers after starting the year with a 9–32 record, and he needed something to do. PRISM hired him for the remainder of that season—we worked in tandem for the pregame and halftime shows on the 76ers broadcasts—and the following year.

Thanks to Erving, my friendship with Daly started on the fast track. We did everything together. He took me golfing, to the Italian market, to these fancy stores where he bought tailored suits. He taught me about the league, sports, people, and life. He took me everywhere, like on his championship runs with the Pistons, and then as his guest with the original Dream Team. We used to talk at all hours, right up until a few days before he passed.

He even introduced me to my wife.

The future Mrs. Frann Vettor-Gray worked for the NBA in the licensing and marketing group. I first met her in 1988, on the streets of New York City, while I was working for CBS. As fate would have it, Daly reintroduced us a year later at the 1989 NBA league meetings outside San Diego. He asked me to play in the golf tournament the next day, but we discovered the foursomes had already been finalized. Chuck said not to worry, he knew the woman running the tournament and she could surely remedy the situation. He meant Frann, and she did take care of it. That night, after the tournament, I asked her to join us for dinner. I found her both kind and attractive, and I wanted to get to know her better. She declined, as she thought it would be frowned upon by her bosses. She joined us afterward, though, and we hit it off and started dating. When Frann and I married in Maui in 1996, I was flanked by Erving and Daly, with my father as my best man.

Meanwhile, at the end of that '82–83 NBA season, the 76ers won the NBA title. I was so happy for Erving, who had lost in the finals before. Daly and I did the local broadcast for most of the season. We later rode in parade floats down Broad Street, while I reported on the mayhem for ESPN, then partied at the Ervings' mansion late into the night. My career would soon take off, in large part because of these friendships and where they had led.

While in Philadelphia, the Silas connection I had made during those Denver days led to a side gig—a brief stint as a scout for the San Diego Clippers. That's right. Jim Gray worked *in* basketball, not just around the game. Silas served as the Clippers coach from 1980 to 1983, and he hired me in '82 to evaluate players for him and Pete Babcock, his future general manager, and I did that while putting together all those shows for PRISM back in Philly.

Friends like Silas and Daly and Erving led to more introductions as all the best players in the NBA eventually swung through Philadelphia. I met and interviewed Magic Johnson, Kareem Abdul-Jabbar, and Bob Lanier. Some 76ers, like Moses Malone, treated me with more respect once they saw that Julius liked me. PR directors noticed, too—and so did coaches, executives, and owners. It opened so many doors and helped in setting up interviews.

In the summer of 1983, I moved to Los Angeles to work for Greenspan on the Olympic Games that would take place in Southern California the next summer. PRISM was being sold by Twentieth Century Fox, and since I was a Fox employee, my job would likely have ceased to exist. Since Fox had the rights to the official film of the 1984 Olympics, which they called, *16 Days of Glory*, I went west.

Bud trusted me to do a number of interviews for his films, with important and historic Olympians including John Carlos, Tommie Smith, Edwin Moses, Carl Lewis, Mary Lou Retton, and Bob Beamon, among many others. He schooled me in the importance of writing to augment the reporting. He'd often note that "they say a picture paints a thousand words" and counter with, "I say a word paints a thousand pictures." Another thing he said stuck with me. "I knew I was good when I could look at other people's work and admire it."

Working on various films for longer time periods, however, pushed me back to live sports. I liked the immediacy, rather than toiling on something for years for ninety-five minutes of screen time.

After moving to Los Angeles, I hopped on another ride—and one I had never expected to take, with Al Davis. Growing up in Denver, the Raiders, naturally, were the enemy of the people. Their owner had seen me on ESPN, as a freelancer, interviewing the 76ers and Lakers stars. I also reported on his antitrust lawsuit against the NFL, where Davis sued the league to move his team from Oakland to Los Angeles.

For years, I had watched Davis from afar and admired his willingness to wade into the fray and challenge the establishment and work not just as an owner but also as a commissioner, general manager, and coach. From what I could observe, it appeared he never wavered in his principles. I first introduced myself just outside a bathroom at the courthouse, during a break. "Mr. Davis, I'm Jim Gray," I told him, mustering the courage. I later covered the verdict in that same building, reporting from the steps outside the day the jury ruled that Davis could move the team to L.A.

Soon after that, ESPN sent me over to the team's practice facility in El Segundo to watch the Raiders practice and conduct some interviews. Davis remembered meeting me at the trial, and he spoke in that great accent. "Ah, Jimmy, goddammit, I know who you are," he said. "You don't have to introduce yourself to me. Ah, Jesus Christ. Huh. I remember what you said when we won the trial. You weren't afraid." More than anything, I was just astonished that he knew who I was and was watching my reports. Davis knew exactly where everyone stood. He had an amazing mind and could recall even the most minor details.

Davis invited me to sit down in his office. We hit it off, and that led to him letting me watch practice whenever I wanted. He would call at all hours to talk football. He gave me so many tips and stories over the years, hand-delivering numerous scoops, pearls that enabled me to shine at ESPN, then at CBS on *The NFL Today*, and later at NBC on *NFL Live* and the *NFL on NBC*. My bosses were consistently astonished, left wondering how I had obtained all this information. This was back in the days of the NFL pregame wars. The competition was fierce, with networks battling each other for interviews, news, and breaking stories.

The Raiders hired me to do preseason games, and Al invited me to hundreds of dinners, and let me into his box for other contests. He allowed me into his world, gave me his insights, and shared his knowledge and wisdom. His friends became my friends. He would regularly let me sit in his meetings or would introduce me to other owners, like Alex Spanos, Eddie DeBartolo Jr., and Jerry Jones. He made it clear they should cooperate with me whenever they could.

The flip side of my loyalty to Mr. Davis is that he had his enemies, and therefore they looked at me with great suspicion, as if I were guilty by association. Some of them were so distrustful that they tried to harm and damage my career.

It was all a bunch of nonsense, though. At times, it seemed hard to overcome. But that didn't dissuade me. I wasn't going to allow others to bully me or influence who I chose as friends and contacts. Al was accountable for his behavior, not me, and he never seemed uncomfortable with the choices that he made.

Davis never cared much for the perceptions that swirled all around him. He wanted to win football games. "Just win, baby" and all that. Even then, he was generous to his friends, former players, and employees. He couldn't attend our wedding in Hawaii, but he wanted to be there, and so when we flew from Atlanta he asked us to stop in L.A. and had us picked up in a car and taken to his office. He then spent a few hours preaching to us about married life. That's right. Al Davis gave us marriage counseling. He harped on the importance of staying together, being united, never doing anything to embarrass each other and continuing to pursue our own passions. He went far out of his way that day to share his wisdom with us.

Now, Davis could be your worst enemy, too; he could get upset for reasons only known to him, and he held grudges. But he was a genius and a brilliant football man.

Al didn't look at things like other people did. One night, we were having dinner, Al, Frann, and me.

"Hey, Jimmy, what do you want in life?" Davis said.

"What do you mean by that?" I asked him.

"Well, there are only five things," Davis said. "Money, fame, glory, power, or love."

I told him I had never thought of life that way.

"Well, you better hurry up and pick one," he responded. "Or else you're gonna have nothing."

So I flipped the question and asked *him* what he would choose.

"Ah, that's easy. Power," Davis said. "Because if you have power, you have money. If you have power, you're going to be famous. If you have power, you probably achieved something glorious, and I don't give a fuck about love."

Davis had asked the same question in a meeting with me and Alex Spanos, the late Chargers owner. Spanos had answered love. "I love my team, I love my community, I love my family," he told Davis.

To which Al responded, softly, "Alex, if that's how you feel, then you've won more championships than I ever have."

As the NFL celebrated its one hundredth season in 2019, *Sports Illustrated* selected Davis as one of the most important and seminal figures in the history of the league. *SI* wrote that "no single figure has done more to shape the NFL." It saddens me that not everyone sees Davis that way, that so much of his legacy has been questioned or overlooked after his passing. He is remembered during every Raiders home game, by his son Mark, the new owner, with the lighting of a torch kindling an eternal flame.

I will also never forget Al's words at the celebration for the star I received on the Hollywood Walk of Fame. In his speech, he said that

I was a maverick in my field, that I captured the imagination of sports fans all over the world and that I gave credibility to the organizations that I worked for.

"I say to you, Jimmy, you represent our link to the past and our link to today . . . you represent the future. The truth of the future . . . Today, Jim Gray becomes the standard of excellence by which all people in his field will be measured for years to come."

Al imparted his particular brand of wisdom to me on a regular basis. He would tell me, "Just get it right, Jimmy." Or he'd say, "I'd rather be right than consistent." Al never backed down. He always held true to his beliefs. He also had a twist on an old saying, "Don't treat people the way you want to be treated. Treat them the way *they* want to be treated." That's a better Golden Rule, and it underscored his brilliance.

He should be credited—*we* should be at least partially credited—with inventing one of the most famous nicknames in sports history, and not in football. Davis already had been given credit for the mottoes

"Commitment to Excellence," and "Pride and Poise." But he also helped create another moniker that few people know. Remember those great Pistons teams known throughout the world as the *Bad Boys*? Well, let me tell you a story.

It was 1988. NBA Finals. Pistons versus Lakers. Hall of Fame guard Isiah Thomas had badly injured his right ankle, and since Detroit was at that point physically in Los Angeles, he needed to find both the right doctor and whatever treatment might assist him in getting healthy enough to play Game 7.

The Pistons coach? Chuck Daly. He asked for my advice. He didn't want to go through the Lakers. So I sent him to Al.

"Aw, Jimmy, just bring him over to the Raiders, we'll take care of him," Davis said, in that familiar Brooklyn accent.

"Well, he's a Piston," I said, giving him fair warning. "That's not going to go over well."

"Ah, I'm not really going to worry about that," Davis responded. "Goddammit, the kid needs help. Bring him over here."

So we did. Thomas received treatment from the Raiders. He visited that El Segundo facility, and the Raiders put Mike Ornstein, then their marketing director, in charge of this odd rehabilitation project. Davis's medical people used a combination of methods, from whirlpool baths to massages to draining fluid from the ankle and cycling fresh blood back in. All along, Davis had felt strongly: the best players should compete for the championship. They nursed Thomas back into the starting lineup, if not to full health. The Lakers won the title anyway. But in the time that Thomas spent around the Raiders, he grew to embrace the Davis ethos. Davis, meanwhile, adopted the Pistons in return.

After the Finals, before the start of the next season, Davis sent the whole Detroit team white sweaters and black hats and those fancy Starter jackets. Ornstein says they shipped something like $100,000 worth of Raiders product. The players wore it everywhere and adopted the style, made it their own. Orny, Isiah, and his Pistons teammate John Salley started saying that what the Raiders were to the NFL, the Pistons were going to be to the NBA. Thus the *Bad Boys* were born.

A web gets tangled. It doesn't move like a straight arrow from A to B. My web is no different. Who would have ever thought, for instance, that I'd ride John Madden's bus? He's one of my all-time favorite people. I had gotten to know the Hall of Fame coach well in the early 1980s, because of boxing. Madden loved the sport and he was the closed-circuit operator (when big fights were shown in theaters before fans could purchase pay-per-view in their homes) in the Bay Area for all the bouts. He would regularly show up in Vegas for championship bouts, too, doing interviews for CBS. We used to sit for hours in the lobby of Caesars Palace and talk fights and football, arriving Tuesday for Saturday events. I was working for Bob Arum, Don King, or ESPN doing interviews. Madden didn't fly so he would come by bus early and stay all week.

We grew so close that when I went to work for NBC in 1987, I stayed for a few years at Madden's apartment in the Dakota, the famous co-op located at Seventy-Second and Central Park West in Manhattan. It was a roomy apartment, one he only stayed at from time to time during football season, when he had a game to call on the East Coast. Most of the time I was there alone. Gilda Radner, the sketch comedian who performed on shows like *Saturday Night Live*, was the prior owner, which was clear when you stepped into the master bedroom.

She had a dream where she could soak in the bathtub and watch television in front of a fireplace. So, she designed a bedroom with a huge white tub in the center, nearby said fireplace, next to this huge console with a TV. Madden kept the setup, although I don't think he ever reviewed film in a bubble bath.

I set up in the guest bedroom. On nights when Madden was in town, he and I would eat dinner at the kosher deli Fine & Schapiro, Dallas BBQ, or Ray's Pizza.

Madden was so kind to me. In an effort to reciprocate, I invited his son Mike to stay at my apartment in Marina Del Rey while he worked for the Raiders. It wasn't a fair trade. Imagine living in New York, across the street from Central Park, in the middle of all that glorious

Manhattan chaos. I'd always keep a close eye out for Yoko Ono, who lived in the Dakota with her husband, John Lennon, until his assassination at the entrance of the building in 1980. She has remained there ever since. I'd wake up most mornings and slug some orange juice and sometimes, when fate aligned, Ono would be standing there, maybe sixty feet away, at her kitchen sink, across the courtyard. I probably waved at her dozens of times over the course of those three years. She must have thought I was one of Madden's kids or something. And, one day, in an act of sheer randomness, our paths finally crossed.

I was walking back from the NBC studios through Central Park, traversing Strawberry Fields of all places, and I bumped right into her. I introduced myself and we exchanged small talk for a few glorious minutes.

Finally, sensing the end of our confab drawing near, I said, "Well, it's nice to meet you. Perhaps we should have a Coke one day, or maybe I'll see you again."

She didn't pause, responding only, "I prefer to wave."

It wasn't a mean-spirited response, but it *was* an instant classic. *I prefer to wave*! About a week later, I was in the kitchen and looked out the window and there was Yoko. I sheepishly *did* wave, because I was sort of embarrassed and afraid she would totally blow me off. But she managed a big smile and gave back a warm and prolonged wave.

There were other unexpected encounters. One day I was walking down Seventy-Second Street and up pulled a sedan with dark tinted windows. I couldn't see in. The driver rolled down the window and asked if I was Jim Gray, to which I responded the only way I know how. Yes. I crossed the street, considering this situation too strange for my liking, and lo and behold, the same car pulled up again. The driver asked the same question. I gave some version of the same answer. Then, he says, "Would you come over here, please? President Nixon would like to speak with you."

A man rolled down the back window. And there he was, Richard Milhous Nixon. He asked me to get into the car and immediately started talking sports, without stopping for forty-five minutes. I wished I had my camera and a recorder. He knew all these baseball statistics. He wanted to know everything I did about football's New York Giants. His statistical recall and the depth of his knowledge both stood out. He'd say things like, "Let me tell you about the circumstances that occurred when Lefty Gomez came up to the plate and he hit a grounder to third or what the count was with Pee Wee Reese in a critical game in the pennant race." He was like a sports version of Siri; you asked, he knew. He went into a deep dive on the all-star game of 1949. It took place in Brooklyn, at Ebbets Field. That game marked the first time Black players, like Jackie Robinson, were included. He scored three runs. Nixon's recap would have made Vin Scully smile.

After the limo encounter, I skipped dinner and rushed back excitedly to tell Madden about the encounter. He clearly didn't believe me. "Don't ever shit Madden," he kept saying. "I've heard BS from everyone, from John Matuszak to Otis Sistrunk, and this is right up there with that nonsense they used to feed me. You can't shit Madden." Then he walked out, while shaking his head and chewing on an unlit cigar, as was his habit. I wasn't hurt by that, more just confused. Why would he think I made something like that up?

A year later, I'm sitting in the apartment and Madden bursts in. Just like he appeared on TV. Like one of those old, great Miller Lite commercials. Breaking through. . . . Boom! He's all excited. "I'm sorry I called you a shit," he said, referencing the year-earlier conversation. I didn't know exactly what he was referring to, but then he explained . . .

"You're not going to believe this," he said. "I was walking down Seventy-Second Street, and this car pulled up, and they have tinted windows and they ask me to come over. And I wave and keep walking. And the back window goes down, and boom, Gray, it's Richard Nixon. We spent an hour talking Giants football. He must be stalking this place or something."

Nixon, meanwhile, agreed with me that Madden should have run for president. There had been a joking sign to that effect that television cameras captured at one pro football game in our nation's capital. "Madden would be a good president," he said. "He's not only a unique personality, but he connects with the public." His words taught me an-

other lesson, that certain qualities apply to any vocation, from analyzing football games along with tastes-great-less-filling beer commercials
to serving as president of the United States. Nixon 1972. Madden 1992.

*President Nixon was an encyclopedia of sports knowledge.*

I first met Jack Nicholson that same decade, while covering the *Showtime* Lakers, interviewing Magic and Worthy and Kareem. And there,
always, standing close to the action, growing increasingly frustrated at
the referees, giant grin spread wide, stood Jack in all his glory. I was
never a big movie guy but of course I knew his work. Everyone in America knew Jack. I had seen him in *One Flew Over the Cuckoo's Nest, Easy
Rider, Chinatown, Terms of Endearment,* and many other films. He had seen
*me* report for ESPN on pro basketball, which, in hindsight, doesn't seem
like an even exchange.

I came to learn, along with the rest of the sports world, that Jack
loved basketball. He'd tape the games and avoid the recaps until he
could really watch them, and not as his version of background noise,
but rather tuned in, studying, looking for wrinkles or trends. He came

to know many of the best players in the league. He even referred to them by nicknames. *Nothing beats the old Captain with that sky hook. Shoot it, B—* meaning Byron Scott. Jack loved to talk to the refs and opposing coaches. Anything to help the Lakers find a perceived edge. "I am always working an angle," he'd say. "Mainly, I just want the coaches to sit down. I have to remind them that I paid for this seat."

Jack is a loyal fan. He liked to call at all hours, sometimes well after 2 A.M. I'd answer the phone at my apartment in Marina Del Rey, after returning to Los Angeles. He'd ask things like, "What do you think that coach is doing here in the third quarter? I'm just not following him."

"Jack, you're watching tape at two A.M.," I'd respond. "You're out of your mind."

On one of those wee hours calls, he started a different way. "How you doing, Scratch?"

"What do you mean by that?" I asked him.

"You got a little scratchy with those people tonight digging for a story," he said. "Just keep digging, Scratchy. I always am in the corner of the performer. But I like what you did tonight. Keep being Scratchy." Jack called me that all the time. In fact, he referred to me by that nickname so often for so long that it stuck. Employees at the various golf courses we would play began to refer to me by that moniker—they thought it was due to my ability on the course, until they saw me hit the ball. I embraced the handle, and even made it into the name of my company: Scratchy Productions. All thanks to Jack.

There isn't anybody like him. We must have played hundreds of rounds together. Usually with his buddies, and he had nicknames for them, too: Ed White (Mr. Decency), Rudy Durand (Looote), and Rick Dees (Long Ball). Jack was a decent golfer. We were playing at Sherwood Country Club one day in Ventura County, along with John Black, the Lakers' longtime PR director, and Rudy. Jack hit a ball off a rock, that skimmed the lake, bounced into a trap, went off the rake, and trickled back into the water. "Well, Scratch, even I have to take a penalty on that one," he said.

Another time, we played at Riviera Country Club with the actor

Billy Crystal. Billy just reveres Jack. After one particular hole, with Jack keeping score, he asked Crystal what he shot. "An eight."

"I've never written one of those on my card," Jack said.

"Well, that's what I got," said Billy.

"I've got a very forgiving pencil," Jack said. "No snowmen on my card."

"No, Jack, write down an eight."

"I'll give you a six," Jack says.

To which Crystal responded: "I'll go to temple."

As the round neared its end, sweat dripped down Jack's forehead. He used his putter as a walking stick. "Fellas," he said, "I'm exhausted."

"Jack," Billy said, "if I hit 420 balls today, I'd be exhausted, too." Jack loved to hit an extra shot, or two, or three. He made the game so much fun, but the poor caddies had a lot of balls to keep an eye out for. Jack would also continue to hit his ball as if he were not playing with partners; he always had his own style, never mind golf etiquette.

All those rounds and late-night phone calls led to an ease on-camera. Jack almost never appears on live television, but he did five interviews with me. In one, we discussed his two favorite things—basketball and the Lakers; in another, he explained why he couldn't hate Larry Bird, who ranked among his favorite players.

He always reserved a special space, however, for Kobe.

The legendary actor met the legendary baller for the first time in 1998 at Madison Square Garden during an interview I did with Kobe at his first all-star game—a segment that Jack had interrupted, with a basketball in hand. "Mr. Bryant," he asked, "would you mind signing an autograph for me? Nice to see a man with dignity who will actually sign an autograph and go on television instead of those bad men like Jack Nicholson. He won't even go on TV."

Did he have any advice for Kobe? "Go heat up," Jack said. "Heat up and get loose!"

Over Kobe's twenty-year career, the two rarely spoke, despite their close proximity. I asked Jack why. "I love Kobe, but I'm not a backstage guy," Jack said. "I don't go into the locker room. I'm not looking to hang out with any of these guys, or interfere in anyone's life. I like it that he is all business all the time. He wants to win. And I want to watch. This is my entertainment, not my social circle. I always hated when someone would come into my trailer during a movie, or want to come on the set. It's a distraction. I'm trying to concentrate on my job. So I didn't ever want to interrupt, for the same reason I didn't want to be interrupted."

He thought Kobe was our "modern-day Babe Ruth." "We're watching Babe Ruth while it's happening," he'd say. On the night Bryant retired after dropping sixty points in 2016, I did one of my favorite interviews with Jack. "It's an emotional night for me," he said. "It's hard to see him leave. I haven't had this feeling, really, ever, because he's been so spectacular and so great; it's been my entertainment and it's going to be sad to see him go."

"How would you describe his career?"

"As good as it gets," Jack said.

I first met Bill Walton when he played for the San Diego Clippers, back in the early '80s where so many of my relationships were formed or now tie back to. We didn't know each other very well back then, but when he went into broadcasting, we grew closer. I'd run into him at *Up Close with Roy Firestone* on ESPN and my respect for him grew when, on the program, Walton bravely discussed the stuttering issues he had overcome, how much work and speech therapy that took, and how that led to his second career as a broadcaster. Funny thing about Walton now: he has never stopped talking since.

We've had so much fun on-air. Walton is a special guy with a quick and quirky brain, and he comes up with all these crazy, outlandish sayings like "just missed" on an airball, or "when I think of Boris Diaw, I think of Beethoven," or "why does Larry Johnson wear that special belt," when his jock strap was exposed. Classics.

One time, I said to him, in way of a friendly reminder, "Bill, we've got a game." Meaning the action unfolding right in front of us.

"Don't worry about the game, Jim," he responded. "The people can see the game." So he dove into the Grateful Dead and politics and all this other random stuff. Walton always kept it fresh, but what I noticed up close that may not be as readily apparent is he has this fertile, brilliant mind.

We broadcast together for several networks, and we'd often ride to games when we worked for CBS, NBC, and ESPN. During those rides, without fail, he would call his college coach, the legendary John Wooden from UCLA, every single day. Walton would tell the Wizard of Westwood where we were, what game we were calling, the weather in whatever city we happened to be in, or what he might describe to the audience later that night. He would, naturally, just keep talking until finally you could hear Coach Wooden pick up the phone and say, "Yes, William. How are you?"

"I'm just calling to check on you," Walton would respond.

I'll never forget the incredible concern he showed. He made sure that Coach Wooden was up and moving and working out. Walton would urge him toward doctor visits and to spend more time out of the apartment. He loved to make his old coach laugh, and Wooden's reaction often fell somewhere between considerably amused and mildly annoyed. That relationship stood the test of time, gaining strength over more than fifty years.

Walton had a horrible issue with his spine and had undergone dozens upon dozens of operations on his feet, forcing him to retire from basketball and live in pain every day for the rest of his life. His body was such a mess that at one point he couldn't move without feeling stabbing pain in his back, as if he were being perpetually electrocuted. There were times that he so ached, in fact, that he considered suicide, imagining the worst things, like jumping off the Coronado Bridge in San Diego, or telling me that he was going to put a bullet in his head. He had lost his job at ESPN, moved out of his main house, and struggled to survive. His muscles were atrophying; his bank account began to dwindle.

I knew he was struggling, so I'd drive down from L.A. to see him or call him daily, the same way he did with Coach Wooden. *Bill, we're gonna find a doctor. Bill, you gotta get out of bed.* Through my doc at UCLA, the incomparable Dr. Gary Gitnick, we found Dr. Steven Garfin. He performed a complex surgery that literally saved Walton's life, putting numerous rods and bolts in his back. In every speech he gives and every interview he does, Bill is so grateful that he credits me with saving his life, but I have to remind him that it was the doctors that did the work.

I called the Maloof brothers, Sacramento Kings owners Gavin and Joe, and told them that Walton had lost the ESPN job and that his insurance had disappeared along with that paycheck. They hired both of us for their broadcasts, and I worked the sidelines during those games, and helped with the halftime and pregame shows, so I could be with Bill. ESPN eventually rehired him.

He remains one of the most generous, philanthropic people I know. He supports more than fifty organizations and charities in San Diego.

In 2019, Bill gave the introduction for my induction into the California Sports Hall of Fame. In typical Walton fashion, he spoke for twenty-nine minutes without taking a breath. There's no better friend than Bill Walton. I helped save his life because I love him, and he would do the same for me.

You can't talk about the Lakers without talking about Jerry West, an NBA legend. He meant so much to professional basketball that a silhouette of him dribbling became the logo for the league.

Over the past thirty-five years Jerry has taught me so much about the game, giving me insights and analysis on players and coaches. He gave me advice on the job, telling me to be prepared and to treat people with the dignity I'd expect to receive in return. He'll also call me after one of my interviews and tell me I shouldn't have asked a particular question. Or tell me that I was too hard on a certain interview subject. Jerry could be so blunt that his assessments hurt, but they made me better. He'd always say, "We get along because you're the same as me. You tell the truth. And you'll hurt yourself by telling the truth. You won't play the game with all the bullshit. You'll stand up for your audience, you'll stand up for yourself and you'll ask tough questions and hold people accountable."

"And that's why I love you," he'll say. The feeling is mutual.

Over the years, I found that relationships and loyalty matter as much as ability—in my business and in almost any endeavor worth doing. I wasn't necessarily cognizant of that notion when my career began all those years ago in Denver. You start this ride, like with Ali, and you think it's never going to end. But it does. And you pick up another ride, like with Erving, and then another one, like with Daly. They often overlap, and you're on multiple rides at once. And then you wake up, all these decades later, and you can't believe how many rides you've taken and how lucky you've been to take them. They happened organically, one brick stacked onto the next, until you've built the foundation for a career.

The web I've woven together looks something like this: Webster and Silas to Ali to Dr. J and Chuck, to Arum and King, to Al, to Eric Dickerson, to Madden, to West and Mike Ditka, to Charles Barkley, to Tyson, to Walton, to Kobe, to Brady, to Floyd Mayweather Jr., with a sprinkle of Jack, and a touch of LeBron.

Frann and I don't have any children, so our dear friends have become like our family. People often ask me how did I get so close to all these amazing athletes. I often say, I don't know, you would have to ask them. You can't just walk up and say I'm going to be friends with Jack Nicholson or be trusted by Kobe Bryant. It only works when it works both ways. Jerry Richardson used to tell me that "true friendship is reciprocal. If one person is always doing for the other, that's a one-way relationship. Real friendship is a two-way street."

In all friendships, principles matter: honesty, integrity, trustworthiness. I learned that from my dad. I never give up on the people who help me, no matter what happens to them. I guard their privacy, I know what's public and what's private, and I don't let the private stuff seep into the public domain. I don't gossip about my friends or relationships, and I don't get involved in any rumors. I don't post anything. I don't post anywhere.

Any success I've obtained goes back to those same principles. That my business is about people and relationships. And that all comes back to one concept: loyalty, which has formed My World Wide Web.

# CHAPTER 4

# MICHAEL

## (JACKSON) AND THE MIRAGE

I went to a fight at the Mirage Hotel with Julius Erving, Steve Wynn, and their wives, along with Clint Eastwood, in the 1990s. What I remember is not the fight but Michael Jackson walking into the arena with a security guard and sitting down right by us.

Michael plopped down and said hello and draped a blanket over his knees. He looked like . . . Michael Jackson: mask, hat, glasses, the whole deal. After a few rounds, he tapped me on the shoulder with enough force that it startled me. I turned toward him, and he pulled down his mask.

"Hey, Michael. What's up?"

"Jim, Julius, how many innings are in this game?"

We started laughing.

"What's so funny?"

"Michael, it's not a game," I said. "It's a match. There are no innings. It could be over in the next few seconds. Or it could last another nine rounds. The rounds are three minutes, with a minute in between." Here I was, explaining how boxing works to Michael freaking Jackson.

"OK, thank you," he said, as he pulled the mask back up.

The fight did not go the distance and everyone rose quickly, heading toward the exits. I followed the group for sixty, maybe seventy yards. Steve turned around at that point and said, "Where the fuck is Michael?" Only Julius could see over the crowd, and he spied Jackson still sitting in that seat. I ran back, and indeed, he was there, still wearing that mask, still planted next to his security guard.

"Is it over now?"

"Yeah, Michael. Come on, let's go!"

We tried to run out of the arena. This was long before the days of ubiquitous cell-phone cameras, and yet the famous singer attracted a rare fervor, a rabid crowd that closed in all around him, overwhelming that poor guard. People were diving over each other, trying to simply touch him. After a few chaotic minutes, we did exit, and we retreated into a private room, where Michael stood in a corner, lingering next to several palm trees. After a few minutes, he tapped me on the shoulder. "Jim, Julius, I cannot tell you how wonderful of a time I had tonight. Thank you for everything and take care."

Then he walked outside.

# CHAPTER 5

# FIRST
# PITCH

On the same terrible morning that terrorists hijacked four airplanes and crashed two straight into the World Trade Center in lower Manhattan, I was packing my suitcase and watching the clock, less than an hour away from departing for the airport. I was at my parents' house in Denver, and I had spent the night before in a familiar place: working the *Monday Night Football* radio broadcast for Westwood One, on the very night the Broncos opened Invesco Field at Mile High Stadium. Everything about that game, the aftermath, and early the next morning felt normal. I conducted my interviews. The broadcast ended. I went home to bed, woke up, and began readying for another trip on another plane, same as the thousands of jaunts that came before.

My father was stretching in the living room. I tuned the TV to the *Today* show. This was about 6:55 Mountain Time on Tuesday, September 11, 2001. My dad stopped his routine immediately. I forgot about my suitcase. The world had already changed that day. Nothing would feel the same again.

There were Matt Lauer and Katie Couric on the television, both wearing solemn expressions and speaking in grave tones. They said a plane had crashed into the World Trade Center, and while they began to layer in details as they became available, we watched a second plane barrel into the Twin Towers in real time, at 7:03. It was horrifying, and at that moment we knew, we all knew, we just knew—this was not an accident. We watched in disbelief. I felt most for the thousands who toiled in those buildings, who went to work that day, like any other day, not knowing it would be their last.

My wife was at our home in Los Angeles, the city where I was supposed to fly to that morning—until Federal Aviation Administration officials grounded all planes nationwide. My dad went downtown to his office, where he spent a few hours every day to keep his mind sharp, despite having retired from his long and decorated career in 1997. I also went downtown, to Channel 9, the ABC affiliate that once employed a young broadcaster teeming with ambition—me.

I just wanted to watch my old boss, the brilliant TV executive, Roger Ogden, the man who gave me my first job twenty-four years earlier. So I sat there with him, scanning the news hits on all the monitors, seeing the newsroom buzz as editors sent reporters out on assignments. I knew that feeling. I hated this moment, which emphasized the magnitude of the day ahead. We would never forget 9/11. I remember how my parents tried many times to explain to me what World War II was like, what the bombing at Pearl Harbor had meant to them. They told me they had gathered around the radio to listen to the news reports. My mother's parents hailed from Ireland and England, and many of her relatives were killed during the war when the Germans bombed London. This moment felt, unfortunately, like it would become our Pearl Harbor. In the newsroom, adrenaline surged as reporters and producers bolted toward the airport or tried to find closer-to-home angles and make connections, explaining an international tragedy through a local lens.

Like most, I wondered the obvious questions. Who had attacked us? How had they pulled off a crime of that scale, that magnitude? Would there be more attacks? I considered the hundreds and hundreds of flights that I had taken, those planes departing for destinations all over the world, those airports secure, those passengers safe. And I considered: How could anyone take over planes like that, turn them into missiles, and ram them into buildings?

I almost drove to California. That's how long the wait lasted before anyone could fly again. It must have been three days, if not four, before they reopened Denver International Airport. At times, the wait felt interminable, with Frann so far away. But the delay ended quickly enough to avoid a seventeen-hour-or-longer drive.

I continued to ask myself another question en route to the airport. *Who the hell wants to get on a plane right now?* The answer soon revealed itself: almost nobody. Part of me thought the airport would be backed up, with long lines snaking away from the security stations, because so many people had missed their flights and needed to get home. Instead, the whole place was almost empty and the space seemed bigger, without so many travelers jostling for position, wearing their stresses across their faces, furiously wheeling bags toward gates.

Security had changed already. I remember that. I had to check my carry-on suitcase. The searches were much more thorough; they even checked our socks. And it immediately became apparent that the airport had added to its security staff. I remember looking at everyone around me more than normal, thinking suspicious things like, *What's in her purse? Why is he sleeping?* The events of 9/11 had made me mistrustful, which is what the terrorists had wanted, and there I was examining everyone I passed, of every color and every race and every religion, while they undoubtedly did the same to me. Why in the world was I getting on a plane? I tried to rationalize with myself. *I've done this four thousand times. I'm safer now than ever.* But it's one thing to tell your brain such notions; it's quite another to actually believe them.

Still, I boarded a mostly empty aircraft and took my seat. I can't remember what I read or what I watched. I mostly studied the people around me, watching closely. President George W. Bush would later tell me that he wanted to get planes back in the sky as quickly as possible, to send a message to Americans, to reinforce that those cowards wouldn't shake us or rattle our very way of life.

My first flight after 9/11 landed without incident.

Editors assigned me to cover several 9/11-related stories. I interviewed the Yankees and Diamondbacks about the tragedy at the World Series, traveled to Indiana to do a piece with Notre Dame's football program, and covered the Irish's game for NBC the following weekend. Nothing was the same. People everywhere remained in various states of shock and grief. I couldn't find any joy in the stadium; people seemed, instead, to be going through the motions. The same events on the field that would normally draw huge cheers received only mild reactions. It was so quiet. It seemed like many felt guilty for sitting there at that game while the world fell apart.

At *Today*, where I worked as a part-time national correspondent, I pitched a piece on Ray Charles and the song, "America the Beautiful." Every team, in every sport, in every stadium was playing that number all the time. But no one could sing it like Ray Charles. His iconic rendition became something like our new national anthem.

I visited Charles at his studio in Los Angeles for what turned out to be his last interview and one of my all-time favorite exchanges. "Did the events of 9/11 mark one of few times in your life that you felt grateful because you couldn't see?"

"That's a great question," he said. "I hadn't really thought of it that way, but I suppose I'm better off not seeing all this devastation, because I know how it must feel for everybody to see what's going on. So it's probably just as well that I can't."

I wondered what he visualized, at least in his mind's eye. "I see these big, beautiful buildings," he said. I still remember his voice. Talk about beauty; everything he said was melodic.

"And I see all these people out living their lives," he continued. "Going happily about their days and then, all of a sudden, they just collapse into this utter devastation."

Charles also sang "America the Beautiful" for our cameras. I'm not sure I ever heard anything so moving in my entire life. Goose bumps rise on my arms just thinking about that moment.


I went to Yankee Stadium on October 30, 2001, for Game 3 of the World Series between the Yankees and the Diamondbacks. Baseball was back in New York. But the return was fraught with trepidation; there were anthrax scares, rumors of additional and imminent and possibly greater attacks, and a general unease that lingered, understandably, with first responders still sorting through the rubble to the south.

With my friend Eddie Feibischoff, the talented producer at NBC, I visited Ground Zero two days before the game. It was the saddest scene I had ever seen. The rubble still smoldered. Twisted iron and debris lay scattered everywhere. The smell was indescribable. I couldn't shake how loud and how quiet it was all at once, with responders removing the debris and bystanders not saying a word. We stood there for a few moments, taking in the devastation. Both of us started crying.

A few weeks later, I was in Washington, broadcasting Michael Jordan's first home game with the Washington Wizards in his return to the NBA. Before the game, Eddie and I, and some of our colleagues from the *NBA on NBC* crew, went to see the destruction at the Pentagon from the side of the highway. Seeing Ground Zero and the Pentagon immediately after the attacks remains etched in my mind. I think of those moments every time I visit New York and Washington.

It's standard practice now, but when I went to that game, it marked the first time I remember going through a metal detector to enter a stadium for a domestic sporting event. It took forever to get in, but I understood why. We all did. At that point, only a handful of important people knew of the special guest who would soon arrive by helicopter and head down to the Yankees' clubhouse. I heard the blades whirl and knew instantly that President George W. Bush would be in attendance.

That moment remains as powerful and compelling as anything I ever witnessed in my career. Here stood this young president, who had been dealt an awful hand, this terrible tragedy, and he's out there trying to lead the nation. I had no idea he would also throw out the first pitch. Or how the pitch he did throw would change my life.

President Bush exuded courage and strength that night. I couldn't believe he walked out there alone. I'm thinking, *This man is naked out here. This is nerve-racking. There's no Secret Service.*

He waved when he reached the mound, as the crowd chanted as loud as I've ever heard a crowd roar. *U-S-A! U-S-A!* The president wound up, reared back, and delivered a perfect strike. That sent the already amped crowd into a frenzy. Managers Joe Torre and Bob Brenly met him on the infield and took a picture. I was still trying to process what had happened. That moment gave me chills that lasted for forty seconds, easy—just like Ali and the torch; two moments at sporting events that had nothing to do with sports.

The president would later remind us of a sentiment relayed by one of his predecessors, Franklin Delano Roosevelt, who during World War II, after the bombs had fallen on Pearl Harbor, had said that sports would continue, that he wanted the public to know it was OK for the games to be played. "I honestly feel that it would be best for the country to keep baseball going," he said. He wasn't saying that anyone had to stop grieving or lose sight of those who had lost their lives. Just that life would continue on. The old adage "Keep calm and carry on." And that's exactly what happened at Yankee Stadium that night.

"If you're afraid for your own life," President Bush would tell me later, "there's no way you can lead a nation."

The Yankees did not win that series, losing in seven games, but you're damn right they won that night. I can still feel it, how visceral the emotion was. That was everything America could be: sports and courage and memorializing the ultimate sacrifice made by innocent citizens. All those feelings converged at that moment. You couldn't help it. The night went from tremendous melancholy and obvious and warranted trepidation to this incredible lift. I was proud—to be an American, of

our president and of New York and the Yankees and Major League Baseball for how they handled everything.

I had a feeling then that this night would mark the signature moment
of the younger Bush's presidency. That and when he visited Ground
Zero, shortly after the attacks, grabbing a megaphone and speaking
directly to the first responders. "I want you all to know, that America today—America today is on bended knee. In prayer for the people
whose lives were lost here. For the workers who work here. For the
families who mourn. The nation stands with the good people of New
York City. And New Jersey and Connecticut. As we mourn thousands
of our citizens."

Someone in the crowd shouted, "We can't hear you!"

"I can hear you!" Bush yelled back. "I can hear you, and the rest of
the world hears you. And the people who knocked these buildings down
will hear all of us soon!" I'm telling you. Chills.

When I flew home from New York, the airplane was again empty. But
I would soon obsess over a story I had to tell, one that spoke to a greater
purpose than anything in sports.


I got to know the Bush family years before 9/11. I met the patriarch,
George Herbert Walker Bush, at a United Service Organization event in
the late 1980s. That night, I walked up to President George H.W. Bush
and his wife, Barbara, and introduced myself.

"I know who you are," he said, to my surprise. "We watch TV in the
White House."

His wife, Barbara, noticed that we were talking. "What show are you
on?" she asked me.

"He's a sportscaster," the president responded. "George loves his
sports," she said.

She was right about that. The elder Bush cherished golf. His grandfather, George Herbert Walker, created the Walker Cup, a competition
that remains one of the sport's most storied events. Over the years, I
sometimes ran into President George H.W. Bush at tournaments. We

played a round of golf twice, too. Before the first one started, he told me he loved to play and he loved to play quickly. He saw the brilliance in Jack Nicklaus but hated the way he lined up putts for forever, giving casual golfers the license to take almost five hours to play one round. The elder Bush believed such delays were ruining his favorite sport.

I must have interviewed him fifteen times. One encounter took place at Valderrama in southern Spain, at the 1997 Ryder Cup, where I was part of the NBC broadcast. He would have been out of office for four and a half years. Rain poured down in sheets, making it hard to see five feet in front of your face. I took shelter in our golf cart, along with the cameraman Dave "Too Tall" Atkins. All of a sudden, as we made our way to the NBC compound, I saw an older, drenched man walking toward us without an umbrella, wearing one of those black Glad trash bags, in an attempt to stay dry. "Soaked" did not begin to describe his appearance. Three men trailed behind him, wearing serious expressions across their faces. I looked closer. They were Secret Service. And the man wearing the trash bag turned makeshift raincoat? President H.W. Bush.

It struck me just how normal he was. He looked like he had just stepped out of the shower, so we asked him if he wanted a ride back to the clubhouse. *Of course*, he responded.

We did the interview that same weekend. But before it took place, the very next day, the president came back to our compound with the Secret Service detail. Someone flagged his arrival for me, delivering the news via my earpiece. I speed-walked back in the direction of the compound and went straight to George H.W., who desired to find Too Tall. The president, having remembered Dave from the afternoon before, wanted to thank him and hand him a gift.

We played another time, at the prestigious Shadow Creek Golf Course in Las Vegas, with Steve Wynn. By then, Bill Clinton had become both a wildly popular president and embroiled in the Monica Lewinsky scandal. The caddies followed us closely, but at one point they seemed a safe distance out of reach.

"Mr. President," Steve said, "I gotta ask. What do you make of this whole circumstance with Monica?"

President Bush looked over his right shoulder, then glanced over his left. Once assured the caddies remained far enough away, he said, "Reckless. Just fucking reckless." That was the only time I heard him curse.

I believe I was the first person to do an interview where both Bush presidents were together. We did that at the Country Club in Brookline, Massachusetts, at the Ryder Cup back in 1999. Many golf fans remember the event. It's the one where the American golfer Justin Leonard continued to duel the Spanish ace José María Olazábal down the back nine on the final day, tying the match and then clinching victory for the American team when he drained an epic forty-five-foot putt for birdie on the seventeenth hole. The celebration began right then, with players, caddies, and even their wives dancing in delirium right there on the green.

Earlier that week, I had seen President George H.W. out walking the course and asked if he wouldn't mind doing another interview session with me. "Of course," he said. But then Barbara Bush walked up to both of us and interrupted.

"Why are you always talking to the old man?" she said. "How many times do you need to?" She pivoted right there, gesturing at another man who bore a resemblance to both of them standing nearby. There was *W.* "My son right there, he's the governor of Texas," she said. "He's going to run for president next year. Why don't you put *him* on?"

"This one's old news," she continued, pointing at her husband. "This one's coming," she said, motioning at her son.

I had met George W. before, at the Texas Rangers ballpark in Arlington, Texas, where he served as the team's managing general partner. On another occasion, after he became the governor of Texas, we did an interview in 1996 in the middle of a Rangers playoff game. We talked baseball and the Rangers season. Typical stuff. I introduced him to Too Tall, the cameraman, from the golf cart.

Jeb Bush was there at Brookline, too, so we decided to talk with the whole family. Incredibly, both George H.W. and George W. recognized my colleague. That instantaneous recall, exhibited by Bush the father and Bush the son, just blew me away. No one ever remembers the guys on the crew. They did.

When W. ran, I thought it might be cool for him to follow in his father's footsteps right into the Oval Office. We hadn't had something like that in America since the Adams family. I also secretly hoped they never did another interview together, since I'd done the first. But that's not what I wanted most.

On the night that George W. Bush threw out the first pitch, it gave me the chills, but I didn't expect to ever revisit those events. As the years went by, I couldn't stop thinking about that night. People sometimes asked me to choose the greatest sports moments I've ever seen in person, and I always came back to Yankee Stadium, October 2001. I've seen Magic's Showtime Lakers and Elway's famous Drive and Michael Jordan knock down famous championship shots. None of that compared. I imagine that watching the president throw that pitch was more like watching the US hockey team snatch the gold medal in 1980—if you were there, you remembered every detail, right down to where you sat and what you ate and how you celebrated.

Eventually, by 2004 or so, I decided that I *had to* tell the world what had happened on that night. Funny enough, but in that same year, I landed an interview with George W. at the White House days before he would square off against John Kerry in the presidential election. I spoke to both candidates separately and those segments ran on a half-hour ESPN special, titled, "The Issues Important to Sports Fans."

Bush in particular seemed relaxed. He kicked his feet up on a small end table after the interview concluded and asked me several sports questions, like, "What kind of guy is Mike Tyson?" Bush seemed fascinated with him. "I love Mike Tyson," I responded. "He's a lot more than what you might think." I told him about some of the crazier experiences I'd had with Mike, all his chaotic greatest hits. But I also explained that he could recite Shakespeare and *Days of Grace*, the memoir of Arthur Ashe. I told the president that I liked the boxer, a lot, and that despite some of his worst behaviors, he possessed a number of good qualities. W. smiled wide.

Here we were, a few days before Election Night, with Bush headed out on critical trips to Florida and Pennsylvania and Ohio, essential jaunts all, if he wanted to seize another term. And he's asking me about Tyson and the Bite Fight! He also wanted to talk baseball, and we did. He even signed baseballs for the crew. In the interview, we discussed the election, his first term, following after his father, and baseball's steroid scandal. He answered all the questions honestly. I wondered what he made of steroids in sports.

"You know, I have too many of my friends in baseball who believe that steroids (have) enhanced performance among some players," he said. "In other words a singles hitter might've (become a) home-run hitter. In making my statement [in the State of the Union address], I didn't want to accuse any single player of violating baseball rules. But what I was saying to people, as clearly as I could as the president, was that people in these positions must behave responsibly. And that the signal that steroids might be OK is a terrible signal to send to families and kids who aspire to be a major leaguer or a football star."

Could he trust that the great accomplishments in sports like baseball and track and field had been attained without cheating? "My first inclination is to say 'yes' because I've seen some of these great players close up, particularly in baseball," he said. "I've seen their hand-eye coordination. Their incredible quickness. And I think it's very important for us not to prejudge until the evidence is clear."

When the interview finished, I saw my opening. "Mr. President," I said, "you should really tell the story of what happened after 9/11 and you throwing the first pitch." He looked back at me, as if weighing the possibility. He started to tell me the inside story of what had taken place that night. I knew our time was up that day.

"That's the next time I come back," I said. He hadn't said yes. But he hadn't said no, either.

President Bush did win reelection, and every time I saw him afterward, I reminded him of the documentary I wanted to do. He always seemed interested. But, for years, we could never make it happen.

That's the longest I ever worked toward a single project. Eleven, maybe twelve years. I pursued that documentary like Lawrence Taylor chased after quarterbacks, or Usain Bolt barreled down so many tracks.

Steve Wynn factored in again there. I met up with him in 2013, at his hotel villa in Las Vegas, where he wanted to show me a painting of his two German shepherds that the younger Bush had sent over. George W. had taken up the brush as a hobby to pass the time after his second term concluded. This was in addition to all his charity work in Zambia, trying to cure cervical cancer, and working on the George W. Bush Presidential Center, the library and museum he and Laura opened on the campus at Southern Methodist University.

I told Steve about the story, and he grabbed his phone right then and dialed W., who answered after only a few rings

"You know Jim Gray?" Steve asked.

"Of course I do," Bush responded.

"He wants to do this documentary with you," Steve said. "You should consider that."

Bush again said that he would think about it, and he told Wynn that I should contact his chief of staff, Freddy Ford. I did, and we talked over all the particulars for the next year and a half, at least, as I came to admire both his personality and efforts. Then one day, out of the blue, Ford called me. "The president is willing to do this now," he said.

I couldn't believe it. After all the pitches, all the years, all the prodding; finally, we had a chance. Ford told me that Bush accepted for two reasons. (1) He believed that the American public, the majority anyway, had started to forget about 9/11, the lives that were lost that day and the incredible American response to one of the worst tragedies imaginable. And (2) He had opened the library/museum, and he wanted to put together a presidential baseball exhibit there. They saw the documentary as a potential centerpiece. He also had one other condition: Bush wanted the film to be a *30 for 30*; he loved the ESPN series.

I called John Skipper, then the network's president. "John, you've got to make a quick decision," I told him. "I love ESPN, but I don't have a treatment, and I haven't spoken with anyone in your organization about this. Here's the story, and it has to be a *30 for 30*."

Skipper didn't even pause. "I don't have to get back to you," he said. "We're doing it."

The biggest sticking point with ESPN was the overall length. President Bush wanted to make a forty-eight-minute film, and so did I. The network executives insisted on a documentary of no more than twenty-five minutes. I couldn't figure that one out. Brian Bosworth got seventy-seven minutes? And President Bush, after 9/11, couldn't carve out half that time? It didn't make any sense. Ford, at W.'s request, called and lobbied Skipper on our behalf. Whenever another *30 for 30* would come out, we'd bring it up. "How come that guy gets an hour?"

Alas, we ended up with the original twenty-five minutes. It hurt cutting some of that stuff out, but it turned out to be the right call. We were told that the film ended up being one of the most watched and most downloaded of the entire series, at least to that point. Part of that owed to President Bush's silence after leaving office in 2008; he hadn't spoken much directly to the public in so long. He explained to me why eventually. "I owe to the current president my silence," he said. "No one needs to hear what I think. President Obama deserves the opportunity to govern without me chiming in." But this wasn't a political story, it was about 9/11, the moment everyone knew and could relate to, and baseball, the all-American sport that the older generation grew up on and loved.

Beyond that backdrop, W.'s cooperation made the film more real and more poignant. At one point, he admits that first responders viewed him with skepticism, seeing him as "a silver spoon guy." He also asked that all the documents about his appearance that day at Yankee Stadium and the pitch he threw be shared with us. He signed off on releasing relevant information on 9/11, meaning we could speak to George Tenet, then the head of the Central Intelligence Agency, and Nick Trotta, who ran his Secret Service detail, and members of his cabinet back then, like Condoleezza Rice, and his chief of staff, Andrew Card. Those conversations unearthed incredible untold facts. Like in the seconds before President Bush walked onto that field, alone, his detail poised nearby but not close enough to stop a bullet that might be headed in his direction. "Are we going to be OK?" he asked Trotta.

"Mr. President," Trotta responded, "if anybody tried anything, these people here would eat them alive. We're going to be fine. And you've got more help out there than you think." To that end, he also revealed that two of the umpires were actually Secret Service agents, dressed in the familiar blue and positioned near first and third base.

Bush's cooperation also helped in obtaining interviews with famous people who either were involved in the aftermath of 9/11 or lived in New York and thus held unique perspectives on what that moment meant in response to the catastrophe. Freddy Ford rounded up everyone we asked for.

Rudolph Giuliani, the former mayor of New York City, agreed to speak on-camera. He said Yankee Stadium was guarded for two days before the game the president attended. So did the actor Billy Crystal, who had been at the stadium that night, sitting with Yankees owner George Steinbrenner in his luxury box. Crystal joked on camera that 9/11 forced casual sports fans to root for the Evil Empire for the first time ever. Yankees manager Joe Torre pointed out that his sport hadn't been postponed since FDR died in 1945 and that when play resumed "baseball had an obligation" to lift the country up. And shortstop Derek Jeter told viewers to imagine the madness of Manhattan, except the streets empty, minus any cars.

Before we started shooting, I sent over all sorts of information, and we had several discussions over conference calls about the film. Eventually, I flew down to Texas to interview George W. and his wife, Laura.

He made his daughter Barbara available. The interviews lasted two days. We filmed them documentary style, with me sitting away from the Bushes, rather than at an angle off to the side, with a green screen behind them. I could see his face as if looking through a mirror, and he saw me in the same way, looking back. That way the angle the viewer sees is more straight on.

Bush revealed how Commissioner Bud Selig had wanted him to throw out the first pitch for Game 1 in Arizona, a suggestion the president rejected out of hand. "There's only one place to go," he says. "Yankee Stadium." He noted that Selig had suggested moving the entire New York portion of the series to Atlanta. He described warming up near the clubhouse, trying out the bulletproof vest that the Secret Service detail wanted him to wear. Jeter stopped by, watched the president loosen his arm, and Jeter told him to throw from the top of the mound rather than in front of it and joked that if he bounced the pitch the crowd would boo him. Then, there was Bush, striding to the mound, out there, alone; the crowd rising to its feet, delivering a thunderous ovation; Crystal, "the place just went berserk; this is a moment, your politics just go away; he stood up and basically said 'Fuck you.'"

President Bush did most of the interview in almost one take, pausing occasionally if he wanted to rephrase a particular sentiment, or asking a few questions in regard to his answers. At one point on Day 1, he said something like, "I've answered this eight times, let's come back tomorrow." And so we did.

The director we chose, after much deliberation, was Academy Award winner Angus Wall. He asked the questions at the start of Day 2, so that we could glean info from a different perspective. He wasn't in attendance at the game where the president threw the pitch. But he had seen it on TV.

Four months later, Bush saw the film after it was finished, at the premier. Wall had done the editing. We just weighed in with notes. The final version? Even more moving than expected.

It aired on ESPN after a national moment of silence at 8:46 A.M., on September 11, 2015, or fourteen years after the attacks. "That pitch transcended sports, transcended history," Condoleezza Rice says in the film. "It was quite a moment."


People often ask: What most stands out to me from the film? That's easy. Him. *George W. Bush.* The human being, that is. How he cares. He's funny, selfless. He's got courage. He's dignified. He's willing to laugh at himself, and it's those qualities that I admire and respect. I feel grateful to have been part of that documentary and realize the tremendous honor in being trusted by him to tell that story. It's my favorite thing I've done in my career. It's part of sports history and it's part of America's history. I'm tearing up right now just thinking about it.

I was asked by the president to introduce the film at the premier, which was held at the theater at his library/museum in Dallas. That night, I expressed my gratitude to him, becoming choked up. When the president saw my emotion, he wanted to help me get through it. It was so quiet you could have heard a pin drop, but W. yelled "Atta, boy!" and started to clap. As I finished the intro and walked offstage, he greeted me with an embrace. I sat down next to him, forever touched by his reaction. Then he sat back and watched the film for the first time.

The president known as "43" told me several times that throwing the first pitch ranked as the most nervous moment of his presidency. More than the debates, or global policy decisions. He told me, "That ball was really heavy" and confided that he knew how much that one simple throw would mean as a symbol to the nation and the world. I'm certain the nerves and anxiety had never been higher, knowing that he was out there alone on the mound, so vulnerable and heroic all at once. He knew he had to throw the perfect pitch, and he delivered.

I loved all the reactions. A wide range of people reached out, people whom I admired and respected, people who knew baseball, or simply people who were moved by the documentary itself. The broadcaster Joe Buck, who called the game that night on Fox, told me the film moved him to tears and was the best documentary he had watched. The legendary Vin Scully told me it was the best "baseball thing" he'd ever seen in his life—and he had called games for nearly seven decades! I couldn't think of a higher compliment. Jim Nantz, another dear friend who had also put in a good word with W. was elated.

Three days later, I got the ultimate call. George H.W. was on the line, expressing lavish praise, telling me how he and Barbara had loved the film and remained grateful. He said it would serve as a historical document, worthy of preservation so that the public and future generations would be able to fully understand both the context and nuance of that moment.

A few days later, on a routine weekday, I went to my mailbox. Inside, there was a handwritten letter from the president who had thrown that pitch. He had mailed it after the premiere. It reads, in part, "Dear Jim, last night was very special. Thank you for your kind remarks, and for pushing the idea for the film . . . With very best wishes,

George W. Bush."

*President George W. Bush at the White House in 2004.*

# CHAPTER 6

# HAMMERIN' HANK
# MR. DECENCY

The first time I really noticed that records in sports mattered was on April 8, 1974, the date that Hank Aaron became baseball's home run king, smashing his 715th career dinger in Atlanta-Fulton County Stadium.

Growing up in Denver, I respected Aaron, a man who approached both sports and life with a level of integrity that stands out as rare and admirable. Those of us who lived in the shadow of the Rocky Mountains didn't have a Major League Baseball team back then. We did have the Denver Bears, a farm team for several organizations including the Yankees and the Expos, depending on the year, a franchise that featured managers like Billy Martin or future pros like Andre Dawson or Tim Raines.

Even though we lived in Denver, the name Babe Ruth was ingrained in the psyche of every man, woman, and child throughout America. Ruth was a hero, an icon, the Sultan of Swat. I didn't know it at that point, but there were many who didn't want his career home run record to be broken and much of their angst was because of Aaron's race. And yet, as I found later in my dealings with Aaron, the player who broke that mark was more than worthy of owning perhaps the most storied record in all of sports.

Worthy as a baseball player, sure. But also as a dignified human being, a man who grew up in Alabama, confronting poverty, then racism, then death threats, and he encountered all that crap even after he achieved so much success. For those who understand the man and his vast accomplishments, Aaron is now revered everywhere he goes. Strangers pick up his checks at restaurants. Organizations go out of their way to fete him.

Why? Because integrity matters. Always has. Always will. We, as in sports fans, as the people who go to games and obsess over statistics and spend our hard-earned paychecks at these stadiums and ballparks, don't want to see the Astros cheating, or people gambling on games, or contract disputes and holdouts, or recruiting violations. We want sports to be as pure as humanly possible. I've found that the athletes who come closest to that ideal also often exhibit the most integrity, honor, and honesty, even if that means sacrificing everything, including victories, all-star nods, and championships. Hank Aaron, more or less.

As my friend Chuck Daly used to say, "The bad weed themselves out. And if you don't get it by now, Jimmy, I can't explain it to you." But I'll try.

As our careers unfolded, Aaron and I never became friends, but we've always been friendly. He was and remains an impeccable human being. He faced ignominies nobody should confront, like those threats on his life, and he handled everything the worst of the world threw at him with dignity and grace. He deserved better.

Like: in 1991, I ran into Aaron and his wife, Billye, at a restaurant in New York. It was one of those tony spots that sits on the Hudson River, with white tablecloths and stuffy waiters clad in tuxedos, their noses pointed high in the air. Classy and dignified—allegedly. I went to dinner with Frann, and her parents. And right there, near the hostess stand, I spied the Aarons. We spoke briefly, just small talk, before the host sat our party right away. I wondered then why we had been seated and the Aarons had not.

The place appeared more than half empty. It was obvious, at least, that there were many open tables. And yet, every time I scanned the restaurant to see where they had sat the Aarons, I couldn't locate them. After about thirty minutes of looking around, I got up. They were *still* sitting on the bench near the hostess stand.

"Are you guys waiting for some folks?" I asked.

"No, we're just waiting for a table," Hank said.

They didn't want to cause a fuss. But their wait lasted even longer, and by then, the restaurant's treatment of the Aarons had really started to bother me. So I went over to the maître d' and started a conversation.

"How long has this restaurant been here?" I asked.

"Long time," he said.

"If Babe Ruth had come in here, would he have gotten a table right away?" I asked.

The maître d' looked at me funny, started laughing, and then said, "Yes, of course." I asked him the same thing about Joe DiMaggio. He *had* eaten there, the man said with a shrug, giving the impression that Joltin' Joe had been seated right away.

How about Joe Namath? "Love him," the man said, noting that Namath ate there regularly. The maître d' had no idea what was coming next.

"Then why are you keeping these two waiting," I said while pointing to the Aarons.

He pulled back, as if offended, and I'll never forget that image, his smug face. He stammered out something about how he planned to seat them.

"Well, they've been waiting for forty-five minutes for a table and you have an empty restaurant," I told him. "What are you doing?"

"Why is this your concern?" he asked.

"Because they're friends of mine," I said. "And they shouldn't be waiting. And, in fact, if it were up to me, they wouldn't wait."

Then, I added, "Nobody ever should be treated like this. And by the way, this man is the legend Hank Aaron."

Finally, the Aarons were seated at a back table. But not one of the empty ones on the water. Incredible. After all of that, the restaurant still showed one of the most incredible athletes ever no respect or even a little decency. I went to the guy and asked him what the problem was and why they weren't up front. He did reseat them.

I couldn't believe it. This wasn't 1960. This wasn't 1975. This was 1991. *This is awful*, I thought, *and so are people like you who think this way*. We all should have left, and we certainly never went back. But Hank Aaron refused to make a scene. He handled that shameful incident the same way he handled all the others—with uncommon poise from a man who had at that point hit more home runs than any baseball player who ever lived. He could be hurt, and he was, but he was not outwardly bitter. He didn't deserve any of it, and to the best of my knowledge, he never lost his cool. I don't know how he kept his composure when confronted by people whose behavior I found deeply disturbing and offensive. I'm sure he had many similar encounters and handled them all with the same grace.

Shortly after the dinner incident, I interviewed Aaron. I had seen a sample of what he had suffered up close, and I wanted to ask him about race and baseball. I knew he had struggled to get jobs in the game he had played so well. At that time, it was well known that the home run king had not been treated properly by the hierarchy at Major League Baseball and that he didn't have a significant job in the game, despite his obvious qualifications.

The interview opened with a voice-over, in which I noted that Aaron held the most glorified record in sports and yet remained somewhat anonymous to the more casual, younger sports fans. "If it had happened to someone like Joe DiMaggio, Mickey Mantle, or some-body, you know, it would have been a financial bonanza for all those players," he said. "For me, it just happened that I broke the record and that was the end of it. And slowly, if you don't bring it up, some people don't talk about it . . ."

I asked Aaron if he felt like a national treasure that the wider sports world had tried to bury alive. "Sometimes they try to do that, and not only me," he responded. "I think they've tried to do that to a lot of ball-players. You could look at Ernie Banks, I mean you could look at Billy Williams, you can look at even Willie Mays."

It was clear what he meant there: African American ballplayers. I followed up, asking if he felt like the baseball hierarchy had intentionally planned to stop minorities from advancing. He said he had heard that. I asked what he meant by his statement. Ownership? Management? The commissioner? *Ownership*, he answered, adding that he wasn't exactly sure.

"How about the commissioner?"

"I can't say that," he said. "I go back to the same thing, I have heard that baseball itself is not interested in trying to bring, to go into Black areas and bring Black people into the game."

The interview gained a lot of traction after it came out. That's because he was right and honest and willing to say what others refused to admit. "If something happened today or tomorrow that I'm no longer employed by the Braves . . . I'm doing something else, that's still not going to stop me from talking," he said at one point. "I'm gonna speak the truth as long as I can, and as long as I'm speaking the truth, I don't see why people should be upset with me."

That's Hank Aaron, a man who was damaged but not broken; proud but still fighting for the recognition and respect he long should have been afforded. He showed us—he *shows* us—why integrity matters. Racial progress has been strikingly slow, but what has been achieved happened through the persistence and determination of countless men and women like Aaron who have been subjected to the horrors of constant racism and discrimination. Until recently, it was too easy to ignore or not pay attention to indignities like those that Aaron suffered, unless you were directly impacted.

But back in '91, my boss at CBS, Ted Shaker, didn't like the interview. I expected a hearty round of congratulations when he called me into his office. He had not indicated there was a problem, but the expression on his face—stern, unsmiling—told a different story. During our twenty-five-minute conversation, he took me off the World Series, just for that one year. He thought I was inciting or leading Aaron to a place I should not have. He considered the segment bad for baseball. I was confused because he oversaw the show and approved putting it on the air. I wasn't aware of any concerns before it aired, and if there were issues, Shaker could have demanded changes. I assumed he had gotten an earful, probably from then-commissioner Fay Vincent.

Shaker assigned me to *The NFL Today* instead. I was upset about being reassigned and told him I didn't think it was right. I asked him why he would punish me for Aaron's words and feelings? They were not only newsworthy, they were his, and they were right. Shaker would not say exactly, although he did indicate that CBS was in its infancy broadcasting MLB games after NBC's long run had ended a year earlier. Shaker didn't like the fact that baseball was upset with him over the segment and MLB felt it was no way to treat a "partner," by putting Aaron on and attacking the institution and more overt racism in the sport. I will always maintain that what Aaron said needed to be heard.

I actually found Aaron honest in that interview without being accusatory. He had been inside the system for so long that he had learned how to deal with it. That didn't mean that he accepted it. He thought it was wrong, and when he had a chance, he said that out loud, hoping to push change. He was proud of the interview. He just wanted his voice to be heard. Almost three decades later, Aaron told me that all the pain and anxiety he suffered never left him. "That was the hardest thing for me," he said. "If all of this [racism] wasn't going on, God knows how many more home runs I would have hit."

Ali once said of Hank Aaron, "He is the only man I idolize more than myself."

I understand why. Aaron would later be awarded the Presidential Medal of Freedom, the highest honor that can be given to a US citizen.

# CHAPTER 7

# YOUR ROSE,

## MY THORN

I didn't think too much of the interview I had just finished with Pete Rose during the World Series in 1999. I was covering the games for NBC, doing my job, asking questions—and this occasion, a celebration of professional baseball's All-Century team before Game 2, marked the first time that Rose had been allowed on a major-league field in ten years. The network had made the request for an interview. Had Rose said no, I would have spoken to the Hall of Fame slugger Hank Aaron instead. That would have been fine. But that's also not what happened. Rose said yes.

After we finished, I walked back to my post near the Yankees' dugout. As I reached the steps, though, I saw three players standing together: Paul O'Neill, Tino Martinez, and Jorge Posada, who said: "What you just did to Pete Rose wasn't right."

I didn't say anything. *Okay*, I thought, *you're entitled to your opinion*. I wasn't made nervous by their comments. I know how it works. When something goes wrong for a player, the others surround him and prop him up. They're going to protect their own.

It wasn't long before the cell phone in my pocket started to vibrate. I pulled it out. It was Frann, who had just changed jobs and relocated to Los Angeles with our German shepherd, Rave. She usually watches my interviews and afterward we talk, as I'm always interested in her opinion. While generally upbeat, she's forever honest.

"I just don't think that one went over very well," she said.

"What didn't you like?"

"He got that big ovation, you kept pushing him, then he got upset with you. It wasn't comfortable to watch."

That was as honest an appraisal as I was going to get.

My cell phone wouldn't stop vibrating. I thought about turning it off. But I didn't in case somebody needed to communicate something important. I really didn't have time to talk. I was working a ball game, and, not just any ball game, but a World Series contest. My job was to look around the dugout and report on conversations and interactions that the camera couldn't capture.

By the fourth inning, the Yankees were up by six runs when O'Neill turned to me and said, "Why don't you quit looking in here?" I decided not to respond to him, not wanting to exacerbate any potential conflict, not sensing what was to come. But then he said, "Why don't you get the fuck out of here?"

A comment like that is so rare that usually you just ignore it. The problem was, he said it loud enough to embarrass me in front of the camera people and his teammates.

"Hey," I said. "I'm just doing my job. Sorry that seems to interfere with your concentration on the game. But I'm going to continue doing my job. You can either be bothered by that or you can get over it."

By the fifth inning, Tommy Roy, our executive producer, said in my ear, "Jim, you haven't commented on anything since the pregame interview. People think we've taken you off the air."

"People?" I asked. "What people?"

"Well, we've gotten a lot of calls."

I wondered what that meant.

"You've got to come on-camera and say something."

"But I have nothing to report," I said.

"I don't care if this is the first time in your career that you're speechless, but you're coming on at the half inning."

So I did a brief report. To this day, I can't remember what I said.

The question—at that moment and in the days since—is, How in the world did I end up there, in the Yankees' dugout, with not only pro baseball players but thousands of sports fans upset with me for the questions I asked Rose? I've never told the whole story from my vantage point before. Here goes . . .

Can the accomplishments of a man be measured against his lack of integrity? Few people have stood closer to that question than I did on that day, October 24, 1999. I thought I was doing an interview. But it was more like standing on the fault line of an earthquake. I had no idea of the outrage and death threats that would follow, nor of the supporters who'd come to my aid.

I was not out to get Rose when I spoke to him that evening. But I also knew the background. Everybody did. When Pete agreed to his own banishment from the game in August of 1989, he claimed it was not an admission of guilt. But let's be clear: it was. He'd signed away his right to have anything to do with Major League Baseball under a mountain of evidence that he'd bet on games. When I say mountain of evidence, I'm imagining the Himalayas. A report assembled by John Dowd and investigators for Major League Baseball documented bets Rose made on fifty-two Reds games while he served as the team's manager in 1987. Only the evidence didn't stop there.

It's hard to stoop much lower in sports. When every major-league player, coach, or manager walks into a clubhouse, he passes a sign over the door. The sign reads: NO GAMBLING BY ORDER OF THE COMMISSIONER. Now, take into account that Rose played in roughly thirty-five hundred regular-season games, as well as twenty-four seasons' worth of exhibition contests, as well as eight years of postseason affairs. Add in the other 786 games he managed over six seasons. Now, think about all the times he walked past those words to get dressed, to take batting practice, to play the game, to get medical treatment, to greet well-wishers, to go home. Simple math says Pete strolled passed that sign at least fifty thousand times.

The sign doesn't say: No steroids.

It doesn't say: No amphetamines.

It doesn't say: No domestic violence.

It doesn't say: No sign stealing.

For Rose to bet on games as he walked past that very sign shows a blatant disregard for the very institution that defined his life. But that's a nice way of putting it. By gambling on baseball, Pete spit on what mattered most to him.

No one ever proved that Rose bet against his own team. People actually came to his defense for this reason. They were then, and remain, in denial. If he bet on his team fifty-two times in a season, what about the other hundred and ten times that he didn't bet on them? Didn't that send a signal to the bookies? Didn't that show that Rose did not think his team would win those games? In essence, by not betting on his team one hundred ten times, he was betting against it. And how do we know that he wasn't manipulating his pitching rotation so that he had a better chance of winning the fifty-two games that he did put money on? Wouldn't that mean that his team would be weaker when it played the other games?

There's only one reason that anyone allowed Rose on the field that night: *money*. Major League Baseball had sold away control of its All-Century team to a credit card company. Mastercard owned the rights to the celebration and set up a ballot enabling fans to choose the team. But Mastercard had never banished Rose.

To anybody who wanted to put on a blindfold and overlook the gambling, Pete was a shoo-in for the Hall. He could boast of more hits than any other player in history. He'd won three World Series rings, three batting titles, a Most Valuable Player award, two Gold Gloves, and a Rookie of the Year award. He'd made seventeen all-star game appearances at five different positions. But it was the style in which he accomplished all this that set him apart. After a walk, Rose ran. When he stole a base, he did it like he did everything else in life—headfirst. Even if you rooted against Pete, you had to respect his Charlie Hustle style and mastery of the game. I know I always did.

But I couldn't ignore the gambling, and so, for me, Rose evolved into the ultimate paradox. The same guy who symbolized the zest and focus with which baseball was meant to be played was also a cheater and a liar. When fans voted Pete onto that All-Century team, Major League Baseball was in a bind. It had no recourse but to welcome Pete to the celebration taking place at the World Series. None of us could have expected what happened next.


Long before that interview, I came to know Pete well. Our relationship started when I was working in Philadelphia, shortly after Rose had signed with the Phillies as a free agent after his decorated stint with the Cincinnati Reds. The contract he signed, for $3.2 million over four years, shows you what happened to money in sports. At the time, it made Rose the highest-paid Major-Leaguer. The Phillies won the Series a year later and made another run in '83. So I must've interviewed Pete more than a hundred times over the years. Not only that. While hosting his own radio show, Pete would call me to comment on a big event I covered. I wouldn't have called us friends. But when Pete and I saw each other in a hotel lobby, we'd chat cordially.

If our interview came off well after the All-Century team celebration, it could have been helpful to him in regard to getting an audience for reinstatement. Pete obviously wanted to return to the game he loved. The Mastercard vote had brought his situation before the public and created an opening for healing. But there could be no healing until he told the truth.

About that. Rose had been obstinate from the outset. When the gambling charges first surfaced, he refused to appear at a hearing with the commissioner at the time, Bart Giamatti, and then he filed a lawsuit alleging that Giamatti had prejudged his case.

After the *Dowd Report* came out, Rose cut a deal with Major League

Baseball. While he made no direct confession of gambling on the game, he did admit to reasons for his banishment. The allegations against Pete naturally attracted a federal investigation. It turned out that Rose had not listed income generated from autograph signings and baseball memorabilia on his tax returns. Those false returns led to a five-month prison sentence. Shortly after his release, the Hall of Fame slammed its door on him. It voted to exclude anyone from induction while they were banished from the game. This had to be particularly painful for Pete. He had conducted every at bat in his career as if the outcome would determine whether or not he'd get to Cooperstown.

Time passed. The landscape changed. Just eight days after Rose had been banished, Commissioner Giamatti suffered a heart attack and died. His replacement, Fay Vincent, was deeply affected by his predecessor's death. Word was that Vincent believed the Rose controversy had contributed to the stress that brought on the attack. Maybe that was true. Maybe it wasn't. Only Vincent can say what he truly felt. Either way, he took a strong stand against Rose. But Pete also knew the score. The deal he'd signed with Major League Baseball gave him the right to apply for reinstatement a year after his banishment. He never did apply while Vincent was commissioner.

Vincent received a no-confidence vote from the team owners in 1992 and was replaced by Bud Selig, who was one of his chief detractors. The shift didn't seem to have much impact on Rose at first. Selig didn't even respond when Pete finally applied for reinstatement in '97. But two years later, in the face of the Mastercard ballot and Rose's unrelenting popularity, there were signs that Bud might be softening. People close to Bud told me that he was considering a meeting with Rose. Nobody implied that Rose would be reinstated—just that the door had cracked back open.

I'd prepared questions for Rose and went over them with Costas in Bob's hotel room. He was handling the play-by-play for the World Series, and he helped me refine a few of my questions, then added some of his own. Bob said, "Everybody has asked Pete about this before. You'll be the greatest reporter ever if he cracks. He's never going to admit to gambling. But you've got to try."

We went over the questions again at a production meeting, believing that Rose would agree to the interview. There wasn't a single person in the NBC sports hierarchy—not President Dick Ebersol, not producer Sam Flood, not Bob or Joe Morgan (for what it's worth, Pete's former teammate on the Reds) in the booth—who voiced any issues or concern.

I lived in Atlanta at the time, about a half hour from the Braves' home at Turner Field, and I was excited as I drove over. The Braves had lost the first game of the Series to the Yankees, but the city remained pumped for the second and the All-Century team celebration added to the thrill.

I wasn't looking for a Perry Mason moment. I never believed that Rose was going to crack and say, "Yes, I bet on baseball. I'm sorry. I'm begging for mercy."

I thought he might say something like: "I've tried to line up a meeting with the commissioner. But it hasn't worked out. There are some things I'd like to say to him that I don't want to mention in public. But after ten years my feelings have changed, and I'd like to let him know that I've made some mistakes."

Saying something along those lines might have opened the door. But only if Pete recognized the moment and rose to the occasion. When Richard Nixon did exactly that after Watergate, we buried him with a twenty-one-gun salute. The man had destroyed our nation's trust in government, and yet, if we didn't get over his transgressions, we did move on. We certainly could do the same for Rose's betting on baseball. And the truth would set him free.

Officials set up a room near the clubhouses to host the greats that night. There were thirty players on the All-Century team. All eighteen living members were in that room. Walking into that space was something special. Willie Mays. Sandy Koufax. Hank Aaron. Brooks Robinson. Bob Gibson. Ernie Banks. Stan Musial. Yogi Berra. I'll never forget when Ted Williams came in. Ted has been called the greatest hitter of all time, but now he was eighty-one years old and frail, and everybody's eyes turned to him at exactly the same moment. Joe DiMaggio had died earlier in the year and you just knew what was going through the minds of everyone in that room: *How much longer will we have Ted?* It's hard to put the feeling into words. But in that moment, more than anything, I felt grateful.

Rose milled around with his agent. I walked over to say hello and ask about the interview. I told Pete it could be good for him. Mike Schmidt, one of Pete's teammates on the Phillies and another member of that All-Century team, stopped by and agreed.

Pete said it would be fine. He didn't ask me to go over any specific questions I planned to ask. I certainly wouldn't have told him. But he did say, "Is this about tonight's celebration or my life?"

I didn't want him to feel blindsided. "Pete," I said, "it's about everything, everything that's gone on in your life"—meaning, including his banishment from baseball and gambling.

"Okay," he responded. "No problem."


The All-Century celebration unfolded differently for me than it did for everyone watching the broadcast at home. Not seeing what's coming across the television screen while you're working can be problematic. A producer can relay information through your earpiece as you're looking into the camera. But occasionally, you're going to be out of sync with the viewer because you're not seeing the same images or hearing the same music or feeling the same ambiance—which is pretty much what happened that day.

I watched the celebration from my reporting post near the Yankees' dugout on the third-base line. A huge black stage had been set up over second base for the introductions. At the back of that stage was a video screen that unspooled the same highlights filling televisions in homes across the country. I could see the highlights on that screen—but not well.

The magical voice of Vin Scully, the Dodgers' announcer, made everyone feel at home when he took the microphone to announce the team. Vin called it "a precious moment, a moment we will not relive in our lifetime." And he was right, though looking back I can only wonder how the crowd would've reacted if Scully had made the exact same introductions ten years later, calling out names like Mark McGwire and Roger Clemens, due to their respective steroid scandals.

As Scully announced legendary pitchers Sandy Koufax, Bob Gibson, and Warren Spahn, I could feel the warmth of the crowd's ovations. But from where I stood, the ceremony seemed somewhat flat to when I later compared it to what the fans had experienced at home, where the broadcast showed footage of the glory days set to a symphony. Anyone who makes movies will tell you it's the background music that evokes emotion. Violins can inject the sadness of lost youth into an image and trumpets can produce a sense of nobility. You don't even realize where the feeling is coming from. The viewers at home could sense that; in the stadium, I could not.

I could understand why people became emotional at home, while sitting comfortably in their living rooms, when they saw Musial introduced. At home, fans saw the sweet swing of DiMaggio, a close-up of the stadium's misty-eyed applause for Williams, and the fresh smile of a young Mickey Mantle. From where I stood, the ceremony seemed more like a recital of names followed by ovations.

When Scully got to Rose, though, the dynamic inside the stadium did change, as the crowd sensed the momentousness of that moment. As soon as Vin said, "He was known as Charlie Hustle . . ." the ovation grew like a wave. I could see Rose lift his cap. The wave kept gaining force, and Pete lifted his cap a second time. I certainly grasped the power there. But I didn't see the moist gratitude in Pete's eyes the way fans did at home.

The ovation given to Rose lasted far longer than the one for Williams, or Babe Ruth, or even Aaron, the hometown hero. The symphony's cymbals crashed after Vin presented Aaron. Patti LaBelle belted the national anthem out of the park.

As I set up to interview Pete near the third-base line, everybody tuned into the game on NBC saw—what else?—a Mastercard commercial. You might remember the campaign. More or less, experiences are priceless.

When we returned from commercial break, television viewers saw Aaron throw out the honorary first pitch. Then Hannah Storm sent the broadcast down to Pete and me.

The interview was scheduled to last approximately two and a half minutes. That was longer than usual. Sometimes, I have only forty-five seconds to get to the heart of an issue. When you're working in that time frame, there are no second chances. You never have a second to lose.

Gray: "Pete, congratulations. That was quite an ovation."

Rose: "Heart-stopping."

Pete had just summarized the ovation in two words. There was no reason to dwell on it. It was time to get to the essence.

Gray: "Pete, let me ask you now. It seems that there is an opening, the American public is very forgiving. Are you willing to show contrition, admit that you bet on baseball and make some sort of apology to that effect?"

Rose: "Not at all, Jim. Not at all. I'm not going to admit to something that didn't happen. I know you're getting tired of hearing me say that. But I appreciate the ovation. I appreciate the American fans voting me on the All-Century team. I'm just a small part of a big deal tonight."

Rose wasn't the first guy to lie to me on camera. He won't be the last. But this felt like such an extraordinary circumstance. Why wouldn't he at least recognize what everybody else knew for fact? He would eventually admit to almost *everything* in his own autobiography, titled *My Prison Without Bars*, which came out in 2004.

I persisted.

Gray: "With the overwhelming evidence that is in that report, why not take that step?"

Rose: "No. This is too much of a festive night to worry about that because I don't know what evidence you're talking about. I mean, show it to me . . ."

Wow. Pete had not only just lied to my face in front of millions of people, but now he was standing there, telling me I didn't know what I was talking about. He was so used to sliding in headfirst and bowling people over, he thought he could do the same with me.

But I'd read every page of the *Dowd Report* when it was first made available and then gone over it before the interview to refresh myself. I was prepared, and I just wasn't going to let him run me over. At the same time, I was there to interview him, not get into a fight.

Gray: "The *Dowd Report*. But we don't want to debate that Pete—"

I was trying to open the door to more comfortable ground right there. But Pete slammed it right back in my face. Before I could finish the sentence, a challenge came out of his mouth.

Rose: "Why not? Why do we want to believe everything that he says?"

Now, he was calling me naïve. As if I were the only guy on the planet who didn't know what was going on. I needed to establish a baseline of truth.

Gray: "You signed a paper acknowledging the ban. Why did you sign it if you didn't agree?"

Rose: "Yeah, but it also says I can apply for reinstatement after one year, if you remember correctly . . . Matter of fact, my statement was: I can't wait for my little girl to be a year old so I can apply for reinstatement. So you forgot to add that clause that was in there."

If only I could find an honest point we could agree on. I continued trying.

Gray: "Well, you've applied for reinstatement in 1997. Have you heard back from Commissioner Selig?"

Rose: "No. And that kind of surprises me. It's only been two years, though. He's got a lot of things on his mind. But I hope to someday."

My producer, Sam Flood, was saying something in my earpiece, but I was so focused on Pete that I didn't hear what Sam said. I couldn't afford to miss a word that came out of Pete's mouth. (Later, Sam told me he was saying, "Try to turn this into something positive." But I don't know what I could've done if I had heard him.)

So I decided to wrap the interview around to where we started. After what Pete had said, I wanted to leave on a point that couldn't be disputed.

Gray: "Pete, it's been ten years since you've been allowed on a field. Obviously the approach that you have taken has not worked. Why not at this point take a different approach?"

Rose: "When you say it hasn't worked, what do you exactly mean?"

Now, he wanted to turn the tables! He was the interrogator, forcing me to defend the most obvious truths.

Gray: "You're not allowed in baseball. You're not allowed to earn a living in the game you love. And you're not allowed to be in the Hall of Fame."

Rose: "I took the approach—that was to apply for reinstatement. I hope that Bud Selig considers that. He gives me an opportunity, I won't need a third chance. All I need is a second chance."

Well, there it was. He finally made his feelings known. He wanted baseball to give him a second chance without having to acknowledge what he'd done wrong in the first place.

Gray: "Pete, those who will hear this tonight will say you have been your own worst enemy and continue to be. How do you respond to that?"

Rose: "In what way are you talking about?"

Gray: "By not acknowledging what seems to be overwhelming evidence."

Rose: "Yeah, I'm surprised you're bombarding me like this. I mean I'm doing an interview with you on a great night, a great occasion, a great ovation. Everybody seems to be in a good mood. And you're bringing up something that happened ten years ago . . ."

Gray: "I bring it up because I think people would like to see you—"

I wanted to say have a chance to be back in baseball and be able to move on with your life. But Pete wouldn't let me finish.

Rose: "This is a prosecutor's brief, not an interview, and I'm very surprised at you. I am, really."

Now, I heard more clearly the words coming through my earpiece. "Get it back to Hannah," Sam said. It's customary to summarize the interview before sending it back to the booth. But there was simply no way to sum this up.

Gray: "Some would be surprised that you didn't take the opportunity. Let's go upstairs to Hannah. Congratulations to you, Pete."

I have to admit, my congratulations came wrapped in a touch of sarcasm. When I threw it back to Hannah, the camera angle on the broadcast shifted and nobody saw Pete and I shake hands. He didn't appear mad or irritated. It would take forty-eight hours for him to see the advantage to be gained in coming out against me.

Right after the interview, he asked matter-of-factly, "Did it all have to be about gambling?"

"Pete," I responded, "you steered it in a direction where it became unavoidable."

"Well, I didn't do it," he said. "I'm not going to tell you I did something I didn't do."

Back in the dugout, after the interview and Posada and O'Neill and the call with my wife, my cell phone continued to vibrate. The fifth inning went by. During a commercial break, I pulled the cell phone out and checked the caller ID. It said: PRIVATE. I picked up.

"Scratchy . . ."

It was Nicholson.

"Jack, how are you?"

"I saw that interview."

"Yeah."

"Just remember a couple of things."

"Okay."

"If you say yes, they can say you said no."

"Excuse me, Jack."

He repeated it slowly. As only Jack Nicholson could, drawing out the syllables. "If you say yes, they can say you said no."

"What are you talking about?" I asked.

"Don't say anything to anybody because they'll twist it into what they want you to say," he said. "If you don't say anything, then they won't be able to say you said anything. Then they're just lying. The other way, it's your word against theirs. If you don't speak with any-body, you can say, *That's not true. I never spoke with anybody.* They won't be able to twist your words."

I was trying to take all this in. Jack wasn't through.

"The second thing I'll tell you is, for the next twenty-five years, no matter where you go, if you're in public, you'll hear about this."

"You really think so?"

"Trust me. You've taken the golf club and put it through the wind-shield," he said, citing a road rage incident from his own past. "You do that once, and they never forget it."

The conversation ended, and I paused to try and grasp the situation. But I couldn't understand it beyond the obvious. Which was: *Whoa, I've really touched a nerve here.*

By the seventh inning, I could see photographers start to fill up the well next to me. Their cameras were no longer pointed at the dugout. They were aimed at me—and they were snapping away.

My cell phone kept vibrating. I pulled it out during a break and checked the caller ID. A Cleveland number. I don't know many people there, and so I instantly figured out who it was: Don King, the fight promoter. I'd done interviews at his events since the '80s. I picked up.

"Is this Jim Gray?"

"Yes, Don. How are you? I'm doing the game."

"I know you're doing the game. I'm watching the game."

"What do you need?"

"Oh, no, no, no," he said. "I don't need anything. *You're* gonna need people. Because you're going to be treated poorly for a long time, and you better get used to it."

"In what way?" I asked.

"Brother, I can handle the questions," he said. "I don't know if you know if the others can."

"Was it *that* bad?" I asked.

"You've been a lot worse on me," he said, unleashing that trademark cackle.

I wasn't sure how to take that. I knew it wasn't good—and it was definitely a warning. He was chuckling. But it wasn't funny.


One of the moments nearly every older baseball fan remembers about Rose is when he tried to win an all-star game in 1970 by barreling over catcher Ray Fosse of the Indians during a play at home plate. Rose did smash through Fosse, and he did win the game. In the process, though, he separated Fosse's right shoulder and ruined his career.

It was completely in character for Rose to justify the collision. *That's how baseball is meant to be played.* But I never bought that. It was an exhibition, after all, and I can't remember someone getting injured like that at an all-star affair before or since. Pete took some heat at the time, but it ended up just another chapter in Charlie Hustle lore.

Here's the twist. Suddenly, *I* was being made out to look like the Pete Rose who'd bowled over Ray Fosse. As if I were a bully with an agenda to mow Pete down. The strangest part: my comments after the interview sounded eerily similar to what Pete said after that game. *I was simply doing my job the way it's supposed to be done.*

Some people thought that I had succeeded in doing for Pete what he never could've done for himself. I had transformed him into a sympathetic figure.

The NBC switchboard went haywire because affiliates around the country had splashed graphics on the screen directing angry callers to New York. The network's internet server had crashed. Ed Markey, NBC's sports publicity chief, hustled down to meet me as I left the field. "We'll set up a teleconference tomorrow," he told the press that stood between me and my car.

On the way home, I tuned the radio to the sports-talk shows. That my interview had overshadowed the game became obvious immediately. I'm thinking, *The postgame show of the World Series is about* me?

I flipped toward a local station that I'd helped out for a couple of years, the first all-sports station in Atlanta, still in its infancy. I'd occasionally call in to report from big events like the Masters for free. That night, though, the host was rabid. I can't recite his diatribe word for word. But I can give you the drift: "We've had a hands-off policy on Jim Gray even though a lot of us don't like him. The reason for this policy is because he calls us from the big events. But after this debacle, I guess we don't have to keep our hands off anymore. I know I'm not going to."

A guy like that could be expected to kick a man when he's down— and to wear a big boot. Look, I understand how it works. Callers have every right to express their opinions. But this felt more threatening, more menacing. This was: *If I ever see Jim Gray in a bar . . .*

That caught my attention. Amid all the insane calls came the commentary of a columnist at the *Atlanta Constitution*—Prentis Rogers, a writer I always found fair and measured. I didn't always agree with his opinions, but I respected them. When I heard Prentis question the way the interview came off, it forced me to calmly replay everything that had happened. First, the call from my wife. Then, the call from Jack. Then, Don King. Then, the cameras in my face. And now, people were threatening to beat the crap out of me over the radio.

I know that some part of me wanted to think: *Ah, this will blow over in a day.* But I also was mindful of the venom. I know that because when I stopped for a cheeseburger at Atlanta institution The Varsity on the way home, I remember my head swiveling around, as if to check if the coast were clear. I wanted to make sure there weren't any angry people who'd seen the game at a bar and would be out to get me.

Fortunately, the restaurant was almost empty. *This will definitely blow over*, I both thought and hoped.

I had no trouble going to sleep that night.


I woke up figuring the incident had passed. I would soon realize I had never made a worse assessment in my life.

People continued to call my home to check on me, as if I'd been in some kind of accident. As Gavin Maloof says, "Don't worry about your enemies bringing you bad news, your friends will do just fine." One wondered if he needed to send security for my protection. I laughed it off, at least until I checked my NBC voice mail. It was loaded with two things: threatening messages or interview requests.

One of my producers in the truck, Feibischoff, called to check in and offer support. Everybody loved Eddie. "Boy, that was some kind of interview," he said. "That took a lot of guts." But he didn't say if it was good or bad—and I didn't ask. If I'm being honest, I didn't ask because I didn't want to hear a negative response. It felt better to assume his comments were positive.

I was supposed to fly to New York that morning. But with my phone ringing off the hook, I stayed home to do a conference call with the press. Network czar Dick Ebersol phoned beforehand. Dick had put out every kind of fire imaginable in broadcasting over the years, and he could sense how this one had begun to spread out of control.

Yankees coach Don Zimmer had been quoted in the *New York Post* calling me a scumbag. . . . among other things. Joe Torre, the team's manager, intimated that I had lost sight of the word *respect*. One of Torre's players, Jim Leyritz, who grew up rooting for Rose in Cincinnati, added that some action needed to be taken against me because of what I'd done to the integrity of the game. "If he is smart," Leyritz warned, "he will avoid some of us who are Pete Rose fans." That was *exactly* the type of veiled threat that encouraged others to pile on.

Ebersol wanted to stamp out the anger among players and fans as quickly as possible. He was staring at a complicated puzzle. On the one hand, he wanted to protect me along with the network's journalistic standards. On the other, he had to respond to the fury and anger of our sponsor—a certain credit card company. "Jim," I remember him telling me before the telephone press conference started, "don't inflame this any further."

The ironies were really beginning to bloom. This had started with me wondering if Rose would make an apology so he could possibly ease his way back into baseball. Suddenly I was the one being asked to apologize for offering him the chance.

The situation became more ridiculous by the minute. Not only was I being asked to say that I was sorry, but I was being asked to apologize by Mastercard. Oh, the irony, the corporation that charges customers 19 percent interest rates had bought off the integrity of the game!

I'm always aware and respectful of our sponsors. They're the ones that pay the freight so that I can go to work and the fans can watch the games. I get it, and I appreciate it. But that doesn't mean they can make me look away from or distort the truth. The more I thought about it, the more incensed I became.

I didn't back down during that press teleconference, with dozens of writers on the line. Nor did I apologize to Pete, or for my questions.

Shortly afterward, I got a call from Ebersol. I'll never forget his reaction. "That," he said, "wasn't exactly what I had in mind."

I was fortunate to be working for Dick. He showed himself to be the model of how a boss should handle a situation like that. He had to steer the network through this difficult situation, but he also did everything he could to protect me—and that includes trying to shield me from myself.

"Jim," he said. "Have you seen the interview on tape?"

"No."

"I want you to look at it," he said. "It's important for you to see the interview the way the fans saw it, not the way you remember it. You've got to be concerned with the fans. You don't want this getting out of control. Let's get together tomorrow morning and watch it together."

Game 3 of the Series was scheduled for the following night. I flew to New York unaware that police were looking into death threats, even though I was later told I had continued to receive them.

I could see Ebersol's points when we reviewed the tape. The emotion of the ceremony came through in the replay with a force I hadn't felt in that stadium, in the present. I could understand how some viewers might be upset by the intrusion of gambling into such a special ceremony. They had just seen the best in baseball, and I had brought up the worst. I also recognized how fans might have felt the interview had gone on too long. But I didn't get it when Dick brought up the idea of a public apology. I didn't think it was wrong to ask Pete those questions.

"The apology wouldn't be to Pete Rose," Dick said. "It wouldn't be for the line of questioning. It would be to the fans that were offended, and it would be about the timing of the interview. The quicker you apologize, the quicker we can all move on."

I wasn't happy about that. I didn't feel comfortable knowing that it would seem like we were bowing to the credit card company. If I had it my way, I wouldn't have done anything. But I knew Dick had my best interests at heart. The first thing he'd done was send a message throughout the company that I had his full support, and that any problems were external. Privately, he let me know how much he valued my work. And you can imagine how I felt after he told the *New York Times*, the *Washington Post*, *USA Today*, and others something along the lines of: "Jim Gray is the best TV sports reporter of his generation—perhaps (of) all time." I saw no choice but to follow his approach.

Much time went into crafting the statement. I agreed to recite it on-air before the game started.

When our car pulled up to Yankee Stadium, three beefy guys came to greet me. A former FBI agent, a plainclothes policeman, and a uniformed cop walked me into the stadium. They never left my side. I don't want this to sound overdramatic, like I needed a bulletproof vest and riot gear. But wackos are wackos, and you just don't know if someone would take a swing, or do something even more crazy.

I had another security guard with me—the most powerful guy in television sports. Ebersol had learned from the man who basically created the medium in the '60s at ABC—Roone Arledge. Over time, Dick became the Roone of his day. Not only was he in charge of sports and Olympic coverage for NBC, but he oversaw *Saturday Night Live* and the *Midnight Special*. He was looked upon as a champion, which is why it was so surprising to see him sitting down next to me on some milk cartons near the television trucks outside of Yankee Stadium.

"The guys say you're a loner," he said.

I didn't think I was, and I told him I didn't quite understand what he was getting at.

"You're not going to be alone anymore," he said.

Dick stayed at my shoulder as we walked on the field, hours before the first pitch. As we headed to my usual spot by the dugout, he encouraged me to go about my job. But that would be impossible with the horde of press surrounding us and wanting to interview me. Dick had asked me not to speak to the media before the game. The apology would be my only statement. So he answered the questions, deftly responding without saying sorry or offending.

I've got to admit it, though: sitting in that dugout without being able to respond while cameras snapped away ranks among the most uncomfortable moments of my life. I didn't know where to look, or how to look. As I peered out from the dugout at the reporters, all I could think was, *Why doesn't anybody follow up?*

Keith Olbermann came over, sat next to me, and threw himself into my defense. I'll always be grateful. By doing so, he made it possible for other people to put forth a different point of view.

Batting practice ended and the press scattered. I got ready to head to the Yankees' clubhouse for the pregame meeting. Our crew generally met with the manager of each team in his office before the game, so he could review the last one and offer some insight into the one upcoming.

Word soon arrived from Rick Cerrone, the Yankees' public relations director. I wasn't welcome at the pregame meeting in Torre's office.

As if everything already wasn't enough, now I was even more upset. Torre won't let me in his office? Torre says I've lost sight of the word *respect*? What does Torre respect? A guy who betrayed the game and then lied about it? A convicted felon?

But there was no time for that. All I could think was, *I can't do my job*. I looked over to Ebersol.

"What do we do?"

"We're going to let everything slide today," he said. "Whatever happens today, we'll correct for tomorrow. Let's tamp this down and get tonight behind us."

We went back to the NBC trailer. Feibischoff was there. "You have to hear this," I told him, playing the messages on my voice mail. I needed to see someone else's reaction.

A computerized voice said something like: "Your mailbox is full. You have two-hundred fifty new voice-mail messages."

I played a few. People were screaming at me. Calling me a piece of shit. Threatening me. With Eddie, I could laugh. Alone, they were scary.

All I had to do was tap the digits 337 and the entire bunch of messages would be deleted. I tapped 337 and called my voice mail to check that they were gone. The computerized voice said:

"You have no new messages."

A few minutes later, I called my voice mail and heard: "Your mailbox is full . . ."

This had to be stopped.

The apology took place in an auxiliary room near the clubhouses, as if I had been banished to a baseball dungeon. The security detail waited outside. The producers sat in the truck. I was alone with the camera crew. I gave a report about the availability of a Yankee infielder, Luis Sojo, who was returning from the funeral of his father in Venezuela. Afterward, Costas said, "All right, Jim, just about everyone watching tonight saw, or has heard, about your interview with Pete Rose following the All-Century team celebration on Sunday night in Atlanta. You had something you wanted to say about that."

I rarely memorize or read anything over the air. But I had done that with the apology. I didn't want to say a wrong word. "Yes, Bob, after reviewing the videotape I can understand the reaction of many baseball fans. I thought that it was important to ask Pete if this was the right moment for him to make an apology. If in doing so the interview went on too long, and took out some of the joy of the occasion, then I want to say to baseball fans everywhere that I am very sorry about this."

It's hard to know whether my reading came across as heartfelt. You can't be what you're not—and I'm not a phony. It had to appear somewhat orchestrated because it was memorized. When I watch it now, it doesn't seem too sincere. I just wanted to go back to doing my job. I remember coming out of that room and wondering if that would be the end of it.

The security guys didn't want me wandering around because of the threats. I felt trapped. I stayed in my spot by the dugout and waited to do the postgame interview. The game wrote me the perfect scenario.

Yankees outfielder Chad Curtis hit a walk-off homer in the tenth inning to put New York up three games to none. Curtis had hit only five home runs during the entire regular season. On this one night, he'd smashed two, and his game winner fulfilled the dream of every kid who'd ever swung a bat. The hometown crowd went crazy as Chad's teammates mobbed him at home plate.

Chad made his way over to me, shook my hand, stood by my side, and waited for a minute during replays. Elation filled the air.

When we went on live, I congratulated him and asked him the most neutral question that could possibly have left my lips. In fact, I didn't even ask a question. "Chad, tell us about that pitch . . ."

"I can't do it," he said. "As a team, we kind of decided because of what happened with Pete, we're not gonna talk out here on the field."

He had waited by my side for a minute to say this on the air—simply to embarrass me. Then he added: "I do want to say it was for you, though, Grandma, thanks." He turned to walk off.

"Chad," I asked, "you don't want to talk about the home run?"

He was gone.

What could I do in that situation? "All right, Bob," I said. "Back up-stairs to you."

I stood there in disbelief. A ballplayer dreams his whole life of hitting a home run to win a World Series game. He achieves his dream. Is his first thought afterward really going to be: "*Screw Jim Gray*!?!?"

Now, my ability to do my job was being threatened in front of the world. One of my duties was to moderate the presentation of the World Series trophy and conduct interviews during the victory celebration. How could I do that if the Yankees wouldn't talk to me?

I had to know if this was careening out of control. I went through a hallway to look for Ebersol. He was pissed. If the Yankees didn't want to talk to me, why didn't they let us know? Why did they have to blind-side us? Ebersol and Bud Selig are good friends. But Dick wasn't holding back when he talked to the commissioner.

"We will not present this trophy to the World Series winner on the air if Jim is treated like that tomorrow night," Dick said. "We will fade to black, show cartoons, and you can present the trophy during spring training." I'll never forget the stunned look on Selig's face.

Bud threw out a compromise. "How about Hannah?"

"I decide the pitching rotation on my team, Bud, and it's Jim who'll be presenting the trophy," Dick responded.

Bud turned around and saw me. "Not right now, Jim," he said, trying to make the conversation private.

"No," Dick said. "This is about him, and he can hear it."

I really have to hand it to Ebersol. He could've taken the easy way out. He didn't have to fight the Yankees. He didn't have to fight Major League Baseball. Didn't have to fight Mastercard. Didn't have to fight the public. He didn't even have to fire me to satisfy my detractors. All he had to do was take me off the World Series. Or let Hannah do the interviews. He could've said, "We're trying to present the World Series and unfortunately Jim Gray has become a distraction." Nobody would've blamed him. But he stuck his neck out, and he stuck with me.

I will never forget that.


I headed back to the hotel with Costas. The security guys trailed behind us, as Bob tried to lift my spirits. But at the same time he seemed to be disappointed in himself for not coming to my defense at some point in the broadcast.

As Costas and I arrived at our hotel, we saw George Steinbrenner, the Yankees' owner, step out of his car. He kept an apartment at the same hotel. Bob and I waved, then headed inside. A security guard followed me into the elevator and stationed himself in a seat outside my room.

I changed my clothes and got ready for bed. At about one thirty in the morning, I heard a knock on my door. I thought it was the security guard. Maybe he needed to use the restroom or something. I opened the door.

It was Steinbrenner.

"Jim, can I come in?"

"Sure."

Still in his suit and tie, not a hair out of place, he took a few steps inside.

I stood there in my shorts, stunned.

"I want you to know a few things," George said. "First of all, I didn't think that interview was that bad. Second, what happened tonight at the stadium doesn't represent the way the New York Yankees organization feels about you. It doesn't represent my feelings. You are always welcome at Yankee Stadium. And don't worry about that player and what he said tonight. He won't be around here much longer."

He continued. "If we are fortunate enough to win this series—and I'm very cautious about counting on anything before it happens—there will not be a single Yankee who will act inappropriately during the trophy presentation. Every New York Yankee from Joe Torre on down will treat you with respect and courtesy. You have my word. You've done a great job for a long time. I will stand beside you for the entire ceremony."

He held out his hand and we shook. You find out a lot about people in situations like that. You find out what they are beneath the images presented by the media. George was, of course, a polarizing figure, a man forever known as the Boss—and the nickname cut both ways. He defended traditional values. Players on his team couldn't wear long hair or grow beards. One of his favorite expressions was, "If you don't have a hernia, you're not pulling your fair share." But he also became a caricature, firing twenty managers in his first twenty-three years as owner and once posing as Napoleon on the cover of *Sports Illustrated*. Those loyal to him will point to the seven World Series championships secured during his tenure. His detractors bristle that he did little more than buy them by luring free agents with outrageous salaries.

That night, when he stuck out his hand, George Steinbrenner was simply a man who could be trusted. I'll never forget that, either.


I can't say everything changed at that moment. Jimmy Carter, the former president of the United States, would come out in support of Rose, as did a man I deeply admired, Congressman John Lewis, a leader of the civil rights movement. The threats didn't stop. A week after the Series ended, I called in to Jackie, the NBC switchboard operator in New York. In her voice, I heard concern. "Oh, Mr. Gray. I'm so glad to hear you're all right." Not many people ever became aware of the threats that poured into the mailbags at NBC for weeks, or the invective flooding my voice mail or the letters that even found their way to my home. But anyone who encountered me on the street for a long time afterward couldn't miss the German shepherd by my side.

Still, after Steinbrenner shook my hand, I started to feel the counterbalance of support. "I tip my hat to Jim Gray," said John Dowd, who headed the investigation. "The most courageous and honest interview that was ever done in sports." Fay Vincent, the former commissioner, stood up for me as well. "Jim Gray had more guts and impenetrable integrity," he said. "He is to be credited and applauded for his questions and wanting honest responses from Rose. Unfortunately, Rose continues not to tell the truth." Don Sutton, the Hall of Fame pitcher broadcasting in Atlanta, came out for me loud and clear. Aaron, Johnny Bench, and Cal Ripken Jr. all pulled me aside privately to offer their support. Sandy Koufax called. Joe Morgan worked tirelessly behind the scenes. Joe hated the whole thing. He didn't want to be in a public spat with his former teammate or pitted against his NBC partner. So he never once presented a public opinion. But he spoke with writers and baseball officials in the background. He knew Pete was lying, and that I'd been dragged into Pete's cesspool. He told people that I shouldn't be vilified.

After the Yankees won Game 4, sweeping the series, Steinbrenner *did* stand at my side through the trophy presentation. The platform was cordoned off and Zimmer, O'Neill, Curtis, and a few others who'd attacked me were nowhere in sight.

Torre got past his negative feelings and remained cordial. At the end of the interview, he said, "Thanks, Jimmy," as if we were old friends. Mariano Rivera, the Most Valuable Player, was humble. Derek Jeter was classy. Bernie Williams and David Cone spoke articulately about how difficult the year had been for the Yankees and how much the triumph meant.

Champagne sprayed when I stepped off the podium. A player walked over to me. It was Orlando Hernández, the pitcher from Cuba known as El Duque.

Orlando couldn't speak English very well. He had been one of the great pitchers on his native island for years. After his half brother, Liván, defected in 1995 and joined the Florida Marlins, El Duque was detained by state security agents and interrogated. Soon after that, he was banned from playing baseball in Cuba.

Liván helped pitch the Florida Marlins to a World Series victory in '97. I had worked those games, and somehow El Duque had seen them in Cuba. A few months later, on the day after Christmas, El Duque got on a boat with a few others and risked his life by speeding out to sea toward freedom. He was rescued by the US Coast Guard off Bahamian waters.

"Very brave," El Duque said to me.

"Thank you," I said. "But why?"

The interpreter with him translated his words. "Because if you speak up in my country and hold principle, you are persecuted. You are very brave. I really admire you."

"Muchas gracias," I said.

He tapped on his heart. "Mi amigo."

I can still hear those words in my head, knowing they were spoken by a guy once held back by a regime. It still touches me now.

The man who understood me the most was a man who knew what free speech meant.

Several weeks after the interview Jack Nicholson had his famous neighbor reach out. Brando—Marlon Brando!—had been reading all the negative articles about the interview. He wasn't a big sports fan, and he asked Jack why there had been so much fuss, and if he knew me. Jack said he did know me and suggested that Brando call.

His message made me almost drop my phone. "This is Marlon Brando, please give me a call, I want to talk to you." I heard and ignored it, thinking it was one of my friends playing a joke. Why would Don Corleone, *The Godfather* himself, want to talk to me? A few weeks later I was playing golf with Jack and he asked me how my conversation went with Marlon. I told him I thought it was a prank. "Nobody doesn't call Marlon back, you better not let another day go by," Jack warned.

So I called him that evening, apologizing and explaining I didn't believe it was actually him. Mr. Brando laughed, put me at ease, and said to me that he didn't understand why this Rose interview hit such a nerve. This was pre-internet, so he read several newspapers a day. "May I offer you some advice?" he asked. Of course. "I have come to the point in my life where everything that they say about me is true. I hope you can get there."

I asked him what exactly he meant by that. "When somebody says something about me on radio or TV, or when they write articles in the papers or tabloids, I don't combat it, and I don't try to correct it. I give no credence to any of it. I just let it become their reality. I know it's not true, but that becomes the image that is created. It really doesn't matter what a bunch of people I don't know think of me. My family and my true friends know who I am."

I told him that I wasn't in that space mentally. That all this criticism had indeed stung. "Eventually you will get there," he said. I thanked him for calling. It was the only time we ever spoke. Twenty years later, I must say, he was right. Everyone has opinions, and they can express them and think whatever they want. That doesn't mean they are right. Jack always liked to remind me of that fact, laughing and echoing his famous neighbor. "Just let them have their say," he'd remind me. "You're better off just letting it go."

Jack was also right on the night of the interview. I have heard about the Rose interview for decades; if not every day, then certainly every week. I hear from strangers who didn't like the tack I took and others who found it brave; I hear from people who noticed that Rose did admit to almost everything when his book came out and others who tell me he owes me an apology; I hear from a lot of folks who live in Ohio or Kentucky, places that love Rose more than anywhere else. Sometimes, they're still upset. They're usually not mean, or nasty, but they'll let me know. *Yeah, we love Pete.*

Rose wrote in his book that he had no reason to apologize to me, that to admit to gambling so publicly—and without a book to sell—wouldn't have done him any good. Which is fine, I suppose, except that had he actually admitted his wrongdoing, he might have been back in baseball, in some capacity—and saved me a lot of grief.

I saw Rose a few years back at a Mayweather fight in Las Vegas, while walking into the arena with Al Bernstein, my broadcast partner at Showtime. Al considered Rose a friend and seemed worried about our random encounter. I thought, *Oh, shit*. I planned to stand there and not say anything. But Pete reached out and shook my hand. "You don't have to be afraid of me," he said. "I'm not going to bite you."

"Perhaps the other way around," I countered.

He laughed, and we made small talk and, believe it or not, Mike Tyson walked right up in the middle of the conversation. He gave me a big hug right in front of Rose. Now, Tyson and Bernstein have some issues that date back years, so we all found ourselves in the most uncomfortable of moments, four people who have had their run-ins, shaking hands, saying hello. Talk about awkward.

The very next day I was walking with Frann inside Caesars Palace Forum Shops when I bumped into Pete again.

"Hey, Jim," he said. "What's your take on the fight?"

I didn't see him until I had turned around. Rose! Again! "Come on over. Let's talk about the fight."

So I did. And we did. It bothered me still that he had not apologized for the lies he told and for the damage that he had inflicted upon my life. But I didn't say anything, and we both acted as if nothing had taken place all those years ago. It was "a good fight" and "I enjoyed it" and all that.

Fast forward to 2019. Cancer society fund raiser. Los Angeles. They're honoring Mike Tyson, and I've been asked to introduce the famous heavyweight. I had no idea they were also honoring Rose until that day. Organizers sat him at a different table, but he did stop by while Tyson and I were chatting with the comedian Eddie Murphy. We shook hands.

"You do a great job," he said. "You really do a great job."

"Pete, you don't mean that," I responded. "I know you don't mean that."

"I really do. You're fantastic at what you do."

Stunned, I thanked him.

Then Tyson stood up.

"Mike, who do you think would have won that fight?" Rose asked. "Me or Jim."

"For sure, Jim," my buddy Tyson said.

Pete continues to resurface, looking for a crack that will allow the man known as Charlie Hustle to slide into the Hall of Fame. In 2020, when the Houston Astros were revealed as the latest modern-day sports cheaters, there came Pete, saying that if baseball's most-elaborate sign stealers hadn't been banned, then he shouldn't continue to be, either. He again petitioned baseball for reinstatement. What Pete fails to see is that just because what the Astros did was wrong doesn't make his transgressions right. His petition to participate in game activities should not be granted. But I'm inclined to agree with those who want to let the Hall of Fame voters decide Rose's fate, should Major League Baseball come to that decision. They can choose if he's worthy, if his accomplishments outweigh his lack of integrity. His achievements are his achievements. What he did should not be erased from the record. The question is: Should he be celebrated?

Look, this happened twenty-plus years ago. But it's impossible to forget. Time marches on. We've both aged. But what Pete did was damaging to me, and the ramifications of that moment have reverberated ever since. Those were his mistakes I had to live with. I could have handled it better, no doubt. But I endured the pummeling and became the villain, because of this guy's lies and deceit and deception. I was never against Pete. I was doing my job while offering him an opportunity. I had a hard time forgiving him, but I have.

# CHAPTER 8

# STEROIDS

## FROM BEN TO MARION,

## THE BREAKING OF BONDS

The Steroid Era almost certainly started long before we knew it, back when the first soon-to-be-doped athlete or soon-to-push-doping coach or adviser looked around at his or her sport, considered the rules in play, and decided to attempt to find a way around them. We'd be naïve to think otherwise. The testers of drug cheats have always been—*will* always be—playing catch-up. The cheaters will always be looking for new and improved ways to circumvent the standards of any given sport. Such is life, unfortunately.

For too long, sports fans watched as leagues and commissions and sanctioning bodies looked away. They may not have encouraged doping, but they didn't do a whole lot to discourage it, either. Some argued that everybody sought an edge, lumping steroids and their ilk with other more acceptable performance enhancements. When those same leagues did design tests or prevention systems, they often, almost always, fell behind the science deployed by cheaters. So even when they wanted to stop rising drug use, when it became apparent just how many elite athletes were not clean, they often failed to.

Look at the East Germans, the Soviet Union, and China. Doping has been going on forever, unabated, to the point where Olympians from Russia were banned from the Winter Games in 2018 (although some competed under the Olympic Athletes from Russia banner), and the next two Olympics and the World Cup in Qatar. Their cheating was state sponsored, government sponsored. Win at all costs. I once read a survey known as Goldman's dilemma, where a physician named Robert Goldman asked elite athletes whether they would be so tempted to use a drug that would guarantee them overwhelming success in their chosen sport, but—the catch!—they would also be dead within five years. About half the athletes said they would happily take the remedy. Subsequent studies found lower rates and researchers questioned the dilemma's results, but still. Those numbers, as they relate to doping, are significant.

More recently, in 2018, the US Anti-Doping Agency surveyed Olympians, asking similar questions to those posed by Dr. Goldman. Sixty-five percent of 886 athletes who responded said they felt pressured to win medals. Sixty-one percent agreed that "when I am failing people are less interested in me." But only 9 percent said they would use performance-enhancing drugs in any of the scenarios, which still seems significant.

You're talking about young, elite athletes who don't have a ton of perspective, who desperately want to win, who are defined by their chosen sport. Of course they're still figuring out ways to beat the system. Of course, the system will always be behind.

Because what we've also seen, what I've witnessed up close in my career, is that most, if not all, drug cheats get caught eventually. So let's take a little trip through the Steroid Era, based on my interactions with Ben Johnson, Barry Bonds, and Marion Jones.


For the 1988 Olympics in South Korea, NBC executives hired a group of ambitious journalists and tasked five of us with covering the games.

My boss, Mike Weisman, called us the Seoul Searchers, and he sent us off to find the best, most interesting, most important news stories we could land.

Doping, as noted earlier, had been going on forever. But at the Seoul Olympics, the practice would be highlighted and scrutinized in ways it had never been examined before. There had been rumors in the past of other sprinters and other Olympians who might be taking drugs to enhance their respective performances. But this scandal centered around the world's fastest man—and I found myself, again, right in the middle of it.

I saw the Canadian sprinter Ben Johnson win the 100 meters in that Olympics. I saw him beat Carl Lewis, one of the greatest sprinters ever. Johnson darted down the track so fast that he recorded a time of 9.79 seconds, besting his own world record of 9.83 seconds, which he had registered at the world championships the previous year.

I also saw what happened next. I went to leave the stadium and head back to the athletes' village, and I saw Johnson and his team scampering through the hallways in the bowels of the stadium. Three officials trailed him. I couldn't be certain anything was wrong, but he didn't seem overtaken with joy—even though he had just beaten *Carl Lewis* and won the race that conveys mythical status as the fastest man on the planet.

Security was tight in Korea, but it wasn't as strict back then, all those years before 9/11. While we did see machine guns in Seoul, it was pretty easy to maneuver around the stadiums with my NBC credential. Much easier than it is now.

Johnson wasn't going to leave until he got his gold medal. But the officials weren't going to allow the ceremony until he had taken the drug test. A few minutes later, I saw Johnson walk back into the locker room. He stayed in there close to a half hour. He couldn't or wouldn't pee. He consumed liquids, including water and, believe it or not, beer, in order to give a sample. He did submit to a drug test, and we know that . . . because he failed it.

I went back to my post at the athletes' village, then on to my hotel, the Lotte Jamsil. Soon after, out of nowhere, in the middle of the night, Weisman called me.

"Jim, get out of bed right now," he said. "I want you to go to the airport. I have a tip that Ben Johnson is leaving Seoul and going back to Canada. I'm sending you with a camera crew, and I want you to try and find him."

I asked him if this had happened because of steroids, and he said he didn't know because the tipster wouldn't say. He would only tell him to get to the airport immediately and camp out by the next flight to Canada or New York. He said the information came from a consultant to NBC, so I immediately assumed we had received the tip from Alex Gilady, a member of the IOC. I knew it had to have come from someone in that type of position, and I figured the whole episode stemmed from a failed test. Weisman was putting all his trust in me to find Johnson. I felt tremendous pressure to produce, as this was my first network assignment. It was that kind of opportunity for me to show Weisman his trust was warranted.

We sped there immediately. I noticed other reporters and other crews, so I knew we weren't alone. But, as luck would have it, we happened to set up in the right place, the camera pointed at the perfect angle. We were the first ones to catch the now-disgraced sprinter as he made his walk of shame into the terminal to catch a flight to New York City, before connecting to his home in Canada. We landed right at the front, before the crush of media descended. Johnson didn't stop for an interview, but the footage was compelling. He kept walking while I asked him if the IOC had taken back his medal due to a failed drug test, and he glanced at me and gave a half nod, without saying anything. I took that as a yes. I called Weisman and told him, "We got it." When we broke the story, that moment of silent shame reverberated around the world.

We won an Emmy for journalism for that segment, my first. Weisman said the whole world followed our lead and our reporting.

Johnson was disqualified. Lewis won the gold by default, because he didn't cheat, and his time of 9.92 seconds would eventually become the new official world record—the clean version. That victory marked

Lewis's second-straight gold medal triumph in the most famous race in track and field. He had won but sports had lost.

The whole episode felt horrible. It brought shame to the Olympics, to the host country, to Canada and, of course, to Johnson. I was sad for the institution of track and field—and sad for the wider world of sports. This was the 100-meter dash, the race to become the fastest man in the world, an event steeped in history and held in the highest of esteem. It mattered.

If the winner of such a spectacle had doped, then it begged a whole round of other questions. Who else had? Did these nefarious practices extend to the women's events? That seemed likely. To the 200 meters? More probable than not. To other sports? Almost certainly. We could wonder more than ever at that point whether the greatest athletic exploits we've seen resulted from which trainers could find the best juice, or mix the right chemicals. The Ben Johnson saga cast the very core of sports into question and kicked off an era of disgrace that lasted for years and years. That, on some level, is ongoing.

Right away, I knew the lens with which we viewed our favorite games had changed. What everyone had suspected was now reality, out there, in public, right in front of our faces. We shouldn't have been surprised. But maybe we were, a little. Maybe we held out hope that sports could be played with integrity and dignity by all. That's hopelessly naïve, of course. What we learned from Ben Johnson is that someone else, somewhere else, was doing something else to try and circumvent one rule or another. That's the safest bet in sports.

Ben Johnson wasn't the first drug cheat caught by Olympic testers. But he was the first who had won the 100 meters and become a celebrity and wowed sports fans across the world. That day marked when every elite athlete started to fall under a growing cloud of suspicion. It became fair to wonder: What's real? And what's not?

My flare-up with the baseball legend Barry Bonds took place a few years after those Olympics. I was working for CBS back then, and living in Atlanta, and my bosses assigned me to cover the National League Championship Series, featuring the Atlanta Braves against the Pittsburgh Pirates. The Braves would advance to the World Series after winning in seven games.

Bonds and I had quite the go-around that year. The slugger had managed one hit in something like his last eleven at bats, and the producers wanted me to talk to him about that stretch of futility specifically. We conducted the interview before a game in the middle of the series and when I asked him about his slump, he said, "What slump?" Then he got upset and walked away.

Bonds returned about forty-five seconds later, and he was upset, pointing his finger at me. "Jim Gray, if you put that on the air, I'm going to kick your ass," he said.

How does anyone respond to that? I remained calm, hoping he would cool down.

Right away, my producers asked me to inquire if Bonds would like to do the interview again, putting together a more civil version. I went back into the clubhouse and approached him. "We can do this better," I said.

"OK, fine," he said. "You're right. We can do it again."

Bonds told me to meet him in the dugout after batting practice. So I did. We set up there, near the far end, while BP unfolded. Bonds ran out to hit, took his cuts, hung out in the field, and came back. He didn't say a word to me the whole time. We're now thirty-five, maybe forty minutes from the first pitch being delivered. I was sitting on the bench in the dugout when he passed.

"Barry," I said, "are you going to do this?"

"No. If you put that on the air, I'm going to kick your ass," he said again, eyes narrowing.

"Barry," I tried again, "you're really not going to do this?"

"No," he said. "Fuck you. I'm not doing it."

I didn't respond, but I told my boss, Rick Gentile, who said, "Well, we have no choice. We're going to put it on the air." That's when Bill White, the National League president, went into the production truck and begged Gentile to reconsider. He argued that the interview wasn't in the best interests of Bonds, baseball, or the broadcast.

"Well, if you get him to do it again before the game, we're willing to do that," Gentile told White. "But if he doesn't do it, we're going to air it." Gentile meant as is.

Bonds, unfortunately, declined again. The segment did run, playing my questions and Bonds's surly answers on TV screens all across the country. I ended up sitting at the same end of the dugout while the game took place, and the whole time, whenever he wasn't playing, Bonds just glared at me, muttering under his breath. I caught phrases like "you motherfucker" and "airing this shit."

The game ended, and the producer said to go interview Bonds after the commercial, as he was the star of the game. So I approached him, on the field, after the Pirates won and forced the series back to Atlanta. I was concerned after he was so pissed at me earlier and he had let me know during the game as well. I asked him if he wanted to do the post-game interview to clear things up. He looked at me long and hard and then revealed something unexpected. "Jim Gray, you're all right with me," Bonds said. He did the interview, and all went well.

What?

I can't explain why he did that. Part of me wonders if he liked that I didn't back down. Maybe he respected that I and we (CBS) didn't just concede to his unreasonable and threatening demands. Or maybe it was because he just knew we should move on.

It's funny what happened next. I came to like Barry Bonds. He seemed to like me and those feelings remain mutual. He had lived through his own steroids scandal, faced his own disgrace, and when he did that, he always talked to me on-camera. I came to see a side to him that he didn't reveal to many people. He was introspective and open and had this funny part to his personality. When he broke the single-season home run record, he talked to me. When he broke Babe Ruth's HR mark he did a one-on-one interview with me, and then, after he set the career home run record, passing Aaron, same thing. We had formed that type of relationship; one built on a very public argument and, ultimately, trust.

What people forget about Bonds is what a great baseball player he really was, and I mean early in his career through almost the entirety of it. This guy made fourteen all-star teams. He won eight Gold Gloves and seven National League MVP awards and twelve Silver Slugger honors. He remains one of the best hitters to ever swing a bat and one of the most complete players to ever don a baseball uniform. He played all those years in Pittsburgh, then all those years in San Francisco. He was a great player, and while he got very close, he never won a championship.

I was there, on that night in 2001 when Bonds broke the single-season home run record with his seventy-first dinger. I was also in attendance four years earlier in St. Louis, sitting in the stands right behind the family of Roger Maris with Costas when McGwire broke Maris's single season record with sixty-two homers. I wasn't thinking about steroids at that time, but between that night and what Bonds did in '01, with all the rumors swirling about performance-enhancing drugs, and the obvious changes in Barry's physical appearance, I came to suspect that Bonds was being aided. So did most everyone else.

The reputations of everyone from Bonds to McGwire to Sammy Sosa had fallen under assault. Deservedly, in hindsight. Soon enough, they would be accused of being a bunch of drug cheats. The whole thing smelled.

Steroids and sports had become intertwined in ways that made everyone uncomfortable. Including, I would find out, executives at networks.

Covering the steroids scandal as it unfolded wasn't easy. What happened with Marion Jones, the gifted and marketable American sprinter, became regrettable proof. Jones would win three gold and two bronze medals at the Olympic Games in Sydney, Australia, back in 2000. We didn't know yet that she would have to give them all back. Or that her career would end in another steroid-fueled disgrace.

What we did know was that Jones's then husband, the Olympic shot-putter C.J. Hunter, had been outed by the international governing body for track and field after having failed a drug test at a competition in Oslo that year in July. The International Amateur Athletic Federation said Hunter had tested positive for the steroid nandrolone. Hunter had withdrawn from the Olympics two weeks before they started, but news of his drug use broke just before his wife was set to run another race in Sydney (she had already won the 100 meters).

I was working for NBC, reporting on the Games at the track-and-field venue, when it fell to me to interview Jones shortly after the news had broken. Ebersol, remember, had been so great to me through the Rose ordeal and other instances. But in this case, I didn't agree with the call he made. He wanted the viewers back home to enjoy the Olympic experience, and because of that reasoning, he decided he didn't want my interview with Jones to turn into a cross-examination about steroids and sports and whether all her success owed in part to what she had ingested or injected. He told me that whenever we interviewed Jones, we couldn't ask about her husband, his disqualification, or whether she knew of his steroid use. Ebersol and other execs wanted the interviews to focus on the events.

The network did have its anchors read a disclaimer every time we spoke to Jones, so that we had some plausible deniability in the event she joined her husband in the pantheon of shamed Olympians. Whoever introduced me in the broadcast would read something brief mentioning Hunter and what had happened. And that was the end of that. I'm not sure how the arrangement was made, but Jones agreed to speak to us as long as we focused only on the events that she competed in. We should never have agreed to her conditions.

It's easier to say that now, of course, given that Jones has been caught cheating, acknowledged doping, and gone to jail, stripped of all her medals. But back then, the decision to not question her seemed wrong at the outset. It hurt our credibility. I had a bad feeling whenever we put her interviews on the air, period, and that's because she had this great smile and a long list of accomplishments, and yet her husband had been thrown out of the Olympics for the very thing many would eventually accuse her of. It made for an uneasy mixture.

My feeling was: Ask her once and be done with it. Get her rebuttal on record. If she denied everything, fine. At least we had done our duty. At least we had asked. I knew in my heart we were making the wrong call. But I also knew that Ebersol had been such a great boss to me; he had put me in myriad positions to be successful. Dick loved the Olympics, and I knew I wasn't going to win an argument with him over Jones, and even if I did, it would be me asking the questions, and the audience could accuse me of going all *A Few Good Men* on her. I had conducted the contentious Rose interview a year earlier, and the backlash I had received still lingered. So even though I knew I should ask Jones about steroids, I didn't want to be seen as taking away her shining moment, like with Rose.

I'm sure we took some heat for it, but I never saw the papers. Remember, we were in Australia. This was 2000, and the internet was still in its infancy. Either way, forget about what anyone else thought. I knew it was wrong. But I loved my job, and I respected my boss. So I went along with it. It wasn't like Jones would admit everything right after she had won one medal or another. We weren't going to land some big mea culpa. I've never been about securing those gotcha-type moments anyway. I want to ask the right questions, ground them in empathy and fairness, and inch closer to the truth. Still, it's regretful and upsetting, because we could have done it better. That was a tough thing, to punt.

I wouldn't rank the Jones interviews among my great career regrets. I often reflect on my interviews, try to learn from them. But here, I simply disagreed with the decision.

When the news eventually broke and all her transgressions came to light, I was mostly just sad for her. I liked her. I knew she was talented. And I felt for both track and field and the wider world of sports. Here was another steroid-tinged blemish that struck to the core of the integrity we assume most everyone competes with. Here was another reason to question every athletic achievement ever reached.

Jones followed what had become a familiar pattern: deny, deny, deny; then get caught. She went to jail and tearfully apologized. It was stunning and tragic. Having gone from a medal around her neck to a bracelet around her ankle. From global glory, to a prison cell.

On August 4, 2007, I visited with Bud Selig in the commissioner's box at Petco Park, the baseball stadium in San Diego, just before Bonds tied Aaron's record. Selig was uncomfortable and anxious and didn't want visitors hanging around. Then Bonds took his first at bat of the game in the top of the second inning, and one sweet swing produced home run number 755. The commissioner stood up but refused to clap. He actually put his hands in his pockets! He did acknowledge the milestone in a lukewarm congratulatory statement but he wanted to distance himself from the achievement even though he knew that moment was historic. In fact, three days later, when Bonds hit home run 756 in San Francisco to break the record, Selig was not in attendance.

Personally, I am very fond of Selig. I see him as a well-intentioned and earnest man. But I didn't agree with his actions in that moment. The commissioner, the owners, the teams, they let all of this go on for years. It appeared as if they looked the other way or that they didn't want to know. They wanted to bank all the profits from the home run chases. They saw the epidemic coming, saw the statistics ballooning, saw all those batters with biceps that Popeye would envy, and they did almost nothing to head it off, while the players' union put up significant roadblocks to protect its members. Now, at *that* moment, he wanted to be all holier than thou? The guy who had presided over the whole thing?

Also: He's in the Hall of Fame and Barry Bonds is not? Come on. Selig now wants to take credit for cleaning up the game. We're not sure it's clean, for one, and if it is, he doesn't deserve the plaudits for the change. He watched baseball rise in popularity, watched the value of franchises soar, watched a nation of sports obsessives fall back in love with the long ball. At that point, he did . . . virtually . . . nothing. I found—I *find*— his later stance hypocritical at best. Bud and the entire institution did very little until federal investigators uncovered the nefarious activities at BALCO, at which point Congress got involved and made baseball look foolish. Lawmakers drilled Selig and others. Only when pushed and embarrassed did MLB begin to clean up the game and enforce stricter testing programs and apply harsher penalties.

I, too, hate that institutions have been cheated. That the record breakers have been aided. And yet, I struggle with where to place the players from the steroid era in the pantheon of baseball greats. There are Hall of Famers who never faced an African American opponent, who played high on amphetamines, who prospered off other enhancements, like juiced baseballs, or higher mounds. Do numbing agents count? Adderall? Where do you draw the line? What's acceptable and what's too much?

I feel for the great players who didn't dope and lost out on money, acclaim, records, endorsements. I get the circumstances. I realize that holding Bonds up next to a clean player in comparison is unfair. And yet, we shouldn't erase records. We don't live in the Soviet Union. We should not act like a player who played the game at the level that Bonds played doesn't exist. He hurt himself, and he hurt baseball, and now he's paying the price with his reputation. But because enhancements have been around as long as sports, I'm inclined to compare Bonds against the greatest players of *his* era, many of whom were also juiced. For that reason, I'd vote for him for the Hall of Fame. (To be clear, that's hypothetical. I don't actually vote.) Think of all the awards Bonds won, the career he had before the doping. I'd also vote for Roger Clemens, although with less conviction than I have for Bonds.

In November 2007, Barry granted me an exclusive interview. It would be one of the most in-depth segments he ever did. It was sad for me to see him in this circumstance. He knew it would be hard to continue to play, even though he wanted to. His contract with the Giants had expired, and he was a free agent who wouldn't get any offers.

Bonds came out firing at his critics. "I don't think you can put an asterisk in the game of baseball, and I don't think that the Hall of Fame can accept an asterisk in their Hall of Fame," he said. "You cannot give people the freedom, the right to alter history, you can't do it. There's no such thing as an asterisk in baseball."

Gray: "If the Hall of Fame does accept that ball and display it?"

(The Hall subsequently did accept the ball as a donation in July 2008 from a man who purchased the collectible and branded it with an asterisk.)

Bonds: I will never be in the Hall of Fame. Never.

Gray: You mean you personally—

Bonds: Me personally.

Gray: Or as a visitor of your artifacts or your enshrinement?

Bonds: I won't go. I won't be there.

I asked him if he would ever reconsider that stance. "At this time, I will not be there," he said. "That's my emotions now, that's how I feel now. When I decide to retire, five years from now we'll see where they are at that moment. We'll see where they are at that time and maybe I'll reconsider."

I don't subscribe to the theory that Bonds's answers in that interview give critics more reason to not induct him. Politics should not be involved here. I understand where he's coming from, why he wouldn't want to go.

He went on to say that he would leave it up to his lawyer if he planned to participate in the investigation being done by former senator George Mitchell, who was digging into steroid use in baseball. He couldn't answer anything until the BALCO case concluded. As far as the perjury charges he was facing went, he said, "I have nothing to hide, I have said that before and I will say it now, and I will look you in the face, I have nothing to hide, nothing. So look all you want to."

In his book, *For the Good of the Game*, Selig wrote in 2019 that the experience with Bonds was "unpleasant for me" and that Bonds "wasn't likable." Fair enough. That feeling was shared by many members of the media. Barry could be difficult. But as I said, we only had one negative encounter, after which I enjoyed his company, found him engaging, and listened to his stories about the art of hitting; his godfather, Willie Mays; and his father, Bobby.

Bonds was adored in the Bay Area because of his on-field performance. But outside of San Francisco, he could have helped himself by showing some humility, revealing to the world the person I had come to know. He can be funny. One of his close friends was the comic Robin Williams. They used to hang out and Bonds introduced Williams to me a few times. Bonds would spend holidays with Williams and his family. Williams would genuinely belly laugh with Bonds. The actor found that the athlete could be entertaining. Yet this was a side of Bonds the public and media didn't get a chance to see. For whatever the reason, Barry didn't want to show that he could laugh, smile, and let his guard down—that he could be human, more or less. Perhaps that would have helped soften his image if this had been more widely known. The public has demonstrated that they can be forgiving if they like you or feel that you want to be embraced, but Barry never gave people the opportunity. He never did apologize. I wish he would have.

At the time, Bonds told me he was at peace. But in 2020, he told *The Athletic* he feels that baseball has given him a "death sentence." "My heart is broken," he added. "I feel like a ghost."

The harder part to reconcile is what steroids have done to sports. We now have eyesore after eyesore and blemish after blemish and years of failed tests and scandals. It seems to be getting worse, wider, or at least more public. You start wondering whether anything is real. Did they all do drugs? Every truly great athlete? Most of them? Some?

Sometimes, I wonder, *Why are they even testing?* Why not just open the whole thing up and put the heinous behavior in the open? For athletes, it's their body and, you could argue, their choice. It's also the wrong one.

Here's the problem with that. What if it's all fake? Isn't sports then just professional wrestling, an event manipulated to reach a certain result? We pay to watch these games. We should be able to know they're real. But will the testing programs ever catch up to the cheaters?

If the Steroid Era has shown us anything, I wouldn't bet on it.

# CHAPTER 9

# TIGER

## HOW A LEGEND
## BECAME HUMAN

I first became aware of a young golf phenom many years ago, while I worked for ESPN as a freelancer in Los Angeles. I was reading the old *Herald Examiner*, checking out the agate section. Remember those? Small type. One-stop shopping. You could find out who won, who lost, who got hired, who got fired—and all in the same place. Anyway, on that particular day, in that particular section, I noticed that a nine-year-old named Eldrick Woods had managed to hit a hole in one at a club near his home in Cypress, outside of Long Beach in California. The item noted that this particular hole in one marked his third total. *Wait, what? Seriously?* That had to be a misprint. I cut the agate box out and placed it carefully on the desk in my office.

Eventually, I called down to Cypress.

It wasn't a misprint.

"Yep, he's had a few," said the late John Anselmo, a local teaching pro. "He's down here every day."

"Who's he with?" I asked.

"Comes down here and gets lessons, and he's with his dad," Anselmo said. "His dad is teaching him."

The father was Earl Woods, Anselmo said. And everyone called his son by the same name: Tiger.

At my own expense, as a freelance reporter, I hired my own camera crew and went down to see for myself. I found Earl and asked him if he would let me tape an interview, which might lead to a story. *Sure*, he said. *No problem.*

Tiger began to do his thing. He hit something like fifteen balls out of a sand trap and at least four of them rolled right in the hole! This little kid. I'm thinking, *Unbelievable.* Then we went to the driving range. He's hitting balls, and his dad is giving instructions, and Earl is jingling change and throwing coins at him and Tiger is still crushing drives. He's totally unscathed. One thing that struck me is that Tiger retained the exuberance of a kid, even as he trained and played like an adult. The game came that easy to him. "It's a fun game, you carry a bag, get good exercise, hit a golf ball, and try and get it into a little hole," he told me. His father knew that his son was extraordinary, or could be. He said, "He has the talent, and he has the desire, and he has that rare competitiveness, that extra gear, that the great ones have." Decades later the proud papa's foresight proved prophetic.

Anselmo, the pro, was equally impressed. He told me, "In all my years of teaching golf I have never seen a boy this age do it and play this well." At the time Tiger had just finished fourth grade and was one of the top students in his class. He practiced golf twenty hours a week.

As the interview ended, I jokingly asked Tiger if I could be his caddy. He joked back, asking if I could read greens. When I said yes, he said he'd hire me, for the basic 10 percent take that caddies receive from purses. I jokingly accepted on-camera, and we shook hands. Over the years, we've laughed about how I should have taken that deal on the spot. I would have made more as Tiger's caddie, that's for sure.

At another point in that segment, young Tiger says, "I think I'm a good golfer, but I need a lot of improvement," pausing before uttering, "I want to win all of the big tournaments, all of the major ones, and I hope to play well when I get older, and beat all the pros." That would become a fairly famous line. I called ESPN and asked if they were interested in this story for *SportsCenter*, or one of their other shows. A few months later they called back and said yes. Then they ran it.

I liked Tiger. He seemed like a nice kid, bright and happy, a full universe away from so many twists the future held. I didn't view Earl as too overbearing. To me, he seemed instructive, not intrusive and totally immersed and invested in his son's career. When the story came out, he told me he enjoyed it. At that same time, I remember thinking I needed to hold on to the tape. I wasn't going to recycle that one. Earl asked me for a copy so I made him one and kept mine. Intentionally. Back in those days, tapes were used over and over again. You'd tape something, edit it, then use it again later, over the original. When you taped over something, it was gone forever. Digital didn't exist. There was not yet any sort of data cloud. In this instance, though, I kept the original. I knew this kid was special.

Who knew what Tiger might become.


In August of 1996, Earl would hand over his own videotape library and photos to Nike, as part of Tiger's lucrative endorsement deal with the sneaker giant. He didn't know that I owned the copyright to that interview specifically. Chances are, he didn't know that segment was on what he gave the executives who asked for everything in the library that the family had kept and collected over the years. Earl was probably innocent in the whole ordeal; he'd just provided the rights to Tiger's likeness to the companies the family had become partners with. But he did not own that particular copyright. I did.

I was getting ready for a Patriots game, at a hotel in Providence, when I first saw the now-famous Nike commercial and heard those same words that Tiger spoke to me all those years ago. *When I grow up, I want to win all the majors, and beat all the pros.* This was part of his Nike campaign, the celebrated one that future marketers would study in college classrooms, and I'm thinking, *That's interesting, where did they get that interview? That's in my closet. I own that.* They played the commercial all day long, for weeks. I couldn't escape it. When I returned home, I went back to my closet and found the raw interview and the segment. Indeed, there it was, buried under mountains of black three-quarter-inch tapes.

The next week, my phone rang. Someone called from Wieden+Kennedy, the advertising agency in Portland that worked with Nike and had put together that particular campaign.

"Jim," the representative said, "this Nike ad that we just did, they've taken some footage from an interview that you did off a tape that Earl had given us." Uh-huh. "Do you know who owns the rights to that?"

I did, in fact. "I think this call is coming a couple days too late," I said.

I told them that I owned it, and that they needed to call my representative, Art Kaminsky. Lawyers got involved. Tiger was represented at that time by IMG and his agent at the firm was Hughes Norton. In addition to Nike, they had already licensed the footage to some other companies, believing that they owned the rights because the Woods family turned over the library to them. IMG lawyers tried to roll right over me, because they didn't want to believe I held the copyright, and I had to hire Williams & Connolly, this high-powered Washington law firm, to fight back and protect my rights. We easily proved my ownership and IMG acknowledged and agreed. Funny how life works. Five years later, I ended up hiring IMG to represent me for the next decade.

Ultimately, it was Mark Thomashow, Nike's head of business affairs, who stepped in and did the right thing. He recognized that a mistake had been made in using my content and wanted to settle amicably. So Nike paid me for the footage and helped get the other companies to do the same. Woods and his father also signed a settlement agreement. I will never forget how honorable Thomashow was and how he stepped in and treated all parties with respect and dignity. I contacted Thomashow (who has since retired from Nike) for this book and asked him about our dealings. "We knew the footage was yours and we didn't want to infringe on your copyright. We wanted to do the right thing by you, Tiger, and the Woods family. Everyone was pleased it came to a happy resolution."

I want to be clear here: Woods's people are the ones who sold the footage, and they're the ones who created the issue. That said, I don't think they had any malicious intentions. They probably had no idea how all that worked. When the Woods camp later asked me for the same footage for a documentary that they planned to produce and own, I said yes and gave them a license for that project, no problem.

The videotape saga did not dent my appreciation for Woods's immense talent, or his meteoric rise to a level of stardom rarely seen anywhere, let alone in sports. Quite quickly, it became abundantly clear that what he had said to me all those years ago would prove true. Tiger did win all the amateurs, or at least three of them, anyway. He did beat all the pros. Now, I'm not sure anyone saw that he'd win fifteen major championships way back then. Or that he would threaten to surpass Sam Snead's record total of eighty-two PGA Tour victories, which he tied in 2019.

Still, greatness is greatness. At that level, at his level, it's unmistakable. You can see it, feel it, sense it, even. I remember one time early in Woods's career when I interviewed Jack Nicklaus and Arnold Palmer at Augusta National. These are two of the greatest golfers of all time, and they said something like, "This kid's gonna win more than both of us combined." I knew Tiger was the real deal when they said that. These aren't two men who run around making those kinds of bold proclamations. They were reserved, but they also knew what they were seeing, and they sent out a signal to the rest of the world that Tiger was going to be special. That he would be unlike any golfer we had ever seen.

That was before Woods won the Masters for the first time, in 1997, by an incredible twelve strokes. He was twenty-one years old. Repeating: *He was twenty-one years old.* It still ranks among my favorite moments, because I knew Tiger as a little kid, because I had seen him coming, and because I liked and respected his family. Despite the mishap we had, they were all still pleasant when I saw them.

I watched as Tiger strode up the eighteenth fairway, toward the green, on the verge of this historic moment. No African American had ever won the Masters, yet the club has a number of employees who are Black. I looked up at the veranda from my vantage point in the radio tower above the green, and I saw so many of the employees who worked in the clubhouse, or on the course, or in security, and they were watching Tiger, witnessing a golfer who resembled them, who was part African American and winning the most storied tournament in golf by the widest of margins. Many of them knew it had only been seven years earlier that Augusta National admitted a Black member, and it would be fifteen more until they would admit a woman. Some of them were understandably in tears. Some of them were laughing and happy, smiles spread wide across their faces. All of them were in disbelief.

My dad was standing there with me. I'll never forget how I got to share that moment with him. I can't remember what we said; just that we were blissful, elated, stunned. We had just seen something historic, something we'd never watched before and something we'd never see again. Nicholson was with us, too. He shared in our amazement.

Jack is one of the world's most well-known actors, and he told me something that weekend about fame that has resonated with me ever since. On Friday, we had followed Nicklaus, who was ahead of Tiger on the course. We were walking down the tenth fairway, and Nicholson turned to me, his expression serious.

"Never trust fame," he said.

His eyes scanned a few holes away at Tiger. "Fame will leave and it's fleeting, and it will jump away," he said. "And you can tell that it has to bother Jack Nicklaus, because all of the attention is over here on Tiger." He wasn't being critical of Jack the golfer. He was saying: *Don't fall into that trap, don't put your trust in fame, or your hopes.* He was saying: *Here's an example; if you trust fame, you're in trouble.* I could tell he felt empathy for Nicklaus. Perhaps at that moment, Nicholson, then a two-time Academy Award winner (now three), had taken a glimpse of his own mortality. Time marches on, even for the great ones.

After Tiger won, after the fist pumps and the celebration, he sauntered into Butler Cabin to do the traditional postmatch interview. He
gave me a big hug and shook my father's hand. He did his usual first
interview, with Jim Nantz, tugged the famous green jacket on over his
shoulders, and then spoke with me for CBS Radio Sports.

Earl Woods came over and shook my hand. Kultida Woods gave me a
hug and mentioned the earlier interview. Could I believe it? "We watch
that tape all the time," she said.

Tiger had predicted all this. That's what I kept thinking. My emotions swung all over the place. I wondered how that had just happened,
whether he could ever repeat it and whether anyone could ever do something like Tiger had done that week at Augusta National.

The phenomenon had begun. Tiger was the best thing that ever happened to golf. He boosted interest to new, higher levels; he introduced
the game to a wider, more diverse audience. He broke barriers. Won
tournaments. Completed the so-called Tiger Slam by winning all four
majors in a row, just not in the same calendar year. Signed endorsements
with the biggest companies. Flew all over the world on a private jet.
Owned a yacht, which he named *Privacy*. He had it all.

Still, the question lingered: How would he handle that type of fame?
The answer would be revealed soon enough.

In 2006, at a match-play tournament in Carlsbad, California, I asked
Tiger if I could speak to him for a moment. We were always cordial,
but it's not like we had numerous long conversations. We would do our
interviews and go on with our lives. He had just beaten some poor sap,
badly, winning with several holes to play via an absolute birdie-fest.
The interview went well, same as always. Then we had our private
moment.

"Tiger, I just want to say this to you," I told him. "And I hope that
you take it in the spirit that it's intended."

I told him about a quote that Nelson Mandela told me. I'm not sure
where it originated, but those words stuck. They were both simple and
genius. Something to the effect of: *People will forget what you say, and people*

*will forget what you do, but no one will ever forget the way you make them feel.*
Still true.

"Tiger," I said, "people feel great when they watch you play. And then twenty seconds after you're done, you blow off the kids wanting your autograph. You walk past the fans and don't shake hands with the corporate guys who are giving you millions. They don't have the same feeling. And I say this to you because I care about you, and I hope you know and understand that."

He just kind of looked at me. Five seconds passed. Maybe six. I felt a little uncomfortable. He just stared back at me, then said, "Thanks, Jim. I appreciate that."

Tiger left the course for the clubhouse, zipping right past the kids and the media and the sponsors. Clearly, what I said had not sunk in. And look, I understand it's impossible to be Tiger Woods. Everyone wants a handshake, an autograph, a photo. Everybody wants something. But you can't just disregard most people you see in your life, either. You can't shut *everybody* out and continue to think people will support you.

I thought about that when the scandals started. Thought about the billboards that would flash those words that theoretically described Tiger: RESPECTED OR ADMIRED OR THINKER OR RIGHT EXECUTION. He was selling himself as all those things, while living a double life. There were other women. There was infidelity. Not to mention Navy SEAL training that contributed to his myriad injuries and so many clandestine trips to party in Las Vegas.

One of Tiger's lives was carefully marketed and expertly crafted and starting to showcase some of the best golf the world had ever seen anybody play. He hid his other life from almost everyone, at least until he spiraled out of control and the scandal became public, spreading across the internet like wildfire, after he ended up driving into a fire hydrant and his wife was said to have shattered the window of his car with a golf club to help him get out. That was the beginning of what was revealed as a series of extramarital affairs that left sports fans around the country shocked and disappointed.

I covered the incidents for the Golf Channel. I tried to be considerate and careful and not take my reporting over the edge. I wasn't harsh on him, but I wasn't easy on him, either. I'm sure he didn't like it. I'm sure no one ever wants someone they know going on television and discussing their sex and drug addictions. It can't be well received, no matter who's saying it, or what exactly it is they're saying.

The whole saga struck me as very sad. I've always believed that people's personal lives should be their personal lives, that private things should remain private. But that would never again be the case with Tiger. So few people came to his defense, despite how much he had done for golf.

That spoke, I thought, to how he had handled himself for all those years. He was living a life where it was all about him, all the time. He always acted professionally with me. He always was a powerful figure in sports. But he never seemed to be able to let others enjoy and share in his accomplishments, to revel in his glory, to soak in his success. Mostly, when I saw that, I felt sorry for him. What a lonely existence, governing by fear—of access or proximity or placement within the inner circle.

What Julius Erving said to me all those years ago still applied here. "Do you know anybody who is truly successful, at the top of their profession, who's really, really great and doesn't have a major flaw in their personality?" Touché. That remains an accurate statement. Tiger's flaw: hubris; humanity, or lack thereof.

When Tiger held his apology press conference, he said he was filled with shame and felt remorse for letting so many people down. He concluded the statement by saying, "Finally, there are many people in this room, and there are many people at home, who have believed in me. Today, I want to ask for your help. I ask you to find room in your heart to one day believe in me again." I wondered if he was starting to borrow his father's most outlandish statements, "Tiger will do more than any other man in history to change the course of humanity. He is the Chosen One. He will have the power to impact nations. Not people. Nations," said Earl while also comparing Tiger to Mahatma Gandhi, one of the greatest men to ever live. And I thought, *Wow, Tiger channeling Earl? Really? Believe in you for what?* The only thing I ever believed about

Tiger was that he could hit a 7-iron better than any other human on the planet. I wasn't taking life cues from him. Nor should anybody else.

Tiger had a few other public issues. Some people felt he ran afoul of decorum, with rules violations that he took heat for. There was a DUI arrest in 2017 where he put other lives at risk. But mostly, it was personal issues that became uncomfortably public. And the reaction to those moments looped back to the same premise: an icon who had sold himself one way and lived a completely different life. Who suffered the most from that? Easy. *Him. His family.* The public that felt let down by Tiger had misplaced its faith in him by pouring their hope into him outside of golf. We should never look at athletes, no matter how kind or accessible or philanthropic, as deities, as more than man or woman. Charles Barkley was right, OK? Let your parents be your role models. Don't search for them in sports. That doesn't mean we can't be inspired or lifted by incredible athletic achievements. Or learn some valuable lessons about hard work, dedication, excellence, sportsmanship, grace, humility, dignity, charity, and a host of other qualities.

At a certain point, I didn't think Tiger would ever win again. Golf is a psychological game, too. I thought, naturally, that he would be damaged by all that he had endured, on top of the physical toll all his back, spine, and knee injuries had exacted. When you swing a club that violently all your life, from age three onward or whatever, it will wear down your body over time.

All of which makes his comeback that much more astonishing. Like in September of 2018, when he won the Tour Championship, at East Lake Golf Club in Atlanta, and then in April 2019, when he completed one of the greatest comebacks—from injuries and self-inflicted wounds—in the history of sports. The world wanted Tiger to be great again. At the Masters that spring, on the course where he first announced his enduring greatness, the old Tiger summoned the Tiger of old, roaring and fist-pumping again.

I really didn't think he would win. I had been told his neck was bothering him. But I didn't discount him, either. I partook in a Masters-related but friendly dinner bet with Dean Spanos, the Chargers' owner, where I picked ten players and he got the rest of the field. I knew I couldn't ignore Tiger Woods at Augusta National, so I included him in my picks, despite the misgivings.

I covered the tournament, doing reports for Fox. As Tiger took the lead, then held it, then kept it, I wondered the same thing as the rest of the world, which collectively paused to watch the Masters for the first time since the scandals started. For the final round, I went out and watched him play holes number ten, eleven, and twelve, then retreated to the press room. When he made a birdie on sixteen and had a two-stroke lead, I left the building for the course. I wanted to view the end from the famous eighteenth green—from near the same spot where I had watched him ascend to sports royalty all those years ago.

I thought about my dad as Tiger approached. I thought about the '97 Masters and our time together and what my friend Jack had said about fame. My father had always loved Tiger, always pulled for him.

I stood behind the green on eighteen, in the media section, behind the ropes. I saw the cautious approach shot, the putt he just missed, the tap in to win the tournament. I saw him celebrate the moment that he himself had doubted would ever occur again. I saw him walk off the green and hug his son. I then saw him wrap his mom in an embrace, the two of them overcome with emotion, and I thought about Earl Woods and wondered if he was up there, looking down.

That day, we had seen the greatest-ever golf lesson completed.

I believe I've witnessed the two greatest comebacks in the history of sports. The first? Super Bowl LI, when the Patriots trailed the Falcons 28–3 and won. The other? Tiger Woods, hands down.

I still see that video sometimes. I still hear his mom, saying, "We watched that tape a million times." I still remember asking Tiger if I could be his caddy. From there to here . . . who could have imagined?

Tiger will always stop when I need an interview and give me a few minutes. He's always professional, always courteous. He shakes my hand. He might ask about the Raiders or the Lakers. I might ask about his mom. But we've never had a real conversation after that one in which I told him about Mandela and that quote. There's no closeness.

It should be clear: Tiger didn't cheat the sport; Tiger cheated himself. But the man I saw at the Masters in 2019 seemed different. Craig Heatley of Augusta National called on me to ask the first question in Tiger's post-triumph press conference, as if to acknowledge the history between us. I asked if he was thinking about his dad as he walked off and embraced his son and mom in the exact same spot and what that meant. And, for the first time in years, I saw gratitude in Tiger Woods. I saw a person allowing all those people who were pulling for him to be permitted inside, rather than keeping everyone at a distance. *This isn't just for me*, Tiger Woods was saying. *This is for you, for all of you, for golf.*

Humility will always rank among the greatest qualities a superstar athlete can possess. When they display their humanity, it's wonderful, because it's so endearing. Finally, I saw that in Tiger again. He had gone through the ringer and come out the other side. I hope that now he can see that people in his life matter, that relationships, even if they're casual, can be valued. You can't do anything in life by yourself.

Walking right behind Tiger from the eighteenth green to the clubhouse, I saw so many ecstatic fans. Tiger waved and smiled and acknowledged them. Before he signed his card, a number of his competitors stood nearby, waiting to embrace him. Only this time, Tiger hugged them back. Brooks Koepka, Justin Thomas, Rickie Fowler, and Bubba Watson. It was a joyous occasion.

I was happy for Tiger and his family. His kids could finally see how other people *felt* about their dad, and as Tiger expressed, it was important for him to have his kids see and share in the experience and joy of their father winning a major championship. Sometimes the clichés are correct. Time brings wisdom. As has been said, "A wise man will change his mind. A fool never will."

His comeback says a lot about Tiger's will and drive and greatness. To have endured the surgeries, the injuries, and the wrath of the public. The arrest. The rehab. Like climbing Everest and falling to the bottom of the Grand Canyon. I've never witnessed anything quite like that. A lot of people would have quit years ago, quit on themselves. President Nixon once famously stated, "A man is not finished when he is defeated. He is finished when he quits." Most people quit on Tiger. But not him. We could watch him and see something we'd like to aspire to. We can say, *You know what? Maybe I can.*

I had seen Tiger a couple of months before the Masters, while I was with future Hall of Fame receiver Larry Fitzgerald at a charity golf exhibition at the Riviera Country Club in Los Angeles. We shot the breeze, looked at clubs. I walked a couple of holes with him. Nothing deep, but he did it with a smile. I walked away feeling good. And that was the point I had tried to make all those years earlier. *People will never forget the way you make them feel.* I felt good about Tiger when I left him in February of 2019. I felt good about Tiger when I left Augusta National. Not only about his golf, either. About the man, the human. About the comeback and the evolution.

*Tiger Woods in 2002. The last man to repeat as Masters champion.*

CHAPTER 10

# UPON FURTHER
# REVIEW

On the early morning of July 27, 1996, I was living in Atlanta but staying at the Renaissance hotel downtown, along with the rest of my colleagues at NBC. We were covering the Olympics. This marked a special event for both me and my family; I loved reporting on all the Games, but I also had made my home in Atlanta, moving from Los Angeles; my better half, Frann, worked for the Olympic committee; my legendary boss, Ebersol, had tasked me with the swimming beat; and my friend Muhammad Ali would light the torch at the end of the opening ceremony.

The swimming portion of those Olympics had just wrapped up. So I went to the hotel lounge that had been reserved for the network throughout the Games. That's where reporters, producers, and executives could unwind over drinks and snacks after long days. I'd go there to relax, and on that night, when I made it to the top floor, I remember the crew congratulating one another. The swimming coverage had gone well. The United States had won thirteen golds and twenty-six medals overall, led by stars like Amy Van Dyken.

While standing at the end of the bar, I noticed Ebersol approach. He walked quickly, and he was headed in my direction.

"Jimmy," he said, "you're coming with me."

Something in his voice told me he was serious. "Where are we going?" I asked.

"Follow me" was all he said.

We went to a corridor by the elevators, where we ran into David Neal, who worked in production as basically Ebersol's chief lieutenant. He carried out Dick's orders.

"There's been a bombing, Jimmy," Ebersol said. "I want you to go over to the park." He meant the Centennial Olympic Park, where so many Games-related events were held.

"You know this city better than anybody," Ebersol continued. "You live here. You know the organizing committee. Your wife works there. You know the police. Go over there. See what you can find."

He wasn't wrong. I did know Atlanta, I had gone to police banquets and games for the police athletic leagues, I did know the executives at the organizing committee who Frann worked with.

"We got the camera crews ready," Ebersol said. "Just get over there."

We hopped into a waiting car, the streets thick with pedestrians and fear, as the news of the bombing began to spread. Fortunately, Dick had one of those special passes that granted him unlimited access to anywhere, due to his position as the most important executive for the Olympics in American television. Dick had made and helped shape an event that takes place every two years into the global behemoth the Games had become. While we headed over to the park, he told me about what it had been like in Munich, in 1972, when members of the Palestinian terrorist group Black September had taken eleven Israeli athletes hostage. They would eventually kill all of them and a police officer. Dick had been there, in Munich, working for ABC. He had even been near the building, part of the broadcast, and one thing he said stuck with me: "I didn't think I'd ever have to face something like that again."

Back in '96, we did have cell phones, the earliest versions, and mine started to ring on the drive over to the park. It was Frann. I told her what was going on and implored her to stay inside. We didn't know any of the details. She was nervous. She didn't think that our going to the park was the greatest of ideas. But, "I'm with Dick," I told her. "We'll be all right."

The car dropped us off at the NBC compound, and I left Dick and rode in a golf cart over to the park. The space had been transformed into something of a town square for the Olympics, and thousands of spectators went there every day. That night, they had assembled for a concert by the band Jack Mack and the Heart Attack.

Fortunately, some of the police officers recognized me from television, and they quickly filled me in on the basics of what had transpired. Shortly after midnight, a terrorist had planted a green military field pack in the park. It contained three pipe bombs and several of those long, three-inch masonry nails, and this gutless criminal had left the pack under a bench near the sound tower for the concert. The bombs, investigators would learn, had been rigged with nitroglycerin dynamite and an alarm clock.

One officer told me that the FBI had received a 911 call roughly eighteen minutes before the bomb detonated. They believed a white male with no discernible accent had dialed in, offering a warning.

Those same cops knew that a security guard had found the bag and alerted local officers in the Georgia Bureau of Investigation. They had called in a bomb ordnance disposal team and began to clear the area. But that's when the device went off—and in two days, that same security guard, Richard Jewell, would find himself under a dark cloud of suspicion. The cops didn't seem to like the timing of when he found the bag and when the device exploded. That made him not only a suspect but the prime one.

The explosion killed one person and injured more than a hundred, while another person also died after suffering a heart attack. President

Bill Clinton would label the bombing an "evil act of terror." And we would report on it all night and in the days, weeks, and months ahead.

I stayed at the park well past sunrise, delivering several news updates to anchors Jim Lampley and Tom Brokaw, working with Roger O'Neill of NBC News. I remained on the air all the way until the next morning.

It helped that I had an identification badge that granted me access into the organizing committee's building, right next to the park. I spoke to Billy Payne, who many described as the "father" of the Atlanta Games, and he was obviously shaken, trying to figure out what had happened, resolved to ensure there would be no further explosions or terrorist incidents. All night, I wondered if another bomb would go off, and everyone I came in contact with seemed to share in that trepidation, Payne included. Police continued to clear the area; starting with the spectators, moving on to the cars. If a vehicle happened to backfire, or if something made even a popping sound, everybody jumped. The mood was that tense.

I managed to land all this news relating to the bombing. I reported on the arrival of Juan Antonio Samaranch, the IOC president, and that no athletes or coaches had been injured. I found out that officials had termed the Games and its athletes secure and that the competitions would continue as scheduled. Samaranch told me that they felt there were no ongoing or existing threats. We continued to broadcast, as night turned into morning and morning turned into the *Today* show.


I felt sad when I finally returned to the hotel the next day. Sad for the loss of life and those injured. Sad for the city of Atlanta and the Olympic organizing committee; sad for Frann and all her colleagues after the years of hard work they had put in; sad for the Games, and how what they represented had been tainted by some terrorist and the bomb he left in that pack under a park bench; sad that the emotional Ali moment had been hijacked by a criminal.

The need to satisfy the news cycle immediately happened next, accuracy be damned. Jewell had been tabbed by some as a hero, for discovering the bomb and helping clear spectators from the park. It's likely that he had saved lives with his quick and decisive actions. But it didn't take long before myriad news organizations began to report a more nefarious story, with Jewell the chief potential suspect. He was never charged—that's important—but that hardly mattered in the immediate aftermath, in the court of public opinion, where Jewell was tried and convicted in short order. His home was searched, his background picked through, his life taken apart and presented back to the American public for mass consumption. All this was done as quickly as possible—too quickly, it turns out.

Eventually, a man named Eric Rudolph would be tied to the bombing and convicted in the attack. He released a statement in April of 2005 saying his motivation for the bombing was political, that he wanted officials to cancel the Games because he wanted the US government to pay for its "abominable sanctioning of abortion." His statement erased any lingering doubts in the court of public opinion about Jewell, who died in 2007, at forty-four, reportedly of heart failure from diabetes complications. In 2019, Clint Eastwood would put out a movie about his life, named after Jewell, and it would receive both critical acclaim and criticism for playing loose with the facts.

Costas conducted himself properly in the aftermath of the bombing. There's nobody better. Bob went on the air and sounded warning signals right away. He told the audience that the judgment had happened too quickly, that perhaps news organizations had jumped the gun in emphasizing the security guard as the only suspect. *Hold on*, he basically said. *Let the investigations unfurl.* Bob contradicted the pervasive and prevailing sentiment at that moment. He pumped the brakes. He said something to the effect of, if it's not him, the damage could be irreparable, and how will Jewell get his reputation back? Bob turned out to be right.

Jewell would sue NBC News, the *Atlanta-Journal Constitution*, and other media organizations for defamation. He reportedly won a six-figure settlement from NBC in 1997. Other cases filed in his name dragged on for years; some even continued after his death. Regardless, he was proven right. Very little would undo the damage that had already been done, almost instantaneously. That was wrong on many levels.

We see it all the time now: leaping to quickly condemn, to be first, if not necessarily right. We see it pretty much every time that an international news event takes place, with outlets from every medium and journalists from all over the world tripping over each other to report whatever information they can find. We see reporters pronounce a public figure dead, like Penn State football coach Joe Paterno, when they're very much alive. We see it with bombings, with mass shootings, with scandal of all kinds. Now, don't get me wrong. The examination of those scandals and the shining of light on the misdeeds of the powerful are important. That's the basis of good, revealing, public service journalism. But I'd add two caveats there: *when properly vetted* and *when done right*.

In the case of Richard Jewell, the public was desperate for information. This was before everyone walked around with small computers in their pocket, before most regularly knew of this thing called the internet that would change the world. So the masses wanted a suspect to be named, they wanted to know the Games were safe, and because somebody like Jewell came close enough to fitting a profile of what the authorities were looking for, the very fact that they looked into him at all sent various news organizations into a frenzy. Being first took precedent over being right, and that's never a good combo.

It's important to remember that our judgment can be poor when time is of the essence. The decisions you'd make after the passage of time are different, naturally, then the ones you'd make while wrapped up in the emotion and immediacy and adrenaline of any given moment. There's pressure being placed on the journalists that are involved, too—from editors and viewers and even what reporters themselves feel deep inside.

I want to be careful how I say this. I don't want to say I've never gone on-air with the exact kind of reports I'm being critical of here. I don't think I have, and I most certainly have tried not to. I try to follow my own guidelines. One is that I never want to report something on-air unless I know that the source has direct involvement in or proximity to the story and has impeccable credibility. In the cases where the information is more sensitive, I try to put the onus on myself, saying something like "I understand" this to be true. If the info ends up being wrong, the blame should fall on me, because my understanding of the events I'm reporting on was off. I have to trust them and their information implicitly; otherwise, there's no point in sharing that info on the air.

I was praised in the aftermath of the Olympic bombing for our coverage of that event as it unfolded. I got my portion right, leading Ebersol to give me additional assignments. That didn't diminish in any way the atrocity of what happened, or lessen the toll the bombing had exacted on so many lives. I wish I'd never had to report on an event like that at all. I hope I never do again.

The point is that great care must be given to all information we send out into the public domain. I'm reminded of a line from one of David Brinkley's books, *Everyone Is Entitled to My Opinion*. Brinkley writes, essentially, that "the news is what I make it." That might sound arrogant, but boy, is it true. Brinkley had twenty-two minutes every night to update a country on what happened in the world, to decide what qualified as news and how to frame the delivery of the information. That shaped how millions of people viewed the world.

That sentiment remains true today. How we present a story is going to shape the public's opinion of whatever event we're reporting on. The baseline there is that we have to be, we must be, we can never not be . . . right. That should forever be the first and most important step in reporting.

How people consume their information in 2020 doesn't change the baseline, but it sure makes verifying the accuracy of that info a lot more difficult. Back then, people relied almost exclusively on the nightly news and newspapers to learn about the world. Now, with various social media platforms, and hundreds, if not thousands of sources of information, there's so much more noise out there. It's all so much harder to verify. It's almost impossible to know what you can and cannot trust.

Back in 1981, I sat in an edit booth in Denver when I found out that Ronald Reagan had been shot by John Hinckley Jr., who had fired at the president as he returned to a waiting limousine after a speaking engagement at a hotel in Washington, DC. Frank Reynolds was the anchor for the evening news on ABC. He was getting all these conflicting reports—the president was shot; he wasn't shot; he was grazed; he was on his way to the hospital; he was on his death bed. Reynolds finally seemed to tire of all the competing information. He had this sheet of paper in front of him, and he looked down. "Damn it, somebody get me some correct information," he said.

Still holds. Get it right.

Fifteen months after the Olympic bombing, I was working the National League Championship Series in Atlanta for NBC. The Braves were playing the Marlins. Between one inning, I heard something unexpected in my earpiece. "Richard Jewell is here," one of the stage managers said. "He would like to say hello to Bob and thank you." The stage manager meant Costas. They let Jewell in. He shook Bob's hand and told him how much he appreciated what Bob had said that night, his plea for the public *not* to rush to judgment. "Thank you, Mr. Costas, for being fair to me, and my mother wants to thank you," Jewell said.

There are a million examples I could cite, but I'm speaking here to two that I was personally involved with and that I saw up close. That one incident happened in 1996 and the other took place nineteen years later shows that not only has this rush not slowed, it has only accelerated. It's worse now than it was then. There are hundreds and hundreds of examples. Which brings us to Deflategate, a scandal that obviously didn't carry the same weight as a bombing but featured similar reporting haste in the aftermath.

Deflategate started back on January 18, 2015, when the Patriots battered the Indianapolis Colts, 45–7, in the AFC Championship game and the losers accused Brady and his equipment managers of purposely deflating the footballs, albeit ever-so slightly, so the quarterback might be able to grip them better and thus throw them more easily in the cold-weather game. What happened next was Watergate without the break-in: a two-year, multimillion-dollar saga, with an investigation commissioned by the NFL, opinions proffered by fake and real scientists, middle-school science projects designed to exonerate the quarterback, a four-game suspension to start the next season, Brady's appeal, and more deep dives than anyone ever wanted into something known as the ideal gas law.

The mad dash to report happened right away there, too, setting the stage for the insanity to come. ESPN reporter Chris Mortensen had it wrong at the outset, and his initial reporting shaped so much of the reporting that came after it. The blame landed on Brady, with false claims that he had hidden his nefarious misdeeds on purpose, while gaining a great advantage from them. Mortensen's inaccurate information colored everything that followed, making Tom into the poster child for rule breaking in professional football, which is beyond outrageous and ridiculous—especially to anyone who knows him.

I'd ask: Over what? Nothing that came close to needing the resources poured into this scandal. It's hard to be Tom Brady versus The National Football League. Think about that. Tom Brady versus The Most Powerful Men and Institution in Sports. There's a perfect line to that effect in the movie *Concussion*. Something about how the NFL is so powerful it owns one day of the week, Sunday, which used to belong to the church. Brady sued the league, while the investigation continued. Enough already. I'll repeat the score: 45–7. They could have played with hot air balloons or feather pillows and New England still would have won. Nobody ever points out that after the Colts complained the officials inflated the same balls for the second half of that blowout and all met the league standard. The Patriots won that half, 28–0. It was the stupidest thing. How did we get to such a strange place?

Look at the misjudgment involved there. The hiring, in essence, of a special prosecutor in Ted Wells. The studying of the Patriots' fumble statistics. The taking of flat-wrong reporting and applying it to said fumble statistics, as if to show that New England always deflated footballs and that very deflating meant the Patriots committed fewer turnovers. On and on it went. The league even challenged Brady in court. Their biggest star, their best player—they made *him* into the bad guy. Maybe the other owners felt like the Patriots needed a reprimand. Ultimately, by moving too quickly, they picked the wrong target.

Brady had to live with the consequences of those accusations and still focus on trying to win Super Bowls for parts of three seasons. Incredibly, he won championships in two of them. The stress was constant and difficult to deal with. Being asked questions for weeks and weeks about the pressure of footballs used in a blowout was utter nonsense, but the fever pitch was so high it caused the quarterback and his family much anxiety and stress.

Brady did triumph against the Seahawks, in February of 2015, when the Patriots won Super Bowl XLIX, 28–24, after the dumbest scandal in sports history had bubbled to the surface. All that hard work and dedication had paid off. It also helped that Malcolm Butler had pulled off one of the most amazing plays in NFL history with his goal-line interception late in the fourth quarter, after TB12 had led the Patriots on a furious comeback, erasing a double-digit deficit.

That night, Brady tied the great Terry Bradshaw and Joe Montana, his boyhood idol, as the quarterbacks to win the most Super Bowls (four). After that title, before the investigation and suspension, Tom seemed overwhelmed. He was trying to process the final minutes—the big comeback that turned into certain defeat that turned into a miraculous victory. I could feel his joy in the postgame interview we did on the field. His emotion was so raw, because of the scandal; I could see tears well in his eyes. As Brady told me, after chasing another championship for almost a decade, he was going to enjoy every moment of this experience and not let anyone take anything from him, because he knew he had done nothing wrong. I believed him then, and I believe him now. He left Arizona with peace of mind. Incredibly but not surprisingly, he gave the red Chevy Colorado truck that's awarded to the game's MVP to Butler.

The next morning, Tom had to get up early and honor the tradition of accepting the game's MVP award again at a press conference with the NFL's commissioner, Roger Goodell. This was beyond awkward—two people who didn't want to be there having to perform in a perfunctory ceremony in front of millions of viewers, which made

Brady uncomfortable. The moment required decorum and civility; Tom needed to bite his tongue, while still appearing gracious. You could feel the tension.

Sadly, this was the beginning of the saga, not the end. It was the prelude to one of the nastier chapters in league history, one that never made any sense. The league did its investigation, proved nothing, and yet the ultimate ruling was that Goodell could suspend Brady if he wanted, regardless of whether Goodell was right, or whether Brady *had actually cheated*. The year after the Patriots beat the Seahawks, the Broncos topped New England in the playoffs and then won Super Bowl 50, sending Peyton Manning into retirement with another ring.

Before the start of the next season, in 2016, Brady found out in July that his suspension would be upheld. He was working out in Montana, where we both have second homes, preparing for another run. When word reached him, he was livid and despondent. He even took a couple days off from training, which he almost never does, then reported to camp and played sparingly in the preseason and was forced away from his teammates for that first month.

Worse yet, his mother, Galynn, was battling breast cancer. She didn't need the extra stress. His whole life, she had rarely missed any of his games, but for most of that season, she couldn't muster the energy to attend.

That's what everyone forgets when they take the news and sensationalize it and slap up any kind of story without the vetting and care that should go into the reporting of sensitive issues. The world moves on. But the damage lingers, especially for the people who are impacted by the stories, like the subjects and their families. The stain can live with them forever, threatening future opportunities, shaping perceptions of their accomplishments. Look at what happened to Mrs. Brady. Doctors diagnosed her with cancer at the same time she was spending every day worrying about her son, just like Jewell's mother had agonized over the accusations. There may not be any correlation there, but his family was shattered to see Tom called the one thing he is absolutely not. You don't cheat your way to Super Bowl championships. You *earn* those rings.

Brady had worked too hard to have the NFL rob him of another chance to win. He was fully supported by his teammates, but the organization ultimately decided not to take on the league, leaving Tom on his own in terms of appealing the charges. So it wasn't the Patriots organization that had to fight the NFL, it was their quarterback. Nobody ever sees that side, the human side, the toll that all this nonsense took, for no reason other than the need to deliver a head on a platter had spun the situation so far out of control.

This lining up against a player rather than a team or a league happens all the time. It's like something Ebersol told me years before Deflategate. "We're not taking on commissioners and leagues here. They control the rights," he said. "You want to go after somebody, go after the players and the coaches." That was a telling statement. It's always the actors, not the studio.

Why would I want to pick on anybody? News is news. Right is right. But that's what went on here. Again: Tom Brady versus The National Football League. Now, none of this is intended to mean that Tom has lived a totally pristine life. I don't think anybody does. But that shouldn't justify the rush to judgment. Or the impact it had on Tom Brady, the person, not only Tom Brady, the otherworldly quarterback.

The next season, the Patriots again advanced to the NFL's championship game, where they faced the Falcons in Super Bowl LI. They would fall behind 28–3, then embark on that historic comeback, winning in overtime, 34–28. Brady had summoned an epic performance. He completed forty-three passes, threw for 466 yards, tossed two touchdowns, and pulled off the greatest comeback in Super Bowl history to claim his fifth title overall and second in three seasons.

Before the final whistle blew, I made my way down onto the field for our traditional postgame interview. James White had just scored on a two-yard plunge in OT, but as the celebration began, we didn't know that the play was under review, because confetti rained down on the field. Brady was just standing there, still locked in, waiting. I headed over in his direction. "Scratchy," he yelled.

"Scratchy!" he screamed again. "Get the fuck off the field!"

"Just me, Tom?" I responded, smiling. "Or the confetti, too?"

Incredible. Brady had all the accusations swirling around him, all these distractions, and he's still in the Super Bowl, still the face of the NFL, still perpetually in the conversation for league MVP. He's reviled by fans of thirty-one other franchises, because he just keeps winning. With Deflategate, the judgment never stopped.

I'm not exactly sure what can be done here. The rush is a permanent fixture on our media landscape. If you live in the public eye, you cannot escape the celebrity tsunami that spits out information rapidly, without the care that used to be involved. When you're in the public life, you have to expect the scrutiny to be heightened. Conjecture becomes truth. Truth becomes crime. Crime becomes conspiracy. See how I just grew that?

The more successful you are, the harder it gets to not have your reputation sullied and damaged over events and instances that aren't true. Everybody has a voice and everybody can shout whatever they want into the world. That's how fiction morphs into truth. That's why we don't know what to believe anymore; we make the facts our friends. People now search for opinions that validate their worldview. They don't care whether the facts are true or not, just that they're friendly. The problem with that is when I read something I know to be false, how can I trust anything else in the same newspaper or magazine or media entity to be true? I know the report on the sports page is wrong. Why would I believe what the same publication wrote about the coronavirus six pages earlier? That leads to a credibility problem that all media must now confront.

The question is: What's wrong with our brains? I don't have an explanation for that, other than we tend to believe what we see or read, and we tend to believe what we receive from journalists, and we tend to believe that people in positions of authority, in charge of higher institutions, are telling us the truth. Instead, we're all getting versions of the truth, and some of those versions aren't true at all. Some entities don't even try to get the facts right. To them, the Orwellian thought applies: truth is treason in the empire of lies.

In the case of Tom Brady versus The National Football League, I happened to witness one of the most awkward moments I've seen up close in my career after the Patriots triumphed over the Falcons. After that victory, Goodell had to hand the Lombardi Trophy to the Patriots and their quarterback, the player he had investigated and suspended and refused to back down from. Only three people heard that conversation: Tom, Roger, and me.

I was standing next to TB12, behind the stage where the Lombardi Trophy is presented. It was about ten minutes after he won the title, and Brady didn't initially go onto the victory platform because he didn't want the spectacle; he had already dealt with so much that season and the game itself had been so draining from all the excitement. He seemed simply relieved that the whole experience was not only over, but that he had come out on top and in spectacular fashion. He wanted the network to finish its other interviews before he climbed onstage to do his part on TV.

We were laughing and smiling and getting ready to do the radio interview when Goodell came up on us. We weren't expecting him to walk over; he just appeared. It caught Tom off guard. When Goodell reached Brady, he extended his hand, and for a brief moment, Tom looked at him. There was a pause. Then they shook.

"Good game," Goodell said. "Congratulations, you were awesome. That was incredible. What a comeback."

Tom looked at him for another second. Goodell tried to pull him in for an embrace. Tom did not move at all. "Thank you" was all he said. He did not go beyond that, and the words he chose to say—combined with what he chose *not to* say—spoke powerfully to the circus and the lawsuit and his triumph. By the way, I thought Goodell was professional in that moment. He walked right up to Tom, and he was gracious.

Brady didn't smile, didn't growl, and didn't frown. He just accepted what Goodell had told him without fanfare or venom or excitement. He wasn't going to forget what happened, or the toll it had taken on his family. He was . . . courteous, and in that moment, regardless of what he was feeling, he managed to keep his composure. And that spoke volumes, too. He wasn't going to let Goodell off the hook, either, more proof that there's not an ounce of phoniness in his body. As we headed to the stage, Goodell patted Brady on the back. Tom didn't turn around. Deflategate was over and victory was finally, mercifully, his.

# CHAPTER 11

# TOM BRADY

## MY FRIEND THE GOAT

I've done a radio show with Brady on Westwood One for ten years now, and he tells me the same thing all the time: "We're not trying to be perfect; we're just trying to win the game." When he said that, he meant the Patriots, even the mighty, win-the-Super-Bowl-like-it's-normal Patriots, will make mistakes, that they're human beings trying to orchestrate the most complex of sequences, that errors were and are inevitable, even in the biggest game in sports.

Brady doesn't think about football the way that mere mortals do. If his mechanics are off, even slightly, he knows immediately when he releases the ball. Sometimes, he makes a more understandable analogy, to golf. "You know how when you hit the ball perfectly, you can hear it?" he'll say. "You can feel it as it comes off the club?" Sure, every golfer knows that feeling, if not the frequency of hitting those kinds of shots.

"I'm trying to do that with every pass," he will continue. "And if I'm a hair off on my mechanics, or my footwork, or I throw the ball low rather than to the outside shoulder, I'll know I have to correct that. I have to get it right." There's a key distinction in what he's saying there. Brady must *get it right*, even though he knows he won't always be able to.

Tom remains obsessive in every way, and it's not a coincidence that he won a Super Bowl at age forty-one in February of 2019. Or that he looks closer to twenty-five than over forty-three. He's all repetition, all preparation, all if-I-do-these-things over and over, I will inch closer to my desired result.

It sounds simple. It most definitely is not. Take Super Bowl LIII, for instance, featuring Brady and the Patriots against the Los Angeles Rams. The game was ugly; the offenses for both teams stalled. And yet, there he was, in the second half of a close game, the score knotted at 3–3, his sixth ring hanging in the balance. He found one of his favorite targets, tight end mainstay Rob Gronkowski, for an eighteen-yard catch that netted New England a first down. Then, three plays later, he lofted a beautiful spiral down the left sideline, to the exact spot where the hobbled Gronkowski lumbered, diving for a twenty-nine-yard reception that moved the Patriots two yards from the end zone. They would score the game's only touchdown to take a lead they would not relinquish. Brady would secure that sixth ring, because he made the exact throw he needed, at the exact right time, and he was perfect because he had given himself a chance to reach that rarest of air through his mind-set and the work that he had put in.

That work pays off. Sometimes perfection is that simple. It's an impossible thing to harness, and it can slip away like a jellyfish held in unsure hands. You can touch it, you just can't hold on to it. The best live for the chance to touch that perfection, if only for one play.

Brady played golf in the spring of 2019, with a professional golfer who has won multiple major championships and ranks among the best players in the world. The pro shot a 79 that day and shrugged, telling the quarterback, "Well, that's just kind of the way it goes. That's the way the golf gods work." Brady didn't say anything right then, but later he said, "Guess what? If that was me, I'm not leaving the golf course. I'm going right to the driving range. Or I'm playing nine more holes. I'm fixing it right now. There's no *just-how-it-goes*."

That's a different level of commitment. One unique to the greats. Anyone can find Brady after a bad practice—he will remain on the field, correcting and adapting and tweaking until he is satisfied that he has done it right. Until there are zero nagging questions left unanswered in his head.

Now, that isn't to say the golfer might have won more majors had he adopted Brady's gonna-play-nine-more approach. Caring *too* much might have made the golfer play worse. He might have crumbled and not won any majors at all. It's more to say that Tom is different. For Brady, the drive to compete, to dominate, to never let up—all of that starts from within.

I wasn't aware of number 10 while he played quarterback for Michigan in college, where he fought for playing time with Drew Henson of all people, spending parts of those seasons on the Wolverines' bench. Or when he fell, quite famously, into the sixth round of the NFL draft back in 2000. It's not often that anyone knows the 199th selection. But everyone knows the slot where the Patriots selected him.

I first became aware of him the next season, after he had relieved an injured Drew Bledsoe. I was watching, along with the rest of a football-obsessed nation, on January 19, 2002, wondering if this young man would be able to perform under pressure, as Brady piloted the Patriots against the Oakland Raiders in a home playoff game.

The winner would land a spot in the conference championship game. The Raiders opened up a 13–3 advantage by the end of the third quarter, despite heavy snowfall in New England that had seemed to turn TV screens across the country white. Brady sparked a late comeback, despite his inexperience. He drove the Patriots downfield near the end of the fourth quarter, at least until Raiders cornerback Charles

Woodson came free off the corner and smacked into Brady, jarring the ball loose. The Raiders recovered the apparent fumble. But not so fast! Officials decided to review the sequence, and somehow, incredibly, decided that Brady had halted his passing motion, attempting to "tuck" the football into his body. Based on that logic, they changed the ruling on the play to an incomplete pass. Kicker Adam Vinatieri booted the tying field goal. New England won in overtime and Tom would go on to win his first Super Bowl (XXXVI) and his first championship game MVP award.

The "tuck rule" became infamous that night in Foxborough, Massachusetts. I hated the call. Most non-Patriots football fans agreed. I had been friends forever with Al Davis, the Raiders' iconic owner, and it bothered me how his chance to win another Lombardi Trophy had been taken away that night, by an official nobody had ever heard of, making a call nobody could understand. That night, I thought, *They're cheating the Raiders; they're getting back at Al.*

As a longtime offensive mastermind and Super Bowl–winning coach in Green Bay, Mike Holmgren said it best at one of the league's annual meetings to his brethren: if fifty people are sitting in a bar, and even the drunk ones can tell that a certain play is a fumble, then it's a fumble. Duh. I used to joke with Tom about that call and everything that happened afterward. The gist being that sometimes even a Hall of Fame career results from a few breaks. "This is a very fragile existence you have," I'd tell him. "If (the referee) Walt Coleman doesn't make that call, if there is no such thing as the 'tuck rule,' we may not even know you. You certainly don't win that Super Bowl. Maybe it's not as easy to get to the second one. We may have never known who you are if not for that guy." Brady would just laugh. I'd tell him, "You should send (Coleman) a bouquet of flowers every year."

I interviewed Brady for the first time two days before that initial Super Bowl triumph, a win over the Rams. We had spoken for the pregame radio show on Westwood One, after he had won the network's player of the year award. I made the presentation to him and lobbed a few questions his way, and I was struck then by how young he was and how normal he seemed. He gave me his cell-phone number right away. Told me to call any time.

After he won and we did our live interview on the radio as the confetti swirled, I asked Brady to come back on the field to do yet another interview for the *Today* show on NBC. It's remarkable how different he looks twenty years later, how easy it was to get him to sit down in the immediate aftermath—and *how similar* he sounds after two decades. He was humble when we spoke, selfless and poised. He deferred all credit to his teammates and coaches. And, in a nonfootball twist, he also felt that the terrorist attacks that had taken place a few months earlier, on September 11, had put this huge spectacle of the game in the proper perspective, not to be confused with more important things happening in America and throughout the world. He had this confidence that you could feel, but he wasn't cocky.

At the time, he was the youngest QB to ever win a Super Bowl. "For me, to be at this age and to really be the quarterback and in control of a group of guys like this, it's something that I'm really proud of," he said.

One year before, he had gone to Las Vegas and watched the Super Bowl like everybody else, anonymously. He would never be that way again.

His life had changed, and I wondered if that embarrassed him. "Yeah," he said. "Because there's so many things that have fallen into place, and I don't feel like . . . you're playing a team game, you don't feel like you're deserving of the attention that you get. I've got to prove it for a lot of years."

Brady said he had taken a nap shortly before kickoff. Who does that? He said the Patriots considered themselves the better team, despite entering the game as heavy underdogs. Had his life changed forever? "It's beginning to look like that," he said. "I've had so many good things happen along the way. I've been awfully lucky."


It's funny to think back to *that* Brady. He carried a few extra pounds. He still ate like the rest of us. He liked to have a good time. He was disarming and, back then, he always said yes.

I quickly saw a determination about this young Californian that I hadn't seen in most athletes, even the greatest ones. A do-not-underestimate-me ethos that bubbled just beneath the surface. He carried his draft status, his uneven career at Michigan, and how his boss at Merrill Lynch one summer told him to give up football as fuel and motivation. He balanced that steely determination with the naiveté of someone who knew he had it good, who not only became a starting quarterback in the NFL, but who won three of four Super Bowls at the end of the 2001, 2003, and 2004 seasons. No team has won back-to-back titles since, at least not through the 2019 season. Tom had become a megastar by the age of twenty-seven.

Still, fame never fundamentally altered Brady, even as so many parts of his life changed. One time, we walked around Los Angeles, with cameras following him everywhere, taking pictures, *click*, *click*, *click*.

I said, "That must be the bane of your existence."

"No, because, I like to use them, too," he responded.

It seems crazy now, especially for Brady and the Patriots, but the Hall of Fame quarterback didn't win a Super Bowl for nine full seasons after securing his third ring in '04. How many players across the league would have given up their firstborn to say the same, to have at least won three? All of them? But this stretch made for the Gap, those years defined by playoff losses, those teams that came close but ultimately lost. It took some time for New England to recover from the 2007 season, after finishing 18–1 and having been defeated after that crazy Giants, David Tyree, pin-football-to-helmet play. Having discussed this with Tom, I don't believe he has ever gotten over that loss. The hole that it created will never be filled. I've found that most of the greatest athletes feel similarly; they can celebrate the wins, but then they move forward, while the losses last forever, the opportunity missed, the feeling of defeat embedded in their souls.

Don Shula had retired from our radio show the following season, which created an opening for an analyst. By accident, I ran into Brady at the Riviera Country Club in Los Angeles on the tennis courts, as he watched his son Jack take a lesson. I expected to hear no from the guy who had always said yes to my requests, but I asked him anyway. Would he would be interested in doing a weekly segment on the *Monday Night Football* radio broadcast, taking the place of Shula and Mike Ditka, who had to step away for a conflict at ESPN. Tom asked for more details—his brain works that way—and a few weeks later, he informed me he wanted to take part. Before we did our first segment, I received a handwritten letter from him. It said, "I'm really looking forward to the season, and you will get the same effort out of me on Monday nights that I give my teammates on Sundays."

As our relationship developed, I watched Brady try and win another Super Bowl. How he managed that time, for almost a full decade, how he confronted two championships lost by the thinnest of margins, says as much about him as any title he ever won.

New England did return to the title game, like after the 2007 and '11 seasons. Both times, they met the Giants, the second time in Indianapolis for Super Bowl XLVI. New York won a close game, this time 21–17, and the Giants were aided by another borderline miraculous catch, this time by Mario Manningham, who stabbed his feet inbounds to make a leaping, twisting grab that set up the winning score.

By then, Brady and I were doing the Westwood One radio interviews every week. We had grown closer, and so I waited for him that night in 2012 outside the locker room. And waited. And waited some more. We still had the postgame interview to do. Eventually, he was the only player left. It was just the quarterback, still wearing his sweat-soaked uniform, and his personal trainer, Alex Guerrero, in an otherwise empty space. I snapped a photo that should have been splashed across the cover of *Sports Illustrated*. But it has never been seen by anyone other than the two of us. That's him, leaned forward, his head in his hands, his cleats still on, a towel draped on his head. This happened at least an hour and twenty minutes after the game had finished and the Patriots had lost. It was almost like Brady was storing that feeling, internalizing that moment, so he could draw on that pain whenever he needed to. He was surrounded by piles of trash and strewn towels, and he wasn't moving. He physically could not. He would later tell me something prescient that related to both his hardest losses and what happened after them. "You can't learn how to win a game in the NFL until you learn how not to lose," he said.

How did he work through those nine seasons? How did he keep playing? How did he become the oldest quarterback in NFL history to win a Super Bowl? It was excruciating for him to come that close and lose, but he internalized the defeat, bottling it for fuel and motivation.

By then, he and Guerrero had started their routines, which led to his emphasis on hydration and pliability and a TB12 empire that spawned workout centers, a documentary series, jealousy, some negative feedback, and even a bestselling book. Brady changed his diet, how he slept, how he stretched, how he trained. He introduced avocado ice cream to the world. He slept in recovery pajamas. He gave up cheeseburgers. He changed everything, under Guerrero's guidance and influence, so that he could play past forty, with his stated goal of playing until age forty-five. He did not want to be seen as the guy who won three titles early in his career and never reached the pinnacle again. All the greatest ever stuff—the greatest quarterback, the single best NFL player in league history—that mattered to him. But not as much as winning another ring did.

Brady liked to tell me he didn't have any hobbies, and that football and family occupied almost all his time. I'd watch him throw with his mechanics coach, Tom House, making minor alterations. It was like they were speaking another language, a mix of football jargon and science and physics. I'd watch him work out with his receivers and see him run in sand. I'd spy him with Guerrero, how they'd practice on the morning of the Super Bowl even if they weren't playing in the game, because that's the date they targeted when they trained. It was all purposeful, done to make him last, to end, once and for all, the Gap, and stave off the End a little longer.

Most summers, he trains some weeks near Yellowstone, in Montana, out in God's country. By our homes, they even mark off a football field, and he invites teammates like Julian Edelman and Danny Amendola to visit. They spend mornings outside, doing the same drills. Sometimes, I videotape the sessions for him. Other times, he needs another pair of hands. We stand there or run patterns and catch passes. Trust me, it's harder than it sounds. He will ask, "What speed do you want the pass to be: A, B, C, or D?" I always answer the only acceptable answer: A. He knows that Frann would kill him or me if I came back to our house with a broken finger, so he always lowers the speed to something closer to a B-. And let me tell you something: it still hurts, and no one is jostling with me for position, or trying to knock the ball down. Sometimes I leave that field with swollen fingers and pain that lingers for months. But in those same sessions, I also became certain that Brady would win again. It was obvious. His commitment to excellence is matched only by Kobe among the athletes I've encountered.

Leaving New England was difficult for Tom, but after two decades, he felt the dynamic wasn't working anymore. You could see this building for a couple of seasons. I asked in May of 2018 if he felt appreciated by the Patriots and did they have the appropriate gratitude for what he had achieved. He responded, "I plead the Fifth." Then, after a long pause, Brady said, "That's a tough question, but in general everyone wants to be appreciated more at work." Was he happy? He paused for several more seconds. "I have my moments," he said. Eventually, he concluded he had to leave to grow in ways he could not have if he stayed.

The Patriots went 12–4 in his final season in New England, but Tom knew they weren't consistent or dynamic enough to truly contend, the way they had for so many years. A deep frustration set in, which Tom expressed to me in person and on our radio show.

When free agency started, there were several teams involved. The Raiders, 49ers, and Dolphins all reached out. Family remained the overriding factor. His son Jack lives in New York and would frequently come to Boston for visits and Gisele's parents live in Brazil, so staying on the East Coast made things easier. But Tom is also from California—his parents and sisters still live there—so the West Coast held its own appeal, with the Niners, Raiders, and Chargers. Ultimately, Brady picked between the Bears, the Bucs, and the Chargers, choosing Tampa Bay.

Before he told the world, he called me on FaceTime and said he had gone to see Robert Kraft, the Patriots' owner. Kraft thought Brady wanted to finalize a new contract, but Tom told him instead that he was leaving. He thanked Kraft. He wanted to thank Belichick, but the coach wasn't available to meet in person, so they spoke respectfully over the phone. That conversation marked the end of the greatest dynasty in the history of the NFL and perhaps all of sports.

Tom told me he had written two statements that he planned to release, and he read them to me. He cruised through the one he had penned to the fans. But when he began to say what he had authored about his teammates, he started to cry and had to stop reading. I sat there silent, soaking in the beauty of the statement and how much his time in New England had meant to him. At the end of our conversation, Tom told me he felt happy and relieved.

In 2004, Olympic legends Sugar Ray Leonard, Mary Lou Retton, Muhammad Ali, Carl Lewis, and Michael Phelps. Phelps felt he didn't belong on the show because he had not yet won a medal. He finished his career as the most decorated Olympian of all time.

Tiger Woods after his victory at Augusta National in the 2001 Masters, which completed the "Tiger Slam," winning all four majors in a row.

Meeting a young Tom Brady in 2002, a couple of days before the first of his seven Super Bowl victories.

The early days of Air Jordan while broadcasting the NBA on CBS.

Among my favorite memories with Kobe Bryant is when he led the Lakers to a three-peat in 2002.

I trust Mike Tyson. Evander Holyfield might not.

In 2003, with eighteen-year-old LeBron James during his first NBA game, after he jumped straight from high school to the Cavs.

You never knew what was going to come from Charles Barkley's mouth, including this kiss after winning Olympic gold in Atlanta.

Arnold Palmer, Jack Nicklaus, and Gary Player won thirty-four major championships, including thirteen Masters tournaments, which made this interview my best foursome ever.

Julius "Dr. J" Erving and his sons with 76ers teammate Andrew Toney, plotting strategy during the first NBA Slam Dunk Contest in Denver in 1984.

The 1992 Dream Team was the greatest squad and coaching staff ever assembled. Head coach, Chuck Daly, and assistants, Lenny Wilkens, Mike Krzyzewski, and P. J. Carlesimo (not pictured).

Ali with Juan Antonio Samaranch, the president of the International Olympic Committee, in 1996, after Ali was awarded a replacement gold medal for his Olympic victory in Rome in 1960.

Thanks to Larry King, I had the honor of spending some time with Nelson Mandela, the most extraordinary and special person I have ever met.

In Denver in 1999, for an interview with Mikhail Gorbachev, who helped end the Cold War and changed the world.

President Ronald Reagan and mogul Marvin Davis. Marvin introduced me saying, "Meet a fellow sportscaster." Reagan laughed, as he was a sports broadcaster in the 1930s.

I loved having my dad with me for this interview with the Bush family at the Ryder Cup.

My family (*from left to right*):
Lorna, Jerry, and brothers,
Gary and Mike.

My wedding party: Jerry Gray
(best man), Chuck Daly, and
Julius "Dr. J" Erving.

Frann is the flame
that burns brightest
in my life.

My coach and
confidant Stedman
Graham with
Oprah and Frann.

The thrill of being with legends Muhammad Ali and "Smokin' Joe" Frazier has never worn off. They captivated the world and helped spark my interest in sports as a youth. Their rivalry defined boxing in the twentieth century.

Shaq and Kobe were one of the best duos of all time.

Michael Jordan and his University of North Carolina Tar Heels coach, Dean Smith. They were NCAA national champions in 1982, a first for both.

President Bill Clinton at the Presidents Cup. He is a sports enthusiast and a passionate golfer.

With President Barack Obama on my birthday, 11-11-11, during an NCAA basketball game played on the USS *Carl Vinson*, a naval aircraft carrier.

Jim – From your fellow basketball fan... all the best!

I call my buddy Jack Nicholson "The Colonel," and he calls me "Scratchy."

I still laugh when I watch the reruns of *The Larry Sanders Show* episode that Bob Costas and I were on with Garry Shandling.

John Madden described this photo with Don Shula and the Picasso as "three Hall of Famers and the painting."

With Joe Montana and Tom Brady, the two best quarterbacks in NFL history, at the NFL 100 celebration during Super Bowl LIV in Miami in 2020.

The 1997 NBA Championship trophy presentation. It was incredible to witness the excellence of Jordan and the Chicago Bulls dynasty.

Kobe left me with indelible memories. This was his last interview in a Lakers uniform, after scoring sixty points in his final game in 2016.

Next? Brady was on to Tampa Bay. I hadn't sensed this type of excitement with Tom in a long time. Yes, he still wants to play until he's forty-five, but he understands the NFL is week to week.

I've often heard Brady mock the idea of retirement. It's just not something he spends much time thinking about. "I'm retiring to what?" he'll ask. "Why does everybody want me to leave?" he'll say. He's not sure what else he would be doing right now, at age forty-three in 2020, if he wasn't playing football. He thinks the masses want him to leave so that someone else can win. He's not wrong there.

I guess I'm biased. I love Tom Brady, Gisele, his children, and his parents, Tom Sr. and Galynn. We've become more friends than broadcast partners. He has taught me so much about football, teamwork, friendship, sharing, humility, and trust. Tom trusts those close to him because he trusts himself. He is willing to give of himself in an unselfish manner and goes out of his way to help others. He is a genuine, humble, caring, and loving man. Not perfect, but striving to be. We enjoy spending time together, whether we're golfing, sharing a meal, or just hanging out. Among his many acts of kindness, Tom threw a family party at his home in Montana, where he acknowledged my induction into the International Boxing Hall of Fame. I had no idea until I pulled up to his house and there was a banner hanging out front congratulating me on my achievement. He and Gisele had spread boxing memorabilia throughout the house.

Many people ask how we became such good friends, this Hall of Fame quarterback and sixty-year-old broadcaster. I'm not sure. Our relationship grew organically. We saw the value in each other as people. Tom came to see I didn't view him as just a quarterback, and he didn't compartmentalize me as a sportscaster, dropping the barriers of mistrust.

I heard Brady say something once about missing out on the rest of his life. The interviewer wondered if he ever worried about all that he had been absent for while preparing himself for football games—

graduations, weddings, birthdays. He had indeed missed a lot of life in twenty seasons. But he didn't buy that notion. He felt good about all he could do for his family and friends and even better when he made it to the Super Bowl and could share his success with them.

I've spent time around many of the greatest athletes to ever play sports, from Dr. J to Be Like Mike to the Greatest of All Time. But to see Brady's career up close, from almost anonymous to the king of the most popular sport in America, from the 199th pick to the man who can now wear six Super Bowl rings, well, I've never seen anything quite like it.

He's still chasing perfection. I tell him it's my feeling that he has touched the concept in a way that few human beings ever will. The group of athletes who can say that is remarkably small. Brady will hedge, displaying that typical humility, but privately he will acknowledge what he has never said publicly. That I'm right. That's what both

*On the field, just after Tom Brady won Super Bowl XLIX, his fourth with the Patriots.*

torments him and drives him forward. He has thrown the perfect pass, played the perfect quarter, and led the perfect comeback. He wants to be able to do it again, and again. But he can't. No one can. You can touch perfection, but you cannot hold on to it, or take it home with you. If you are great enough, you can borrow it, like Tom has.

# 17–0, 28, 50–0 =
# PERFECT

I've been observing the pursuit of perfection ever since I graduated from the University of Colorado in May of 1981 with a degree in journalism. I still remember Gary Hart speaking to me and my classmates. You might remember him. Senator from Colorado. Ran for president in 1984. Lost to Walter Mondale. Geared up for another run in '88 but dropped out. Became a diplomat, author, writer. Hart told us, "We give you a perfect world. Don't go screw it up."

Soon after he said that, Hart found himself embroiled in a 1987 scandal involving a yacht named *Monkey Business*, two women, a trip to Bimini, and an extramarital affair with Donna Rice. This controversy all but took over the tabloids, sinking his second presidential run before it really started. But Hart's speech, combined with what happened to him afterward, taught me something about perfection: that to reach the perfect anything is almost impossible, and to remain in that space isn't realistic. So when we see perfection, when it's right in front of us, we should appreciate it, savor it, study it. Because we know both how rare it is and that it won't last.

In fact, I remember something Kobe once told me. "I understand and know that perfection can never be attained, but it sure is a hell of a lot of fun trying to get it. I know that perfection isn't a real thing. I'm a realist." Not everybody saw perfection in such literal terms.

I've seen three of the most prominent examples of this concept in sports over the course of my career. They happened with three men who couldn't have been more different in almost every aspect of their lives. I should say up front: perfection is a difficult notion to define; it doesn't always pertain to undefeated records; it's not tied every time to wins and losses or money made. But in the case of these three men— Don Shula, Michael Phelps, and Floyd Mayweather Jr.—their records happen to be the most perfect thing about them.

The men have become seminal figures for perfection, whether it's because of the undefeated football season they once navigated, or the famous "0" on their boxing record, or their collection of the most Olympic medals. They're not perfect people. No one is. But they've reached a level of flawlessness, the highest stratosphere of their respective sports, and we can learn from not only how they got there, but why, and why it matters. And trust me, it does matter.


In the entire history of the NFL, there are only four teams that have won every game before the championship contest: Chicago (1934), Chicago (1942), Miami (1972), and New England (2007). Those '72 Dolphins stampeded through their schedule, winning every regular-season game, every playoff game, and Super Bowl VII, 14–7, over the Washington Redskins. To this day, that campaign remains the league's only undeniably *perfect* season. And in order to preserve the memory of that unblemished record, up until his passing in 2020, Shula would actively root against any modern franchise duplicating his historic year, as would his former players. When the last team loses its first game, some members of that undefeated Dolphins squad pop champagne corks, their legacy secure.

In 2007, the New England Patriots became the latest team to threaten to match the Dolphins' magical year. The Mighty Belichicks finished the regular season undefeated and won both a divisional playoff game and their conference championship tilt, advancing to Super Bowl XLII, against the Giants. This made Shula nervous.

By then, I knew the coach quite well. I had covered his Dolphins teams, and even though he was known to frequently lose his patience with the press, he always remained kind in his dealings with me. He would go out of his way to accommodate my requests.

In the final years of his coaching career, whenever Miami fell out of playoff contention, Shula would moonlight at NBC for our postseason broadcasts. We both worked on the show *NFL Live*. One year, we were broadcasting Super Bowl XXIII from Joe Robbie Stadium in Miami. The San Francisco 49ers toppled the Cincinnati Bengals in the final moments, and I was standing next to Shula when Montana lofted a game-winning touchdown to wideout John Taylor right in front of us. I had been expecting that Montana would try and find his top target, receiver Jerry Rice, especially with the championship at stake. But just before the snap, Shula had told me that he believed Taylor would be the intended receiver. As usual, he was right.

Shula became my partner for our Westwood One radio broadcasts during *Monday Night Football* several years after he retired in 1995. He did that for a couple seasons and what struck me about him was that he remained a living legend and yet was so meticulous in his preparation for the show. You could see how he had become such an incredible football coach. Plus, he added credibility, with his two Super Bowl rings and an NFL record 347 career victories. Those numbers, funny enough, were part of his email address.

Shula did not join those who celebrated the 2007 Patriots. He never liked their coach, Bill Belichick, who will surely join Shula in the Hall of Fame. The Dolphins' czar was antagonized by his counterpart in New England. Perhaps it's because Shula was protective of his records and Belichick is a legitimate threat to break them all. Mainly it was because Shula was disgusted by the Patriots' involvement in Spygate, the video-

taping scandal that came to light that season. Shula thought that Belichick had cheated. He publicly called him Beli-cheat. But New England
barreled toward the Super Bowl, and, after beating the Jaguars and the
Chargers to advance to the championship game, the Patriots stood one
win from a perfect season of their own.

Super Bowl XLII took place on February 3, 2008. The game was held
in Arizona, at the University of Phoenix Stadium. The New England
Patriots versus the New York Giants. Shula was my broadcast partner
for the pregame show. We interviewed him before the game and planned
to speak to him again afterward, whether the Patriots matched the Dolphins '72 season or failed in their bid for a truly undefeated year.

I sat with Shula and his lovely wife, Mary Anne. The game was close,
but what I most noticed was not the action on the field but how much
the Shulas lived and died with every play. They did *not* want the Patriots to win. You could see how much the record meant to them, and they
were transparent about their feelings. Most would say something like
*records are meant to be broken; we had our time; their greatness doesn't diminish
our greatness.* To that, Shula essentially responded: hogwash. I had never
seen someone care so much about any one record other than Eric Dickerson, the Rams back who amassed an incredible 2,105 rushing yards in
1984. That's still the NFL's top mark, by the way, and no one knows the
number or its significance better than Dickerson himself.

That night, Shula alternated between terrified and anxious, angsty
and petrified. New England took a 7–3 lead into the half. The Patriots
went back ahead, 14–10, after Brady connected with wideout Randy
Moss for a six-yard touchdown with 2:42 remaining. Shula looked dis-
consolate. The clock ticked down . . .


The "perfect" play saved the meaning behind Don Shula's perfect season. That's the only time I can recall that I've ever seen in a football
game where all twenty-two players on the field did exactly what they
were supposed to do. Everyone on offense did their job. Everyone on
defense did their job. Even the referees didn't screw it up.

This happened with 1:15 left in the fourth quarter. The Giants, down four, faced a third-and-five at their own 44-yard line. Quarterback Eli Manning immediately came under duress, ducked, dodged, and scrambled away from pressure, then chucked a prayer deep down the field. Patriots safety Rodney Harrison defended the pass well, even got his hand on the ball, but a little-known Giants wideout named David Tyree managed to pin the pigskin to his helmet and wrestle the ball away. The Giants scored four plays later, on a pass from Manning to Plaxico Burress for a thirteen-yard, game-winning, season-spoiling touchdown.

The Shulas jumped right out of their seats, hugging, everyone slapping high fives. This was like '72 all over again, minus Don's trip off the field on the shoulders of his players. There would be no perfect Patriots season.

In 2020, Frann and I went to visit Coach and Mary Anne at their home in Miami and enjoyed several hours with them over lunch. Bo Jackson was sitting at the next table over and the coach joked that even

*When the Dolphins won in Philadelphia in 1993, Don Shula set the record for most coaching victories in NFL history with 325.*

though he was confined to a scooter perhaps he would be able to beat one of the greatest athletes ever in a race. Shula, 90, was vibrant and sharp, and, incredibly, he ate 20 cookies. When he gave me one, I understood why. He was excited about the NFL 100 celebration that was taking place at the Super Bowl, and he took part in all the festivities and was honored for his accomplishments. He remained a gentleman, a towering figure of dignity. He died peacefully at his home in May of the same year. I will miss him, his wisdom, and his council. You could say he was the perfect coach.

There *would* be the coronation of Phelps, the elite swimmer turned Olympic god. Phelps competed in five Games, from 2000 to 2016, and he collected 28 medals (or more than many countries over that same span), setting records for total golds (23), total individual golds (13), and total golds (8) in the same Olympics (Beijing, 2008).

I first interviewed Phelps at the Sydney Games, in 2000, where I covered swimming for NBC and he managed a fifth-place finish in the 200-meter butterfly, while also becoming the youngest US male Olympian swimmer in sixty-eight years. He was only a kid then, shy and introverted; he gave short answers to questions but was polite and happy to be interviewed. We would rarely feature a nonmedal winner on national TV, but NBC producer Eddie Feibischoff said, "Let's put this kid on. He's got a big future." Somehow that notion ended up being understated. Nobody could have predicted what happened next.

I spent more time around Phelps before the Athens Games, in 2004, as he attempted to break Mark Spitz's record of seven golds in a single Olympics. Phelps seemed at ease, like he welcomed the challenge and felt zero anxiety. Any doubts he might have harbored were hidden somewhere where nobody could see them. He won his first gold medal in Greece, then seized another five.

Over time, Phelps's relationship to his own greatness, to his perfect career, began to shift. He told me he struggled with fame, with having to always be both on point and on display. He had been basically raised by a single mother, the result of a bad divorce. He had also immersed himself so deeply into swimming that his existence seemed lonely, even to him. He later battled anxiety. He had stared at the same black line at the bottom of the pool for most of his life, day after day, resolute to not only touch the wall first but to swim without making a single mistake. To swim perfectly.

He told me that he had been tortured by this relentless pursuit, and that his internal struggle in regard to his athletic prowess had bled into his personal life. He could not accept anything other than perfection—as a husband, a father, a mentor, a friend. No one could ever be all those things, not at the same time, not perfect, and whenever Phelps considered his actions less than his ideal, it led him to the darkest kinds of places, to addiction and suicidal thoughts.

We forget that part of perfection. The darker part. The harder part. It's wonderful for the public and for sports fans to see Phelps compete, to soak in the indelible victories, the Olympic races won by fractions

*Michael Phelps in London in 2012 right after he became the most decorated medal winner in Olympic history.*

of seconds. But almost everyone who is watching Phelps be Phelps has no real idea what that takes. They have no clue to the devastation that causes someone like the greatest swimmer ever to peer deep inside his soul and find not comfort but angst, not confidence but doubt. All that internal torment has denied Phelps his fullest life, a less perfect and more "normal" one. I hope that in retirement he finds peace but make no mistake, perfection can come at a steep price.

There aren't many athletes on earth who understand the notion of perfection—and the pursuit of it—better than Mayweather, whose mantra was "hard work and dedication." I'm in a unique position, in that I work for Showtime, which broadcasted many of the later fights in his Hall of Fame career. I've seen him chase boxing history up close.

I first became aware of Mayweather in 1996, when he won a bronze medal at the Olympics in the featherweight division. That's actually the last time anyone saw him lose, and the decision was egregious. Still, what struck me about our introduction is that the man who later became known as Money *didn't* stand out, not the way he would later. He conformed. He fit in. He remained exceedingly polite, even after the judges robbed him. There were no hints of the bombast yet to come.

Mayweather always fought with uncanny composure that gave him a chance to respond in moments of peril, to rise and dominate, because of the work he had put in. There aren't many athletes like that ever. All work hard, but few ascend to this level, possessing myopic tunnel vision with blinders, desperately wanting to do more than win.

For most of his career, Mayweather fought on our rival network, HBO, before spending his last four and a half years on Showtime. He won ten bouts, then twenty, then thirty, then started a truly dominant run, topping opponents as skillful as Oscar De La Hoya and Ricky Hatton. Shane Mosley wobbled him with a vicious right in their bout. Victor Ortiz kissed him. Miguel Cotto bloodied him. Marcos Maidana pushed him deeper outside his comfort zone. Ultimately, though, none of that mattered. Mayweather bested world champion after world champion, even after he transitioned personas, becoming driven by wealth, collecting dozens of cars and enough houses for his sizable entourage and enough jewelry to outfit not just a football team but every player on every team in the NFL. He boasted loudly about the spoils of his success.

I never had any problems with Mayweather. In fact, he went out of his way to develop a relationship with me once he signed the megadeal with Showtime in 2013. Sometimes we'd discuss the fight that everybody wanted to see take place, Mayweather versus Manny Pacquiao. Floyd remained consistent when we spoke about the chances that blockbuster would be made. He continued to insist on drug testing before the bout. He stopped short of accusing Pacquiao of anything untoward, at least to me, but he wanted the fight to be both lucrative and fair. He also wanted to preserve perfection. That meant negotiations dragged on for six years, and by the time they did finally square off, in 2015, Pacquiao entered the ring with a torn rotator cuff and Mayweather won easily, to little acclaim.

The fight was a huge financial success, registering a record that is unlikely to be broken, garnering a full 4.6-million pay-per-view buys, the highest number in the history of the sport. I always respected how Mayweather remained in character. He never broke. His act sometimes overshadowed all the hard work, all the dedication, all the important things that really helped him to remain undefeated, so that he could make more cash and win more fights and bank more cash.

I once saw him at a Lakers game. He showed me his betting slip, the $250,000 wager on the first half alone.

"That's a lot," I told him.

Mayweather winked. Not a big deal, he said. Not at all. So he wins, only to bet $300,000 on the second half, and I looked at him skeptically and said something like, "Slow down there, buddy."

At which point, he pulled out a receipt from Bank of America. "This," he said, "is my checking account; just one of my checking accounts." I couldn't believe my eyes. This slip read: $198 million. Sometimes, to someone like Mayweather, *that* is what perfection looks like.

Perfection can take a peculiar path. When dealing with Mayweather, you're on Floyd Standard Time, but he can still be generous and accommodating. I once flew across the country, by myself, on Mayweather's plane. Showtime sent me to Las Vegas to interview Floyd after the Pacquiao fight, after Manny said he wanted a rematch and a chance to win with two healthy shoulders. Immediately following the interview, I was planning to take an overnight flight, to fulfill a commitment I had made to Brady, to interview him at an event at Salem State, outside of Boston, the following afternoon.

By 5 P.M., the Mayweather interview had not yet taken place. Floyd continued to delay, as I continued to press him, telling him that I could not miss my flight. Finally, he called maybe an hour later—only to tell me that he was at the Louis Vuitton store and would be there for a while. Of course.

"Floyd, I'm leaving," I said.

"Blow it off," he said.

"I can't," I said.

"No, you're not (leaving)," he said. "You can take my plane."

To which I responded the only way anyone would respond to such a statement. "What?!?!"

He called back with the pilot on the line and a plan in place. I met him at the store, and he was there with several women, buying expensive handbags. Afterward, he went to a Bentley dealership and bought a car, then went to dinner. The scene was at once outrageous and totally on brand. We finally sat down at 12:30 A.M., after he'd tried on several outfits for the cameras and put on gold chain necklaces. He said he was annoyed that Manny had used the injury as an "excuse." He initially told me that he would give him a rematch but would immediately change his mind after Pacquiao said the only reason he lost was because he wasn't healthy. Floyd said that if Pacquiao refused to give him credit, he would not grant him another fight. "No rematch," he said, firmly.

Sure enough, the plane was waiting when the interview concluded. I would travel alone, on the Money jet, which took off at about 2 A.M. I landed in Boston that morning and interviewed Brady that evening. We rode in a helicopter to the interview at Salem State College, where he addressed for the first time the ridiculous findings that had been made public the day before in the *Wells Report*, the idiotic NFL investigation into deflated footballs. CNN, MSNBC, Fox News, and ESPN all broke in and carried the interview live. Brady said that nothing in that report could take away or diminish his feelings about the Super Bowl victory a few months earlier, the one over Seattle, and that sentiment alone made headlines across the country, just like what Floyd had said about the Pacquiao rematch. Then Mayweather's pilot took me back to Vegas. We won a Sports Emmy for that postfight Mayweather show, adding a television victory to his perfect record.

Two years later, when Mayweather fought Conor McGregor in a silly and lucrative boxing match, I watched knowing that I had helped make the event happen. In early 2016, Mayweather and I were talking about if he would continue his career and, if so, who he wanted to fight next. He mentioned fighting McGregor, and we both agreed an affair like that would do huge numbers; way bigger than anything he might be able to find in boxing outside of the Pacquiao rematch he had already said he wasn't going to do.

I told him I knew the guy who could get the McGregor deal done, or at least get the notion of that blockbuster bout in front of the people who were running the UFC. So I presented the notion to my dear friend, a technology investor who had founded the company Silver Lake, but who has always stayed in the background, never seeking attention. My friend has asked not to be named here. Instead, let's use the nickname I've given him. SMIK, or Smartest Man I Know.

Now, Silver Lake was a major investor in both the UFC and in IMG/WME. I told him that Mayweather didn't want to fight Pacquaio again, that the boxer felt the Filipino champion had been disrespectful with the excuses. Mayweather wanted an MMA exhibition instead. Although SMIK ran Silver Lake, he explained he didn't have direct oversight over the UFC/IMG/WME investments. But he added that he would ask his team to float the idea directly to those entities.

We heard a response back promptly, and it wasn't ideal—they weren't interested. But a month or so later, I emailed SMIK again, emphasizing that this event would bank millions and millions, and there had never been anything like it before. McGregor would make multiples of millions compared with any MMA deal he had ever signed. But the UFC pay structure was actually part of the problem. The company controlled its own labor costs, and so, unlike in boxing, where a fighter like Floyd can make more in any given year than any athlete in all of sports, MMA fighters did not receive the majority of their purses. The UFC did. There seemed to be a concern that a fight like Mayweather–McGregor could threaten the financial model the UFC had long held.

They dismissed the notion again at that point, with SMIK saying that they liked the idea, but still weren't interested, not then. Soon after the second rejection, I ran into Mayweather at a Lakers game. We called SMIK right there, on the spot, and Floyd made a direct pitch, saying they're all in the entertainment business and, with their collective reach and star power, they wouldn't be putting on a fight but rather a blockbuster event. He argued that this bout would give the UFC a chance to go more mainstream at a speed and scale that only a megaevent of this magnitude could enable. SMIK said he was convinced the event should take place. Ensuing conversations with UFC/IMG/WME were more productive, and those talks turned into meetings, and, eventually, everyone got together and agreed to move forward.

I was one of the broadcasters at the event for Showtime in August of 2017. Floyd had been right. It wasn't one of the greatest exhibitions of his career—McGregor wasn't a boxer, struggled to land punches, and tired quickly—but it was an evening. Celebrities flew in on their private jets. Titans of industry mingled with stars and Fortune 500 CEOs. All this solidified Mayweather's genius. He took almost no risk and still banked over $200 million. And he knew it the whole time. Mayweather publicly signaled his intentions when he walked into the ring with a ski mask covering his face. I pointed at the mask, wondering why he was wearing it. "It's a bank robbery," he said. Easy money, more or less. He was right. He also proved that his first love remained the reward, the riches—and by staying undefeated, by keeping that "0" in the loss column, he would continue to maximize his profits. When he easily topped McGregor, he improved his record to a perfect, polished 50–0. He also proved that he could change the paradigm for how athletes in general, but boxers especially, could assume control of the financial part of their careers. He made it so the best fighters could make that much money in one night. And he did that whether fighting against famous MMA champions like McGregor or boxing unknowns like Robert Guerrero.

As for McGregor, he, the UFC, and Silver Lake made the millions that Mayweather predicted. The spectacle printed cash. After the fight that night at the MGM, I brought SMIK into Floyd's locker room. They had never met in person. The man who always stood behind the scenes, who had suggested, cajoled, and pushed in getting the event off the ground, finally got to shake hands with the champ. Floyd, sitting in his trunks back near the shower, told SMIK, "I can't thank you enough." Floyd then asked for a photographer. "I need a picture with my man!" he shouted. I had rarely seen Floyd ask to have a photo taken with anyone before. The fight wasn't perfect. The money was.

Perfection matters more to Mayweather than any other athlete I've ever covered. Why? The boxer is a historian, and he feels slighted by those who doubt his place in the sport's history, who question the opposition he faced, or when he took on older or younger fighters, or the controversies that surrounded some of his bouts. Mayweather always has an answer there, and it's always the same answer: he never lost, not in the pros. He's motivated by the record, because the record is what makes him the most cash. His perfect world is filled with material goods and stacks of hundreds. To Floyd, money also equals perfection.

The "0" became his identity as much as the cash over the years. It also changed an entire sport, forcing promoters to try and protect undefeated records and limit losses, because that's how many boxers began to judge themselves. Gone were the days when the best took on the very best, all the time, without requiring negotiations that drag on for years. Perfection cost boxing and that also derived from Mayweather's influence. He taught fighters how to take control of their finances. He made perfection into a status symbol. But casual fans became less attracted to boxing than they used to be, in part because so many of the matches aren't compelling, because the elite so rarely fight the top-shelf opposition. If fighters don't have a 0 after their win total, they've been diminished by Floyd's greatness and the perception he created. Some might believe that champions can't be that good if someone beats them. Only in boxing do they think this way. All other sports crown champions every year with several losses. We can't expect all contenders to be perfect.

In 2008, I hosted a round table on Westwood One for the Super Bowl broadcast as the Patriots were preparing for those Giants. I wanted to speak to coaches who had finished seasons undefeated, and we chose three: Shula, John Wooden (UCLA), and Joe Paterno (Penn State).

We addressed notions like how tough it was to navigate an unbeaten season. "The end of the season gets a little more difficult," Wooden said, "because the media, alumni, and there's so many others putting so much (pressure) on us."

With that in mind, had perfection satisfied them? "I don't think that you're ever totally satisfied as a coach," Shula said. "I know going through the perfect season, there were games where we won when my players wondered whether we won the game in the first meeting we had after the game. I corrected all the negative things that happened first before I talked about the positive things that we accomplished. There's always something more to learn."

Wooden would endear himself to Shula in that interview when he said that if the 2007 Patriots went undefeated, they wouldn't surpass what those '72 Dolphins had done. Perfection is perfection, after all. But what excellence meant to these men is as different as how they reached it. Kobe was right. None of them were perfect. Nobody is. But in not only striving for perfection but ultimately being defined by that very concept, these men who held almost nothing in common became men who shared the most important thing of all to them.

# CHAPTER 13

# PEOPLE WHO
# CHANGED
# THE WORLD

I've always been interested in great people, true luminaries, deep visionaries, men and women who have altered the course of history. To that end, I've interviewed many presidents of the United States, along with world leaders such as Nelson Mandela and Mikhail Gorbachev, plus astronauts like Neil Armstrong and Gene Cernan. These are the best stories from my time with them.

I first met Barack Obama before he became a national figure, outside the Bulls' locker room in Chicago, back when he was a state senator in Illinois. My broadcast partner Mike Ditka later considered opposing Obama on the ballot for US Senate. Even though Da Coach told me he regretted not throwing his hat in the ring, it was a good thing he didn't. It was obvious then that Obama had charisma and brilliance, that he could move large crowds with his speeches, and that he oozed political potential.

I interviewed Obama and John McCain in 2008 on the eve of their election night, during the pregame and halftime segments for our Westwood One radio show on *Monday Night Football*. Obama was so gracious he even stayed on for a few extra minutes, saying "I'm enjoying this" when aides tried to end the segment.

When we landed on the subject of race and sports, Obama highlighted what these games have meant to the larger world. "I'm not sure that I'm here today as the Democratic nominee if it wasn't for Jackie Robinson," he said, noting that sports is one place where Americans can come together and that he thought *Monday Night Football* was the only show that ranked in the top 10 most viewed among both whites and African Americans. "The point is," he said, "that sports has set the tone."

Three years into his first term, I interviewed Obama again on Westwood One Radio at halftime of the Carrier Classic, an early season college basketball game between Michigan State and North Carolina on 11–11–11, which is both Veterans Day and my birthday. The game was played on the deck of the USS *Carl Vinson*, the massive aircraft carrier that was docked at the naval base in San Diego. The *Vinson* and its crew had helped bury Osama Bin Laden a few months earlier.

Obama discussed how he felt about being with so many troops, aboard this famous aircraft carrier, on Veterans Day no less. He noted how long these soldiers were away from their families. He said he wanted to give them an opportunity to unwind and watch some high-quality hoops.

From there, I wondered how he felt about Joe Paterno and the scandal that was unfolding at Penn State. "Obviously what happened was heartbreaking, especially for the victims, the young people who got affected by these alleged assaults," he said. "It's a good time for the entire country to do some soul searching, not just Penn State. We care about sports, it's important to us, but our number one priority has to be protecting our kids." Obama added that too often we rely on bureaucracy when dealing with human beings. We need to tap into our core decency, he said.

In that same interview, Obama said he wanted to help college athletes cover all their expenses, even as he argued that he also wanted them to remain amateurs, not pros. He also mentioned his daughters and how he wanted to support women's sports.

What most struck me were his comments about how sports could bring our country together. "What sports has in common with our military is that they focus on mission," he said. "They're not focused on who's more important. They're not focused on who's getting publicity. They're focused on getting the job done. What I hope Washington understands is that at a time when the country is struggling and a lot of folks are having a tough time, we should not be politicking all the time, not worrying about the election all the time, and let's focus on actually improving the situation for ordinary men and women across the country."

Still, my most significant interaction with Obama did not result from any on-camera exchange. It happened in October 2015, when I sent the president a letter urging him to award the great Dodgers broadcaster Vin Scully, a man who had spent almost seven decades calling games and was more of a poet than Henry Longfellow and more of an artist than Rembrandt, with the Presidential Medal of Freedom. I wrote that no sportscaster had ever been honored with that medal and that if anyone should ever be considered for one, it was Scully, who represents the best of America and humankind. I heard back from Josh Earnest, Obama's press secretary, who thanked me for the letter and said they would take it under advisement. I asked Costas and Rob Manfred, the commissioner of Major League Baseball, to send their own letters. Both did.

Eventually, I told Scully what I had done, and he was flattered and appreciative. And finally, in 2016, he called me. He sounded out of breath. "Jim, you're not going to believe this, but Josh Earnest called me today. I'm going to get the medal. I'm getting goose bumps. I can't thank you enough for all your efforts."

Earnest invited me to the White House, and I attended the ceremony with Frann, along with Bob and Jill Costas. I shook Obama's hand, thanking him profusely. He said he was honored to award my friend and grateful that I had pointed out Vin's worthiness. When he gave Scully the award, he said, "I thought about having (Vin) do all these citations, which would have been very cool. But I thought we shouldn't make him sing for his supper like that." Everybody laughed.

I interviewed Scully that night at the White House. He described the ceremony as "overwhelming" and said he felt inadequate, having the president of the United States hang a medal around his neck.

He explained what had gone through his mind at that moment. "In all honesty: What am I doing here?" he said. "Did you see all the accomplishments of the other recipients? And then there was me? I didn't do anything that compares to what these people did." We should all have such humility. He told me it never would have happened without me, and that sentiment brought a tear to my eye.

Obama held a reception and then a party that night for the honorees at the White House. Among those he celebrated: Michael Jordan, Kareem Abdul-Jabbar, Tom Hanks, Diana Ross, Bruce Springsteen, and Bill and Melinda Gates.

*My God*, I thought when I first met Bill Clinton in 1994, *he can talk to anyone about anything*. When he spoke to you, you would feel like no one else existed in the world. He never broke eye contact and he exuded this grand charisma and great intellect. His instant recall of history and world news strained belief. Same for sports. He would cite statistics and player records from decades and centuries gone by.

That same year, his beloved Arkansas Razorbacks made the Final Four with their choreographed chaos of a defense, known as "40 Minutes of Hell." I was supposed to interview Clinton at halftime of one game, but the nod went to my longtime friend and colleague Jim Nantz instead.

While the president waited for the interview, we spoke for a few minutes. He talked about how he always found the time to watch all the Razorbacks games at the White House, adding that they had a satellite TV package. He struck me as a real fan.

We built a relationship from that chance meeting and many years later did a long segment for the Golf Channel, where Clinton said he believed golf would become more of an everyman-type sport. He knew so much about the history of golf. He referenced the book *The Greatest Game Ever Played*, about the 1913 US Open, which was won by a blue-collar amateur, an everyman, one Francis Ouimet.

In the interview, Clinton cited Tiger Woods as the greatest golfer he had ever seen in person, adding that Jack Nicklaus wasn't far behind. He mentioned how he considered Tom Watson one of the best links golfers to ever come from the United States. He noted how Sam Snead had won more than eighty tournaments, how he admired Ben Hogan, how Bobby Jones inspired awe. His ultimate foursome: Harry Vardon, Bobby Jones, and Ben Hogan, meaning he picked three golfers who were no longer alive. And his dinner foursome? Socrates, Genghis Khan, and Jesus.

During his time at the White House, I went to see him with the legendary broadcaster Larry King, who had secured his own interview with the president. Larry would include Frann and me in many of his great adventures. Hillary Clinton took us around the White House, showing off the Christmas decorations, pointing out our national tree, taking us inside the Blue Room where we would come back for dinner. At the end of the tour, she suggested we come back for the Christmas Party dinner that night, inviting me, Larry, and both our wives. And we did go to dinner, only, for some reason, when we returned that evening the great Larry King was not included on the guest list compiled by the Secret Service. Now, Larry had a pacemaker, and the alarm starts going off, as ten minutes passed, then twenty, then forty-five. He had spent all day there interviewing Clinton!

Finally he got in, and he made all this fuss about how he was going to rail to President Clinton about the whole ordeal. Larry was so upset, I was concerned he might have another heart attack. We stood in line, inching forward for a picture.

Only when we arrived to the front of the receiving line, Larry's tough exterior vanished. "Mr. President, how are you?" he asked. "It's so great to see you, so nice to be back with you. Thanks so much for having me."

"What happened?" I asked after. "I thought you were going to explode."

He laughed. "I didn't want an international incident."

Fourteen months later, on February 5, 1999, I had been invited by Clinton to a dinner honoring the home run king, Aaron, on his sixty-fifth birthday in Atlanta. This happened on the same day that President Clinton's impeachment trial was taking place in the Senate. He had already been impeached by the House of Representatives and news of the Monica Lewinsky scandal had spread all over the world. Yet the president felt it important enough to not only attend this dinner but to honor one of the greatest baseball players who ever lived. He celebrated Aaron with the honor and dignity that Aaron so richly deserved. He helped drum up support for Aaron's foundation. No one mentioned the impeachment, or the politics, except President Clinton. He stated that his job isn't always much fun, and that he had wanted to come down a day earlier so that he could prepare for the dinner. Everyone laughed. No matter your politics, seeing him there to honor Aaron, amid all the personal turmoil, embarrassment, and shame, he somehow found a way to show humility.

A letter arrived at my house in Marina Del Rey, randomly, in 1988. I almost fell over when I opened it and saw the signature at the bottom of the page. The letter came from the White House and President Ronald Reagan, who had written to praise my news-gathering efforts over the previous year or so. I had broken several stories, from Brian Bosworth signing with the Seahawks to Dan Fouts resolving his contract dispute with the Chargers to the Yankees retaining Billy Martin to Tom Flores retiring as the Raiders' coach. I'm glad that somebody recognized the work. I just never expected that somebody to be the leader of the free world. There would later be a book released about the actor turned president and one of his favorite pastimes. *Reagan: A Life in Letters.* The correspondence I received was typed, not handwritten.

> *Dear Jim,*
> *Congratulations on such a fine year of sports reporting. Your breaking of numerous stories has significantly raised the level of sports journalism. Both Nancy and I are proud of your accomplishments.*
> *As you know, I started my career in sports broadcasting and have a special affinity to your profession . . .*
> *With our very best wishes for every continued success.*
>
> > *Sincerely,*
> > *Ronald Reagan*

I had met the president years earlier, at the White House, when I went with Erving and the 76ers for the celebration after they won the NBA title in 1983. Everyone had to say their name and where they were from. I said, "Jim Gray, Denver, Colorado." He looked at me rather puzzled and kept going. I said, "Mr. President, I didn't play." After about an eight-second delay, President Reagan looked back and responded, "Well, Jim, neither did I."

I would meet him again years later, after receiving the letter, when I went to lunch with President Reagan and several members of Marvin Davis's family, including my longtime friend Gregg Davis, at the Carnegie Deli in Beverly Hills. Reagan had possessed such a presence, both as an actor and a politician, and throughout he told jokes and stories, reveling in his rewarding life.

After his presidency, he also worked, randomly, in the same office building as my father. I stopped by to see my dad after the lunch and, also randomly, ended up in the same elevator as President Reagan, along with our lunch companions. Someone asked if he had enjoyed his meal. "I had a beautiful lunch with four guys, had a really good time," he said. He didn't seem to recognize me at all or anybody else. I learned another lesson in that moment: it's tough to watch great men, great women, great friends . . . grow old. Even presidents. We didn't know it at the time, years before his public announcement, but looking back it's clear this was the start of the dreaded and horrible disease, Alzheimer's, that eventually took his life. This instance made me wonder when the disease had taken hold.

Of the nine presidents I have interacted with, I spent the least time with Jimmy Carter. I did interview him on maybe six or seven occasions at Atlanta Braves games, back in their 1990s heyday.

We once spoke about his decision to boycott the 1980 Olympics in Moscow, where American athletes did not compete. He had done so because the Soviets had invaded Afghanistan. "I have no regrets," he said of the decision. "I asked the IOC to move the games to Greece, and they didn't want to do that. I always felt that international sports brings people together and breaks down barriers. But the USOC agreed with me and voted not to go, and I don't regret the decision."

I understood the reasoning, but his decision bothered me, nonetheless. To deny those athletes who worked all their lives for that one moment in time is always heartbreaking, and that chance can never be retrieved. It would be different if boycotts of sporting events actually stopped wars, as the ideal might suggest. But this boycott had no impact, and the athletes were used as pawns for politicians, robbing them of their lifelong dreams. Athletes shouldn't be weaponized. They deserved much better.

Imagine if the same had been true with Jesse Owens at the 1936 Olympics in Berlin. If our country had decided not to go, the world would never have seen Owens smash Hitler's despicable dream of an Aryan master race. As the sprinter once said, "It was a lifetime of training for just ten seconds. And those ten seconds ended up having a great impact on the world."

That thought—coupled with his performance—always resonated with me. I also asked Carter to look back at the 1980 USA Olympic hockey team that had won in Lake Placid over the Soviets. It's the greatest victory for our country in the history of the Winter Games—

perhaps in the history of sports. Didn't that triumph and the subsequent lift it gave the country make him want to reconsider? "It was one of the proudest moments we had, and I was grateful of the achievement, but no," he said.

On a lighter note, Carter had a peanut farm. When he'd come to the Braves games, he'd bring us bags of nuts. Frann even had one bronzed and framed with the photo from my interview.

*With President Jimmy Carter at the World Series in Atlanta.*

In the mid-1980s, I went back to Vail with my friend Dr. J, who had been invited to play in President Ford's golf tournament, the Jerry Ford Invitational. When we got to the course for a practice round they had room for a fourth, so Julius ran over and grabbed me. We played with President Ford and Fred Haggar, from Haggar Slacks.

Alex Spanos came to the tournament every year. He owned the San Diego Chargers. I had gotten to know him because of my relationship with Al Davis. Spanos knew I lived in California so he asked me if I wanted a ride back to Los Angeles on his private plane. That was a no-brainer. But when I boarded, there was Bob Hope. Spanos told me that we were going to drop him off in Palm Springs. When we landed there, the pilots discovered an issue with the plane. They told us that we were going to have to stay overnight in the desert. Hope said, "No problem, come stay at the house." So now I'm at the home of the great Bob Hope with Alex, Bob, and his wife, Dolores.

The next morning, we drove to the airport, ostensibly to head back to Los Angeles. But I was wrong. Instead, we took our golf clubs off the plane and drove to Tamarisk Country Club. Waiting for us in a cart were President Ford and his Secret Service agents. So now, for the second time in five days, I would be golfing with the former president and his most hilarious friend. Hope was relentless in his teasing of Ford, who was famous for hitting people with his ball on the course. "This is the first time for me to play with the president when I didn't have a paramedic in the foursome." Spanos and I teamed up to beat Ford and Hope. I still have the $10 bill. President Ford would not sign the note, though. He said that was the job of the Treasury secretary.

From then on, every year I would go to his golf tournament. Once, he invited Erving and me to his house in Beaver Creek and we brought Chuck Daly and introduced President Ford to our little band of basketball aficionados. Now, his home sat at over eight thousand feet above sea level, and Chuck met President Ford on his outside deck, after we all climbed a flight of stairs. As he turned to me and shook my hand, he fainted. His eyes rolled back in his head, and I held him up while two members of the Secret Service ran over. We all worried he had died. They carried him to a deck chair, splashed water on his face, and, thank God, he came to. After a few seconds that felt like an eternity, all President Ford said was, "These goddamn, motherfucking stairs." Back in those days, you never ever thought you would hear those words come out of a president's mouth; it's one of only two times I heard a president cuss. He went on to tell us that a short time before he had undergone knee replacement surgery. When we left his house, we were all grateful he seemed OK, and for years after, the three of us would joke that meeting Chuck had nearly killed him.

My favorite on-camera exchange, though, took place after President Ford had left office, when he sat down with me, a sportscaster, at the Beaver Creek compound to discuss not golf, but Watergate, the Vietnam War, and the JFK assassination. He said that the public supported him because he had remained honest and straightforward. He stated that the restoration of public confidence marked his greatest contribution as president.

I asked him how much Watergate had shaken him. "I was badly shaken because I was misled by the White House on what the facts were," he said. "They were dishonest in their dealing with me, so I lost total faith in what I found when I got to the Oval Office."

The interview continued on this way. President Ford said he did not persuade Nixon to resign. He said Nixon never consulted him over whether to stay or go. He tried to explain how it felt to be the only man in US history who became vice president and president without being elected. "It was not something I had planned, because my total political ambition was to be Speaker of the House of Representatives, and I tried five times to achieve that but we never got a majority in the House on the Republican side . . ."

On a lighter note, at dinner one night I asked his wife, Mrs. Betty Ford, a woman known for her candor and courage, if she had a favorite story. Surprisingly, Mrs. Ford said it was about the Queen of England, who she found to be down-to-earth, and she told me why. The monarch had visited them at the White House for a state dinner, and she and Prince Philip had arrived early. The Fords hurried to get ready and invited them upstairs to the private residence. When the elevator opened, one of their kids ran by not fully dressed. Mrs. Ford was so embarrassed. But the Queen put her at ease. "Oh, Ms. Betty, I had the exact same thing happen at Buckingham Palace one time with my Charles. There's nothing you can do other than put your hands on your head and wipe away the astonishment. But know this: it's quite common for all of us."

What's uncommon: for her husband's ninetieth birthday, Betty still saw room for an upgrade in the president's golf game, signing him up for chipping and putting lessons. When he told me, I started to laugh.

"Why are you laughing?" he asked.

"Does she think it's really going to help at this point?" I said.

"It's never too late to improve," he said, laughing, with a wink.

*One of many rounds of golf I enjoyed with President Gerald Ford.*

Most people would ask for a party for their fortieth birthday. Or a new car. Or some new ties. Not me. When my wife asked me what I wanted in 1999, I told her: an interview with Mikhail Gorbachev, the leader of the Soviet Union. The man had changed the world and been vilified at home for it. And not only did I want that, but Frann actually made it happen, with an assist from Larry King. I wanted to host a show titled, "People Who Changed the World." The segment would focus some on sports, some on the Olympic boycotts between the United States and the Soviet Union, and some on world history. Eventually, we found out that Gorbachev would be in Denver, where my family lived, so we set the whole thing up.

The Soviet Union had been such a dominant threat to America throughout my childhood. The way I saw it, Gorbachev had basically ended the threat, making him an international hero and treasure. He rose to power in a Communist regime, where, despite this horrible system, people were guaranteed employment, they were housed and fed, and while their lives were indeed miserable, they at least had guarantees. Look, change is hard. Imagine the courage it took Gorbachev to transform that system, for himself, his people, and his country; think about what it took for him to unravel that bureaucracy, despite public sentiment that had turned against him.

We set up at the historic Brown Palace Hotel. Gorbachev told me I could ask him anything. I took advantage. "When I was in tenth grade, I became a member of the Communist Party, so I was a person who did that because I was very active," Gorbachev said. "And I believed at that time in the Communist slogans."

He then went on to explain how he was different from his "other Communist brethren." In many ways, he said, adding, "We had traveled, we had seen things, we understood that we must change because without that, despite the tremendous resources that the country had and the tremendous scientific potential, something was going wrong."

He called Reagan a "great president, great leader," despite the fact that he had once referred to Reagan as a "dinosaur." "Yes indeed, and he said that I was a dyed-in-the-wool Communist," Gorbachev said. "Sometimes we supported each other, sometimes we were angry with each other."

Given all the problems the Soviet Union faced, I wondered if he had ever put his finger on the nuclear button. He said he had been trained to, but he never actually practiced or attempted to push it. He was frightened of that kind of power and the destruction that he could wreak. "No, just morally," he said, adding that he was deeply convinced that nuclear weapons had to be abolished.

Gorbachev would admit that he had lost control of the politics back home. That nationalists went after him, even while Communist regimes across Europe were overthrown. Eventually, he did win the Nobel Peace Prize, but even as he accepted it, as I noted in the special, his enemies were plotting his downfall. He told me it had been a difficult experience.

"So it still hurts?"

"Yes, indeed," he said. "No doubt. I feel that I am responsible. It hurts that I did not do certain things that I could have done, perhaps I ought to have done. Perhaps I was not tough enough, perhaps I should have been less democratic toward certain people. Nevertheless, I wanted to show a democratic example, to give a lesson to the country in democracy. That we should solve every problem in a democratic way."

We can all take something from his courage and honesty. The man paid a severe personal price for making the world better and safer.

I met Nelson Mandela with King in 2000. Larry invited me to attend a taping of his show in New York City, and I ate breakfast with them both, spoke to Mandela in the green room, and even taped a short interview with him after they had finished. The day left me entranced.

It's funny, but one thing I remember was his handshake. He had these round, meaty fingers, and this beautiful grip that was very firm and very soft at the same time. His grasp wasn't that different from his leadership style in that it was both gentle and resolute. And that struck me, since Mandela had been a boxer, and when he was first imprisoned in South Africa, he had been assigned to quarry duty by officials who wanted to ruin his hands to dampen his spirit.

We connected over boxing. He asked me about Ali and Tyson, and we swapped stories. He said he wanted to bring more cards to South Africa.

He then proceeded to regale me with unforgettable stories. As a political prisoner, he came to know the men who watched over him, even becoming close with one guard. Some of those men were at his wedding, after he finally got out. For quite some time, Mandela was permitted one visitor a year. He could only send out or receive one letter every six months. And yet, after he had already spent several years away, officials came to him and said he could have a conjugal visit.

"That's great," he told the warden, who promised to bring his wife over the next day or the day after that.

"Oh, no," Mandela said he told the warden. "You have to bring eighty-six women."

"Really?" the warden responded, telling Mandela he should think more seriously about the initial offer.

A month later, Mandela gave the same answer, increasing the number to eighty-eight. The warden didn't get it, and neither did the guards.

Two months after that, officials tried again. "You just don't get it, do you?" Mandela told them. "There are eighty-seven other guys in here with me. If they hear me having sex, how are they ever going to follow me again? If I'm treated in a special manner, they're going to resent me, and you're going to create a distance between me and all the other people who are in here for the same reason."

At another point, near the end of his time in prison, officials told Mandela he was free to leave. They said they recognized the ills and wrongs of his sentence, and they planned to free him and reconcile. But there were conditions.

"I'm not leaving jail," he said.

"Why?" an official asked. "Are you not ready to be out on the outside?"

"Of course I'm ready," he said. "Who wants to stay in jail? But I'll stay here as long as I have to be because you need to condition the public that I'm OK and that the African National Congress is also OK; otherwise, you're going to have riots, and all the people who are Black who are going to be in the majority are going to take revenge. We're going to have chaos. And however long that takes, we will save a lot of lives, we will save a lot of heartache. We will save a lot of tragedy, and we will have a better chance at reconciliation, peace, harmony, and coexistence." He wasn't ready to accept their conditions.

He stayed in prison for many, many more months. Talk about sacrifice. About putting your people before yourself. That's what made Mandela such an incredible leader. How did he have the ability to get past the pain and suffering that he had endured and all the humiliation and deprivation inflicted upon him by his oppressors? "What we got in return was reconciliation," he said. "I had to control a lot of my emotions. By doing that I was able to have a better way of life for all of the people."

When I was with Mandela, I felt better about him, better about mankind, and better about myself. During the time we spent together I detected no ill will toward his captors; he wasn't bitter, he hadn't forgotten what had happened to him, but he wanted to look forward; he knew reconciliation would take time. The deeds of yesterday didn't need to define tomorrow. We should all exhibit such grace. "I never lose. I either win or learn," he said. "A winner is a dreamer who never gives up." Of all the people I've met, Mandela stands in a class all his own.

When I put together that TV series on people who had changed the world, I called Neil Armstrong, the first man to walk on the moon. I found him reclusive and reluctant, but I kept pursuing him and, eventually, worn down by my persistence, he consented to a telephone interview. He didn't want credit for anything; he thought the scientists and engineers who worked at NASA deserved the lion's share of acclaim. He wouldn't have walked on the moon without them.

That kind of humility floored me. Armstrong described what it was like to stand there in outer space as the first person to make that giant leap for mankind. "That was an unbelievable experience," he said. "And a great expedition and great accomplishment for America. It showed the world the tremendous scientific advances and breakthroughs that were possible by having more knowledge of the moon and outer space."

I came to know another astronaut, Cernan, quite well. Sometimes, he joined Frann and I at Super Bowls. He was the eleventh and last man to walk on the moon—for now, anyway. He's one of at least three men to fly to the moon twice.

He detailed how he had flown to the moon on a previous expedition, with Apollo 10, as part of a rehearsal, more or less, for Armstrong. They went all the way up but continued to orbit, not having enough fuel to take off again if they had landed. Years later, when Armstrong did land, with Apollo 11, Cernan said he held his breath, knowing that Armstrong's equipment would be beeping because he was coming down on a boulder field.

"We [he and Neil Armstrong] went to Afghanistan together here in the last few years and a young marine said, 'Mr. Armstrong, how did you feel when you only had fifteen seconds of fuel left and you had to fly over the boulder field.' And Neil, in his casual way as only Neil could do, said 'Well, well, young man, you know when the gauge says empty there's a gallon or two left in the tank.'"

"Here we are, forty-five years later," Cernan told me in 2014. "I luckily made those last steps coming up on forty-two years later. We last walked on the moon forty-two years ago. Nobody's been back since."

Cernan didn't think he would be the last man on the moon. "I am for now, not forever." When I asked if he thought people would ever live in outer space or on other planets, he answered, "Yes. I think we'll have habitats on the moon."

As for leaving the moon he told me he looked back at his footprints on the lunar surface. "I knew I wasn't coming back," he said, adding that sunrise remains a special time of day for him. It makes him think of his time traveling to the moon. "All of us can see the sunrise. But how many of us have been able to see the earth rise?"

Can I summarize all that? I'm grateful that I got the chance to meet those people and awed by this incredible collection of world leaders I've interacted with. It's not that I find covering sports boring, but I've always been curious to explore issues with no relation to the playing fields, to see why these great men made the decisions that they made and how those decisions and achievements changed the way we lived.

In most cases, the men above served a purpose bigger than themselves. Many of them dedicated their lives to the betterment of humanity and had tremendous intellectual capacities. They believed in themselves and inspired others. In many instances, they made the world a better place. We can argue policy or politics, but we should examine these men for what they did.

———

As for the 45th president, I first met Donald Trump in 1982, and he came across very much like the Trump you see today: everything he did was the biggest; everything he liked, the best; and every person who wronged him made an enemy. There was nothing in those days that would have indicated that Trump would one day become president. He was a character, an original, a real estate mogul who lived on the back page of New York City's tabloids and dated supermodels and sat in the front row at NBA games. He had the ability to walk in a room and make heads turn. Trump was a publicity machine, and if he wasn't faced with some sort of crisis, he could create one, thereby generating even more attention. Sounds familiar, no?

One note I want to state up front: with the exception of an interview I did with Trump two weeks after he took office, all my interactions with him took place before he became president. I knew him as a pro football owner, an NBA fan, a boxing promoter, and a golf enthusiast. I knew him before he had that kind of power—or that kind of social media reach. My observations about Trump are only from those interactions.

Trump loves golf. He saw the game as both an escape and a way to conduct business. He reveled in the fact that he could play, and did, with famous people all over the world.

In 2009, I filmed a special on Trump for the Golf Channel. The crew flew with him for three days to various courses. It wasn't really an airplane; it was a traveling apartment. Picassos hung on the walls. His name took up the entire side of the plane, so everyone knew who was inside. He could retreat to his bedroom, an ornate living room, or his working office, all of which were decked out in gold.

We had some interesting interactions that week. He wanted to know if I thought he could ever land a US Open or major championship. I told him he would probably need to take his name off whatever course he wanted to enter into that discussion. "That may be right," he said, laughing. "But my name's going to be on it." (He eventually secured the

2022 PGA championship for Trump National Golf Club in New Jersey. He did not remove his name.)

We played every day while filming. Throughout, Trump really wanted me to declare that he was "the best" at one thing or another. This proved more difficult than he had anticipated. Was he the best golfer I ever played with? Well, no. I had played with dozens of pros.

"Am I the best amateur golfer you ever played with?" he asked.

No, I told him. I had played with Tiger Woods before he turned pro.

Later on, Trump asked if he was the best golfer I'd ever played with over the age of sixty.

No, again. I had played with Arnold Palmer after he reached that milestone.

Trump continued in this way until he found a "best" something. It was the . . . best . . . player . . . I had played golf with . . . in . . . New Jersey! I had never played golf in New Jersey before, but still. "That's gotta be in the piece!" he said. Despite the bravado, Trump is a single-digit handicap.

In the interview, I wondered: Did he think his higher profile helped or hurt him with people in power?

"I think both," he said. "It helps with membership tremendously. My courses are all very successful, and they're all full. Probably there would be a group that would say, 'Oh, we don't want to have a certain championship at the course because we don't like Donald Trump.'"

Wow.

In the years that followed, I saw him at some NFL and NBA games, at golf tournaments and a few other events. But president? No. Never did I consider that. The first time he ran, in 1999, we kind of laughed about it.

Then I saw him about two or three months before he ran for real. "I'm going to do it," he said. "I'm running."

I would interview both him and Hillary Clinton on Westwood One's radio broadcast for *Monday Night Football* the night before the election. I had called him a couple of months earlier and asked if he would come on. For the last several election cycles, we had interviewed both candidates during the pregame and halftime segments, with the topics being about sports. It took some coaxing to get Trump on.

During the interview, I wondered if he would let his sons play football, or what advice he'd give them if he did. He said that he would indeed let them play, but he would not encourage them. "I see the same stories that you see and all of your listeners see and there are definitely some problems," he said.

I asked if he expected to win. "I do," he said. "I do."

He did.


Within a few hours of his becoming the president-elect, we spoke on the phone.

I congratulated him, after recovering from the shock. He said that he really liked the interview, that a lot of people heard it. He then told me what he appreciated most was that I hadn't tried to play "gotcha" with him. He thanked me for living up to my word.

Before I let him go, I reminded him that he had promised that if he won he would come back on the air in a few months on the Super Bowl broadcast and do another interview. (He fulfilled that promise, and we haven't spoken since.) Then the line went dead.

Forty seconds later, he called back. "I would never hang up on you," he said. "I'm going downstairs, and I'm in the elevator. Thanks again." I couldn't believe he was still using the same mobile number. He hadn't changed it yet.

Soon after, we saw him on TV, accepting the presidency.

# CHAPTER 14

# DREAM TEAM

## "YOU'LL NEVER SEE ANYTHING
## LIKE THIS AGAIN"

I don't know when exactly I became aware that USA Basketball wanted to do away with the rule that prevented professionals from playing in international competitions. Or when I came to understand that not only would pros play in the Olympics, but that in '92, in Barcelona, the US would field the single most talented basketball team ever assembled. Perhaps it was when Chuck Daly told me that he was being considered for the position of national team coach. My initial reaction to all that news was roughly equivalent to the way the rest of America's sports fans felt. *Whoa*, I thought, *this is cool*.

I knew about the history of Olympic men's basketball for the United States. As a teenager, I watched in horror as officials cheated the Americans out of victory at the Munich Games in 1972, replaying the final play until the Soviets won instead. I covered the Games when Team USA triumphed with amateur players like Michael Jordan ('84, Los Angeles). But the Soviet Union had not participated. I also knew that the Americans had *not* won gold in Seoul four years later, behind another collection of amateur talent. I had covered that Olympics for NBC. Those Games marked the first time the United States did not make it to the gold medal contest, having lost to the Soviets in the semifinals.

The whole experience left a sour taste in the mouths of team officials. But David Stern, when pushed by the secretary general of FIBA (International Basketball Federation), agreed to collaborate, opening the door for NBA players to play in the Olympics. That move was a game changer from a man who always dreamed big. They decided to make a more drastic change—and thus the Dream Team was born.

Now, it's important to remember that other countries already had used professional players. The Soviet Union, for instance, had captured the gold in '88 while using de facto pros that were older and more experienced than their American counterparts, who took the bronze. The pros versus amateurs debate made for an obvious and significant competitive disadvantage. But US officials would close that gap in '92, when a world that had seized on the small chunks of NBA basketball available to them on television got to watch the best players in the universe try to figure out how to form a cohesive team on the fly.

I was excited for Chuck. He had won an NBA championship in '89, secured another title in '90, and tried for a three-peat in '91, only to be swept by Jordan and the Bulls in the Eastern Conference Finals. Chuck sounded thrilled whenever the subject of the national team gig came up.

But one concern did linger, especially after that conference finals series had grown contentious. The Pistons had even walked off the court before the final game ended and refused to shake hands with the Bulls. Chuck loved his team but he was disappointed and embarrassed by their behavior and, in this instance, their obvious lack of sportsmanship. He told me he had zero knowledge of their plans. The attendant concern was how Chuck would handle some of his best players who *hadn't* made the Dream Team roster, like Isiah Thomas and Dennis Rodman.

The legend was that Isiah had been part of the group that had frozen out His Airness at Jordan's first all-star game by not passing him the ball, and Jordan had never forgotten that, because Jordan never forgets anything. But when John Stockton made the Dream Team roster and officials decided to add a college player (Christian Laettner), Chuck knew his Pistons wouldn't take those selections well. There was simply just too much bad blood between the Pistons and the Bulls, and Jordan told USA Basketball officials he wouldn't play with Thomas. So although Chuck had to live with not having Thomas and Rodman, he moved forward with the roster that American officials had assembled. His consolation prize: no better roster had ever been assembled.

In some ways, Chuck's job looked like the easiest task in the world. This wasn't so much an all-star team as an all-history one. Sometimes, I look at the poster hanging on the wall in my home office. It highlights the top fifty players in NBA history from 1946 to 1996. Ten of them played on the Dream Team, out of twelve roster spots. Ridiculous.

In other, less discussed but more prominent ways, the gig required Chuck to find the most delicate balance in the history of sports. He had so many egos to massage—colossal, planet-sized egos—and he had just the right temperament to hold them all together. That's why the American officials picked Chuck. The committee saw how he had turned a team with combustible personalities—Rodman, Thomas, Bill Laimbeer—into a championship squad. Chuck was amazed that he had won those titles. He would tell me, "It takes an act of God colliding with an act of Congress to win a championship. That's how hard it is; it's almost impossible." He described the essence of his Olympic task ahead as figuring out how to keep a group of twelve brilliant CEOs happy, despite the fact they were all more popular and more highly paid. He called it "24/7 crisis management."

I so admired how Chuck was able to get along with everyone. I would often ask him what in his personality made that possible. "Selective hearing," he would say with a chuckle. "Ignore the little stuff. Just move on. I try and take what people do best and accentuate that. If someone does something poorly, or that I don't like, I don't harp on it. If I do, it only aggravates them. So I take what I like and disregard what I don't. It helps me, and it helps them." He would figure out a way to keep all the Dream Teamers happy. He had to. Or America would again be embarrassed in a sport it had dominated since the game of basketball was invented.

I didn't cover those Barcelona Games. I was working for CBS at the time, after switching over from NBC, and my former network held the rights. I went to Europe strictly for the Dream Team, to hang out with my best friend. I went as Chuck's guest.

I read up on the Dream Team as the games approached, noting that not everyone looked at that collection of talent with the same type of awe that basketball folks did. Others regarded the roster the US had assembled as indicative of typical American arrogance. Lose one game in one Olympics and transform back into the bully and all that. Many predicted other nations would have no chance to win, saying that America would stomp all over the competition.

What I didn't expect was the Beatlemania feel that accompanied the Dream Team. They became a collective phenomenon. Bedlam was their constant companion, wherever they traveled or stayed or played. The tsunami was like seeing pandemonium around the Beatles on TV when I was young. The group had a collective star power, a global reach, and the world would indeed take notice. Everywhere Jordan went, people wanted pictures, handshakes, autographs. Same for Magic Johnson. Same for Larry Bird. Same for all of them.

I paid close attention to Chuck and the way he always wanted to come across as happy-go-lucky, stoic, unbothered by the celebrity chaos that unfolded all around them. He would say things like, "My goal here is not to get in the way" and "I'm going to try to not call a timeout the entire tournament." He didn't want to have to call over that cast of players and tell them they needed to regroup. But he also did have to coach, and that experience proved more stressful than he let on.

For one, Chuck had what he called a Magic Problem. Now, to be clear, this was a champagne problem, a first-world problem, because Magic Johnson at that point still ranked among the best players in the world. But Magic had also retired in 1991, after contracting HIV, the virus that causes AIDS. By the time the Olympics rolled around the next year, Magic had all this pent-up energy. He had rested while his national teammates played a full eighty-two-game season and squared off, often against each other, in the playoffs. The Games meant more to him than them. They were a way for him to show the world that he could still play, still lead. He worried that he might die from the virus he contracted, and he knew this might be his last chance to seize basketball glory on an international stage. But Chuck knew that Jordan would have other ideas as to who ultimately would become the team's foremost leader. And Chuck didn't want his players to turn on each other, when their competitive natures got out of hand. In this instance, he again needed to find and strike the most delicate of balances.

To that end, as the Americans prepared for Olympic competition, like against college players in San Diego, they would scrimmage but not all that hard. They wouldn't get out of control. I did not attend the 1992 Tournament of the Americas in Portland, when Team USA won all six of its games by an average of more than fifty points per contest to qualify for the Olympics.

I did see some of the early scrimmages, and when I took note of the team dynamics, I started to notice some unusual pairings. Bird spent all his time with lumbering Knicks center Patrick Ewing, two rivals turned best buds, with Ewing bringing beer to Bird after practices. While many of his teammates gambled, partied, and caroused, David Robinson mostly kept to himself. On a few occasions, he would join Chuck and me on the golf course. Stockton nursed a right fibula injury, hoping to hold on to his roster spot. Laettner remained respectful of his elders. Karl Malone was friendly and gregarious. And Charles Barkley was, well, Charles Barkley. Jordan liked to say to me that Charles "acted and behaved like the rest of us wish we could."

I went with the team to San Diego for training camp, bunking with assistant coach P.J. Carlesimo. The team qualified in Portland, then traveled to Monte Carlo before heading to Barcelona for the Olympics. And I went there with them.

In Monte Carlo, the players spent their trip enjoying the most exclusive gambling enclave in the world, while I played golf with Chuck on some afternoons at the Monte Carlo Golf Club, an average course on a hillside with stunning views of the city and the Riviera, all the splendor spread for miles down below. The Monaco stint felt as much like a vacation as a work trip. Every day, the Dream Team practiced for about two hours. The other twenty-two hours, they enjoyed themselves. Chuck didn't even think about putting in a curfew. Most of the team went to the same nightclub, Jimmy'z, and wouldn't have complied.

Still, Chuck was a coach, and his team's performance against France in an exhibition game concerned him. The officials were terrible that night, but their missed calls should not have mattered. The US would win easily, 111–71, but the team didn't play well, so Chuck called for another practice, just twelve hours later and not long before they would depart for the Olympics. He wanted to ratchet up the intensity. He wanted the players to challenge each other and themselves.

"We're going to scrimmage," Chuck told them.

Both Clyde Drexler and Stockton would sit that afternoon out, dealing with their own respective injuries. The other ten players divided into two teams: one led by Jordan, the other led by Magic. And a routine scrimmage would become the greatest game that so few ever saw.

I only know because I was there.

The contest would feature this incredible display of talent, the likes of which had never before taken the court at the same time. Here were some of the top players in NBA history, some of the top athletes in sports history, and they're making baskets and blocking shots and playing with such fervent competitiveness you could feel it. The intensity in the gym that day was so high that during a careless and unenthusiastic full-court drill before the scrimmage, Magic became so upset, he threw the ball into the stands.

But here's the thing: when Wilt Chamberlain scored a hundred points in a basketball game, he held up a sign afterward announcing his accomplishment; and when Kirk Gibson smacked that magic home run to win Game 1 of the 1988 World Series for the Los Angeles Dodgers, we all heard Jack Buck on the call for CBS radio, announcing, "I don't believe what I just saw." We witnessed these things. We heard these things. We came to know these things.

This basketball scrimmage was different from all those events. This was the greatest game ever played that only a handful of people ever saw. There is a videotape, but only one. Instead, there are the memories of the people who were there, who saw the famous Dream Team play its most competitive game in 1992 days *before* the Olympics started, with American basketball legends pitted against one another, in an almost empty gym, on the other side of the world.

It took place right there in Monte Carlo, a city where money, glitz, and glamour reign, except for inside Stade Louis II. I sat in the bleachers next to Tom McGrath, the associate executive director for USA Basketball. Besides the players and the coaches, there were maybe fifteen other people there. What was noticeable, both immediately and throughout, was Magic and Michael, Michael versus Magic, two of the greatest players ever at two very different points in their Hall of Fame careers.

The details of that day stem mainly from three sources: my memory, the recollections of others present, and the recap of the scrimmage that was written by Hall of Fame sportswriter Jack McCallum of *Sports Illustrated*, who managed to find the only tape that existed and write a lengthy piece that became a chapter in his book about the Dream Team.

The crowd was sparse on purpose, the gym locked down. Chuck's video guy from the Pistons, Pete Skorich, was the only person who videotaped the events of that afternoon. Chuck told his players, "All you got now. All you got."

During an early interruption in play, Chuck came over near where we were sitting and announced, "You'll never see anything like this again. Keep your eyes on this. Pay attention."

Everyone wanted to win, and yet no one wanted to more than the two stars who represented the best of professional basketball's past and its just as glorious present. This was not a practice anymore. This was going to be a badge of honor.

Jordan rallied his team, and, when the clock hit triple zero, they had won, 40–36. But the triumph proved to be more than a simple scrimmage win. Jordan would later tell me that was the most fun he ever had on a basketball court. To me that's because of what the scrimmage represented: a passing of the torch. Michael let Magic know, *It's my day now, get out of the way, here I come.* Message received. A new king had been crowned.

Michael wasn't content with simply winning, either, which was more or less on brand. "Way to work, White," Jordan yelled, so that Magic would hear him. Jordan continued to pace the sidelines. Jordan asked Magic, "How did you all like that ass kicking?" He slugged a cup of Gatorade and began to sing. "Sometimes, I dream . . ." and there it was, from the famous Gatorade commercial, the song "I Wan'na Be Like You" from the animated film *The Jungle Book* transformed into "I Wan'na Be Like Mike."

Even on the bus ride back, Jordan continued his karaoke session.

*I dream I groove /*
*Like Mike /*
*If I could be like Mike*
*Be like Mike . . . Be like Mike. . . .*

Magic later admitted in an NBA Entertainment segment that while he was holding a conversation with Bird after the scrimmage had ended, Jordan interrupted and announced, "There is a new sheriff in town." Magic and Bird both looked at each other. He wasn't lying, they concluded.

The Dream Team arrived in Barcelona soon after that scrimmage ended. Their fellow Olympians aimed a fair amount of jealousy at the NBA all-stars. There was a needless controversy, because officials at the United States Olympic Committee were unhappy over the fact the team didn't stay in the Olympic Village. They couldn't have. Everyone who saw them wanted to reach out and touch these guys. Every time they stepped off their bus at the team hotel, it was like a rock concert.

As the Games themselves approached, Chuck and I went to La Sagrada Familia, the famous church in downtown Barcelona. Designed by the amazing architect Antoni Gaudi, it is one of the most incredible structures in the world. For as long as I'd known him, Chuck had gone to Catholic church every Sunday. He told me his mother used to go to six or seven churches, temples, or synagogues every weekend throughout his youth, cycling through all the different denominations. Why go to so many places? "Well, I'm not quite sure who's right," she'd say. "So I want to cover all my bases."

When we left Sagrada Familia, I asked Chuck what he had prayed for.

"I prayed to God that I don't lose one of these games, because I'll never get another job and that will be the end of me," he said.

"What are you worried about?"

"The only money I think I have is what's in my pocket," he answered. Ah, the mind-set of a man raised during the Great Depression. His friends knew him as the prince of pessimism.

I spent a lot of time with Sir Charles in Barcelona, too. At night, we'd walk up and down La Rambla, the treelined street in the center of town. Barkley didn't have any security. He'd just saunter around, talking to people, grabbing drinks at the bars, making new friends, having fun. Of all the guys I covered, Charles was the most entertaining.

The theme was clear: the hardest game the US team would play had already taken place. Now, it was time for their star turn.

One morning midway through the Olympics, on a day that the team didn't have practice or a game, Chuck told me that Jordan wanted to play a certain course that was a short helicopter ride away from Barcelona, up into the mountains. As the nonworking member of the foursome, it fell to me to arrange the helicopter ride. The concierge made sure we found a pilot with impeccable safety ratings at one of the top companies. And then, one morning, up and away we went.

The group consisted of me, Chuck, Dr. J, and the greatest basketball player of all time. On the ride over, I remember Dr. J saying, "Jim, guess what? Ten years ago, I was one of the most famous players alive. If this went down then, it would have been 'Julius Erving killed in a helicopter crash with top prospect Michael Jordan, Coach Chuck Daly, and broadcaster Jim Gray.'"

*Julius Erving, Chuck Daly, and Michael Jordan in 1992 in Spain. They were my golfing Dream Team during the Barcelona Olympics.*

"Now," Erving continued, "if this goes down, you and I will be lucky to be mentioned. It would be 'Michael Jordan, his coach, and two others.'"

Jordan heard all that. "This helicopter is not going down," he said. "I've got too much to do."

Down below, the mountains were majestic; the Mediterranean, breathtaking. Chuck couldn't believe I had pulled the whole thing off. The ride lasted about thirty minutes. The whole time I kept thinking, *Wow, I can't believe we're doing this.*

We landed on the Mas Nou golf course, took pictures, grabbed our clubs, and set out to play. At that point, the only people we had run into were a couple of pros and a couple kids. That didn't last long. Soon enough, it was like you could sense a murmur in the hills. I had never heard anything like it. It sounded like a river rushing down these mountains, cascading toward the course. We soon came to realize where the sounds were coming from. Every person within what seemed like a several-mile radius was booking it toward us. The crowd that assembled was larger than a gallery at a typical tournament. It was like Jesus had arrived.

Where had these people come from? They were young and old, entire families, groups of friends; a few even carried chickens, like live chickens, to watch the four of us play golf. Jordan shook his head in disbelief. "What is going on?" he asked. But he knew, we all did. This was about him. The longer we played, the more people came. By the last few holes, I started to wonder how we'd make it back to the helicopter.

I found out that day that it's hard to play golf against Michael Jordan. Some fifty strangers became a few hundred, and then the crowd swelled to a number too overwhelming to count. We all wanted to beat Jordan, if only for a hole. Chuck had done just that a few days before, and MJ was not happy with the outcome. The defeat helped Jordan focus, and the forever-swelling crowd didn't seem to distract him. In return, he signed autographs. Waved. Smiled. Everybody just wanted to say hello, shake his hand, or simply touch him. Jordan won the match, and he let Chuck and all of us know. Daly's bragging rights were over.

When we did finish and head back to the helicopter, the scene resembled a war movie, with everyone scrambling on board. It was a little scary, the crowd unruly, the security lax. I thought somebody might get hurt, and there was nobody around to protect us, because we were in the middle of nowhere and no one had expected that kind of crowd would materialize that quickly. These people had come out of the mountains! And that was the really crazy part. Every single one of them knew who Michael was.

As the copter prepared to lift off, all these people stood underneath it, exactly where they're not supposed to stand. The course officials were trying to push them back, but they kept encroaching. Finally, Jordan said to the pilot, "Hey, man, you better lift this thing off the ground." So he did, and we did a spin around. It reminded me of when the president leaves the White House for the last time in Marine One. As we spun, Jordan waved to the massive crowd that had gathered to watch him play a sport he wasn't legendary at.

On the ride back to Barcelona, Chuck said to Jordan, "You know what? God forbid any of us are alive on the day you pass, but if you ever have surgery, or if you die, they're going to open you up and find out you got wires. Because you don't sleep, you don't rest. You're like that Energizer Bunny." That was a big thing back then. Soon after, Jordan fell asleep. Or at least he closed his eyes for the remainder of the ride. "Thank God," Chuck said. "It's the first time I think he's rested." Exhausted by the day's events, we returned to the team hotel.

Except Jordan.

He went to another golf course to get in eighteen more holes.


The Olympics unfolded exactly as expected. The Dream Team was the biggest deal, and they won by the largest margins. Barkley almost caused an international incident when he elbowed a player from Angola. "Charles," I said, "what were you thinking?"

"Well, that might not have been the best thing to have done," he said. "But he was too close."

The most dominant team ever assembled played fourteen games that summer and won each of those affairs by at least thirty-two points. The smallest margin came in the Olympic final, against Croatia, in another blowout. At least the US fell behind in that one. There was tension, if only briefly. I watched that dominance up close, from behind the team bench, with Dr. J. "I've never seen anything like this," he said.

Chuck never did have to call time-out. He came close once in that final but held back.

Before that game, I went to Barkley and Robinson and others and asked if they wouldn't mind grabbing the ball when the final whistle blew in order to give their coach something to remember. Chuck and the other coaches wouldn't receive a medal. Those would only go to the participants. The players promised they would do that. Except, as the final horn sounded, Stockton was dribbling that ball. He wouldn't give it to Charles. He wouldn't give it up, period. I even asked him to consider Chuck and how he wouldn't get a medal, and Stockton said, "I'm keeping the ball." I don't know whatever happened to it.

The Dream Team showed us, reminded us, and highlighted for us what sports can be at their absolute best. This wasn't America trying to show dominance. This was a door that opened to display a unique collection of greatness.

That team and its Olympic run helped propel basketball into a truly global force, a game popular all over the world. Be like Mike, right? Fans on every continent were able to see Jordan, at his peak, surrounded by the other most talented players in the world. And not only that, but everyone could witness how some of the best players in basketball history could play together, giving up shots and playing time in order to better mesh. The Dream Teamers showed tremendous teamwork. I can't think of any team in sports that compares.

That vaulted the NBA on a path to becoming America's greatest sports export. The game played now on basketball courts across America is truly an international one. From Dirk Nowitzki (Germany) to Yao Ming (China) to Kristaps Porziņģis (Latvia) to Giannis Antetokounmpo

(Greece), many of the league's best players have come from somewhere else—and many of them drew inspiration from watching or learning about the Dream Team growing up. If the team had never been assembled, the NBA wouldn't have players from thirty-eight different countries (or as many as forty-two in other recent years), with more than a hundred of them hailing from outside the United States. That's their legacy. Chuck's two favorite words apply, "beyond belief."

# CHAPTER 15

# HIS AIRNESS'S

# GOOD-BYE

On October 5, 1993, I was in Chicago for a White Sox baseball game where the NBA legend Michael Jordan threw out the first pitch. Chicago was hosting the Toronto Blue Jays in the American League Championship Series, and this contest marked Game 1. I was working for CBS, as part of the broadcast team.

Oddly, Jordan wore blue jeans, brown dress shoes, and a tucked-in blue button shirt while he strode to the mound, looking more like a suburban dad than one of the greatest athletes of all time. As he bounced his ceremonial throw low and to the right, a look of shock spread wide across his face. His mouth opened. *What just happened?* Little did we know that he'd hold a baseball again before a basketball, or that the sports world would share his expression that very same day.

After the game started, I received word that Jordan was planning to retire from pro basketball. The murmurs had already begun to spread at Comiskey Park throughout that evening. But even though Jordan was in attendance, he had yet to confirm, or even address anything. His longtime NBA team, the Bulls, had not responded to the speculation. All there was at that point was one report from *Dateline NBC*.

I rose from my seat in the dugout and bolted up toward the suite, where White Sox owner Jerry Reinsdorf, who also owns the Bulls, and board member Eddie Einhorn sat with His Airness. Jordan was camped out, hiding from the spotlight glare. I spent the next couple innings trying to get inside, without any luck. After repeated failed attempts, as my desperation increased, I decided to knock on the door to the next luxury box over.

The occupants of that suite let me in and asked if I wanted something to drink. Instead, I went to the end of the box and stuck my head out the window, over the ledge. I managed to get Einhorn's attention in the owner's suite, and when he came over, I asked him, point blank, "Eddie, is this true that Michael is retiring?"

He nodded his head up and down, indicating a yes.

"Can I put that on the air?"

"It's true, yes," he said.

They told me that I couldn't speak to Jordan, that he was in the back of the box and not planning to move any time soon, least of all for an interview about his future. Reinsdorf also spoke to me, confirming the news account, but he didn't want to go on-camera.

"There's a press conference tomorrow at the practice facility in suburban Deerfield," Einhorn said. "You've got the story."

I had completely lost track of the game that was unfolding down below. I didn't even know the score. Instead, I parked myself and a camera crew outside of the owner's suite, knowing that eventually Jordan would have to emerge, or else he would be camping out there overnight. Eventually, Jordan did leave, and as he walked quickly toward the elevator, he could hear me yelling.

"Is it true, Michael?"

"Is it true?"

He looked back at me but didn't respond. When he climbed into the elevator, Jordan remained silent. We followed him to his car. He turned around once more as I shouted.

"Is this true?"

He didn't say anything, but this smirk came across his face, and he spread both arms wide. He had confirmed the story without saying a word. We reported it that night, and he retired from professional basketball—for the first time, anyway—as scheduled the next day. It all seemed like *bull*shit that the greatest Bull and basketball player ever would be leaving his sport by exiting a baseball stadium.

# CHAPTER 16

# THE TRIANGLE

## KOBE, SHAQ, AND JAX

I met Kobe Bryant when he was an infant, and I later saw him wandering the hallways of that San Diego Clippers organization I once scouted for. His dad, Joe "Jellybean" Bryant, was playing for them at the time, and Kobe would run around on the court after practice.

Frann, having managed Coca-Cola's partnership with the NBA, had known Kobe since he was a teenager and signed him to his first beverage deal as an NBA player. She managed that relationship and was involved in his first Sprite commercial and many that followed.

By the time the Lakers traded for him on draft night, straight out of high school in 1996, Kobe was already a star. I was among the first to interview him in his Lakers uniform, when he arrived to help an iconic franchise return to glory.

He faced some struggles early on. Coach Del Harris wasn't playing him, and Kobe was initially frustrated. But soon enough, he began to play and start and morph into one of the best players in the league. It didn't take long at all.

Throughout all that, I interviewed him. Over and over. Before games and after games and at halftime, and we developed a real rapport. While working all those games for the *NBA on NBC*, the broadcaster Marv Albert used to always tell me, "Kobe checks in with you, as opposed to the more typical route, which is the other way around." Kobe would ask if I needed anything. He was respectful, insightful, and as driven as anybody I've ever been around.

In 2003, Kobe called me. I was taping an interview with Governor Gray Davis about the Cedar and Paradise fires raging in San Diego that had forced officials to consider canceling a *Monday Night Football* game there that I was scheduled to broadcast. Kobe was agitated and deeply upset about his most prominent teammate, all-world center Shaquille O'Neal, whom he had played with since 1996. Kobe wanted to be interviewed, so I called ESPN and made the necessary arrangements. What he said that day in Los Angeles, before the season started, carried a long way and reverberated in many directions. It was seismic.

I started by asking for his reaction to Shaq calling the Lakers "his" team and saying that "everybody knows that."

"It doesn't matter whose team it is," Kobe responded, firing the first salvo. "Nobody cares. I don't, Karl [Malone] doesn't, Gary [Payton] doesn't, and our teammates and the fans don't either. There's more to life than whose team this is. But this is his team, so it's time for him to act like it. That means no more coming into camp fat and out of shape, when your team is relying on your leadership on and off the court. It also means no more blaming others for our team's failure, or blaming staff members for not overdramatizing your injuries so that you avoid blame for your lack of conditioning. Also, 'my team' doesn't mean only when we win; it means carrying the burden of defeat just as gracefully as you carry a championship trophy."

Well, as they say in the movie *Anchorman*, that escalated quickly.

Did Kobe consider Shaq a leader? Again, he didn't hold back. "Leaders don't beg for a contract extension and negotiate some 30 million [dollars] plus per year deal in the media when we have two future Hall of Famers playing here pretty much for free," he said. "A leader would not demand the ball every time down the floor when you have the three of us [Malone, Payton, Bryant] playing beside you, not to mention the teammates you have gone to war with for years—and, by the way, then threaten not to play defense and rebound if you don't get the ball every time down the floor."

I wanted him to respond to all of Shaq's criticism. I reminded Kobe that Shaq had described him as less than a team player. Was he right?

"That's ridiculous," Kobe responded. "I have been successfully sacrificing my game for years for Shaq. That's what Phil [Jackson] wanted me to do, so I did it. Last year Phil told me Shaq was not in physical condition to carry the trust of our offense, so he asked me to do it . . ."

The interview continued on like this. Kobe said his right knee wasn't sufficiently healed to start the season, adding that "I don't need Shaq's advice on how to play hurt." Kobe noted that he had dominated before while requiring IV fluids, and played with a broken hand, a fractured tooth, a severed lip, and "a knee the size of a softball."

I asked if he would leave the Lakers when he could opt out before the next season. He said he would decide later, but added that he had told Shaq he did plan to opt out. It was obvious how hard the feelings were there. Kobe said that Shaq had not supported him during his legal situation in Colorado (Bryant was charged with sexual assault; he denied the charges. The criminal case was dropped and the civil case was settled with an apology from Kobe). He mentioned other teammates who had called or reached out. He mocked Shaq for describing himself as a "big brother" to Kobe.

The obvious follow-up came next: Why not resolve all this behind closed doors? "I asked Phil on Sunday to say something to calm this situation down before it boiled over," he said. "But he backed away, so now here we are. I have been a bigger person every time something happened with Shaq, and I don't expect this to be any different. But somebody in this organization had to speak up, because his unprofessionalism hurt us last year, and I don't want it to hurt us this year."

I knew immediately that the interview would reverberate, that it was volatile. Kobe actually wanted it to be more so. One quote that I didn't put on the air was that, "the guy selling donuts at 7-Eleven has more pride and dedication to his job than Shaq does." I said to Kobe that we were going to edit that out because I didn't think that I would ever be able to deal with Shaq again if that sentiment aired. The interview was explosive enough. Kobe understood. Shaq didn't. He also never knew how concerned I was about how Kobe's words would impact him.

I also knew Shaq and many of their Laker teammates, so I called the "Big Aristotle" and told him the interview would be coming out. I gave him a heads-up, because I didn't want him to be blindsided, and I knew the quotes would spread wide and fast. He declined to respond. But he also got mad that day and remained upset with me for the better part of two years, when he referred to me as . . . Traitor Gray.

Shaq gave me his version of events in 2020. He described the vibe at Lakers practice the day after my Kobe interview as intense. The team had put in a metal detector at the entrance of the players' facility, he said, because they thought that things could escalate, and they wanted to take precautions. Shaq said he told Kobe, "If you say anything like what you said to Jim Gray ever again, I will kill you." Upon hearing that, Kobe jumped up and wanted to fight. "Let's go now! I'm not afraid of you!" he yelled. But no blows were thrown and that situation was defused.

The interview also impacted my relationship with other Lakers. Before games, the broadcasters would often tape segments with coaches, and I showed up one afternoon to interview Phil Jackson, and he flat out declined to speak with me on camera. "Get out of that chair," he said when I sat down.

"Why?" I asked.

"I'm not doing the interview with you," he said.

"Why not?" I asked.

"Because when I see you, I see Kobe," he said. "And I don't want to see Kobe." Then he repeated himself. "Get out of that chair." So I did. I mean, I get it. Things were tense.

Fellow broadcasters Walton and Mike Breen were there when Jackson declined to speak with me. I left the room as Breen stepped in and did the interview instead, while Walton stayed to listen. Bill said it was one of the worst moments of his life. He would later say publicly—and maintains to this day—that he wished he had "punched Phil Jackson in the face and walked out of the interview. I'm ashamed of myself, and I apologize to you."

Jackson never ranked among my favorites. He lived on a constant ego trip, thinking he was better than everyone else, and smarter, too. He deserves credit for being a great coach, and he has eleven championship rings to prove it. Still, he acted like he was above it all. From time to time, I saw him treat players and reporters like they were small, dispensing wisdom from his mountaintop of Zen. David Stern, the longtime NBA commissioner, said to me on more than one occasion that the league office had grown tired of having to deal with all the whining and complaining of Jackson.

I heard from numerous coaches over the years who were annoyed at the distance Jackson kept from his brethren, signifying, in their minds, how he looked down on them, too. He went after the guy who hired him, Jerry Krause, the Bulls' general manager, who he blamed for anything that went wrong in Chicago. He picked on Krause, who had a multitude of issues. In Jackson's defense, there was some professional jealousy from his opponents. And Jordan, the best basketball player ever, said he would *only* play for Phil. But there was also genuine disdain for the way he behaved toward his colleagues, like Jerry West, the Lakers' GM, the NBA logo, who Jackson once asked to leave the locker room after a game. Due to a professional rivalry, there was also tension between the legendary Red Auerbach and Jackson, who was a threat to Red's records. I never forgot a conversation that I had with the legendary Celtics coach. He didn't buy Jackson's stated ethos. "He talks about all of this Zen stuff," Red told me. "Give me a break. He's a good coach. But he thinks he's a genius. But it was luck much more than genius that he was able to have Michael, Shaq, and Kobe. Much of the credit should go to Krause and West; they're the ones who put those teams together."

It also bothered me how Jackson ripped Kobe and called him "un-coachable," taking negative jabs at a guy who won championships for him. In his memoir *Eleven Rings: The Soul of Success*, Jackson wrote that Jordan was more charismatic and gregarious, in contrast to Kobe, who Jackson described as reserved because he hadn't developed social skills in college. Kobe wanted away from Jackson so badly that he asked the organization to trade him. In 2015 Jackson told ESPN, "Often, I could feel his hatred." I was also bewildered by some of Jackson's motivational techniques. Once he reportedly compared the Sacramento Kings' white, tatted point guard, Jason Williams, to a neo-Nazi character, and their mustachioed coach, Rick Adelman, to Hitler in a spliced video with movie clips, in an attempt to motivate one of his Lakers teams.

I was pleased when LeBron James finally put Jackson in his place. It was long overdue. Phil had called James's best friends and business partners a "posse" to an ESPN reporter and James went public over his disappointment with those comments. "To use that label, and if you go and read the definition of what the word 'posse' is, it's not what I've built over my career," James told reporters. "It's not what I stand for, it's not what my family stands for. I believe the only reason he used that word is because he sees young African-Americans trying to make a difference." Well said.

Kobe and I continued to stay connected during his career and after he retired (with five championship rings) in 2016. The fact that he continued to call even after he stopped playing spoke to the depth of our relationship, which continued to grow. The next year I heard from a group of businessmen in Hong Kong. They wanted to fly Kobe over for a question-and-answer-and-picture session, and they had been unsuccessful in reaching him through either his representatives or the Lakers. They wanted to know if I could float their idea to Kobe, and when I did on their behalf, he seemed interested, especially in the seven figures he would make for that one event.

Bryant's rep, Molly Carter, handled the negotiations, ironing out how he would fly (private) and the length of time he'd spend at the event. Kobe stepped in only when the organizers wanted to cut me out of the equation. No Jim, he said, no deal. Our relationship meant that much to him.

Kobe spent more than twenty-four hours on that plane en route to Hong Kong, after his landing had been blocked and the pilot had been forced to detour to Japan, where the plane waited for clearance. He arrived just before the event, which took place at night, and answered questions for an hour on the top floor of the Ritz-Carlton. He also posed for pictures and signed autographs.

From there, the night took a wild turn. We went to karaoke. After Kobe sang *Empire State of Mind* by Jay-Z, I did *Take Me Home, Country Roads* by John Denver, and then Kobe and Frann serenaded me with *Can't Help Falling in Love* by Elvis. We watched the businessmen play poker with pro Phil Ivey. You've never seen so many people happy to lose their cash. We were only in Hong Kong for about thirty-six hours, but Kobe showed us videos on his phone of his daughter Gianna playing basketball, matched up against him. It was uncanny, the resemblance. It was like watching Kobe versus Bryant. "It's so weird how genetics work," he said with a chuckle. I will always cherish that trip we took together—and I would cherish it even more soon after, when it became unbearably clear we'd never take another trip together again.

One of the worst days of my life was January 26, 2020, the date that Kobe Bryant died in a helicopter crash. He was forty-one years old and traveling with Gianna, who everyone called Gigi, and seven other passengers. In the final days of his life, Bryant had sat down for an ESPN+ project with Jackson, the coach who had been so nasty to him. They had come full circle. Kobe had largely forgiven Jackson for what he had written in that book and for the way that Jackson had treated him in general. Kobe was even considering having Jackson come with Jordan to play a role in his Hall of Fame induction in 2020.

I found out about Kobe's death from Stephen Espinoza, my boss at Showtime, while eating lunch in Manhattan.

The text read: "Kobe??? I'm in shock."

"What happened?" I asked.

The worst possible thing. I called Frann, same as always. We were both shocked. Within moments, I was doing a phone interview on Fox, and then I went into the studio, where I talked about Kobe and his legacy for hours. This death hurt as bad as anything can hurt. I'd known Kobe his whole life. My heart broke for his family. I had done more than a hundred interviews with him, including his first game and his last one in a Lakers uniform. I had wondered how he hoped to be remembered. "As a talented overachiever," he said. "Blessed with talent but worked as if he had none." That sentiment remains etched into my memory. But so does his love for his girls (#girldad). I knew his daughter, how much she meant to him, how much life he had in front of him, and how many amazing things he planned to do both inside and outside of basketball, now through his daughter. I had known many of the stories of his countless acts of kindness that he wanted no credit for and the players he mentored and the lives he changed. It hurt, because I would never have expected that this was how his life would end. I'm still mourning Kobe's death.

O'Neal and Kobe weren't good friends, but they had agreed to a detente. I do think Shaq had found an appreciation for his rival/teammate as the years had passed. He was despondent over the crash and had appreciated how Kobe had been in touch with his son Shareef that day. Shaq knows their names will be tied together forever and that what they did was special and that Kobe left us far too soon.

Perhaps there's irony that in the days before his death, Kobe was at peace with Jackson, and any anxious moments with Shaq had long passed. On my end, Shaq and I have resumed the relationship we had before that Kobe interview. As for Phil, especially after Kobe's passing, maybe someday we can end the tension that exists between us.

# CHAPTER 17

# MALICE

## AT THE PALACE

When I first started covering sports, long before email or this crazy idea called the internet, the interactions between the athletes who basked in glory and the fans who showered them with praise were mostly civil and defined by mutual respect. I don't say that to diminish the poor treatment of African American athletes before and after Jackie Robinson broke baseball's color barrier, or to ignore the racial epithets that were thrown their way. Such behavior was and remains despicable. But overall, fan-athlete interaction was much less contentious, and that made for a more innocent time. No trolling on Twitter. No Facebook feuds. Ticket buyers didn't pay as much for seats. They didn't know everything about their favorite athletes. They couldn't follow them anywhere, or on anything, unless they stooped to stalking and even then, the most fevered fans didn't know where, say, Larry Bird had eaten breakfast that very morning. There was no Instagram for that day's superstars to post his latest car purchase, or vacation spot.

Back in that day, fans liked or followed a player and a team based on their style of play, their winning record, or home-team allegiances. They waited patiently for autographs and had nowhere to sell them. Interactions weren't colored by fantasy leagues or social media accounts. Fans didn't judge athletes based on what they liked or disliked away from the arena. The media had greater access to the players. The public? It had less. Players rarely left the court, or the fields, on which they starred. Fans jeered and booed, sure. But for the most part, they stayed in the stands.

All of which sets one incredible stage for the night of November 19, 2004. The Indiana Pacers versus the Detroit Pistons. The game held at the Palace of Auburn Hills. Of all the events I've witnessed in my career, of all the best-laid plans gone awry and moments that flew off the rails, I've never seen anything quite like this. On that day, the dynamic of fan/athlete interaction changed forever, with me, microphone in hand, standing in the middle of it. That night will be forever known by the most accurate of titles. *The Malice at the Palace.*

The broadcast team went to the shoot around that morning. We usually did before we met together to go over the plan for that night, before heading our separate ways, whittling away the hours before tip-off.

I had lunch that day with Chuck Daly. He had moved to South Florida but kept a home in his old haunt, and he happened to be back in Detroit for a few days. He stopped by the Townsend Hotel, where I was staying, to visit his former assistant and current Pacers head coach, Rick Carlisle, who joined us. What an hour. Pacers players Ron Artest and Reggie Miller stopped by our table to say hello. Chuck told us that he didn't know Artest, but the forward reminded him of Dennis Rodman, his former Pistons superstar. Artest struck Daly as the same kind of player, driven by desire, unafraid of doing the so-called dirty work. Chuck added that players like Artest and Rodman were special, but they needed to be coached with great care, because they are sensitive and extreme and prone to wild swings in behavior. "You don't know what can happen with guys like that from moment to moment," Chuck said.

Carlisle listened carefully. He had no idea what would transpire just a few short hours later: an incident that would significantly alter the Pacers' franchise, its forward's reputation, and the relationship between fans and players throughout sports.

I had come to know Artest up close and personal, especially the close proximity that he would inflict upon opponents. Pain defined our intro-duction, which took place during his 1999–2000 rookie season with the Chicago Bulls. I was working an NBC broadcast with Marv Albert and our crew. I was sitting in the front row on the baseline and the whistle blew and the ball went out of bounds. I looked down at the monitor, trying to glimpse the replay, and Artest had attempted to save the ball, only his attempt began a full two seconds after the play had ended. I'm not sure why. I wish to God he had pulled up. But he didn't. Instead, he crashed into me, and his body collided with the bridge of my nose. The impact knocked me from my chair and the back of my head hit the floor, leaving me woozy and concussed.

Yes, Artest managed to complete a service that aggrieved athletes over the years would have liked to perform. He knocked me out. As in, he . . . knocked . . . me . . . unconscious. In fact, Garry Shandling, who I miss on a daily basis, once told me I should have my own show and it should be entitled, *I Can Make You Hit Me*. I didn't do the show. But Garry got his wish.

Now, I've done enough sideline reporting to know the dangers. I've been tangled up on NFL fields, as cameramen backed into me and tack-lers landed on top of them. I've seen my counterparts suffer bruises from footballs and baseballs that struck their faces, seen Gatorade baths land on their suited shoulders, seen foul balls whiz by, inches away. I don't want to overstate that. My suits have been stained by blood at fights. I've also been showered several times with champagne in celebrations— Bulls, Lakers, Pistons, Marlins, Yankees, Braves—of one sort or another.

I've been banged around a little bit but never hurt before that night. Not even bruised. Artest hit me like Foreman hit Frazier. Down goes Gray! That's the first time I met him.

As officials took me back into the training room, my cohorts chortled on the air. Marv loved it! "Our colleague, Jim Gray, knocked cold by the Flying Ron Artest!" I was helped to the Bulls training room. Trust me, it's funnier in hindsight. I came to, both dazed and confused and wondering, *This is where I ended up?* Artest came back to check on me maybe fifteen minutes later. He apologized and told me he would cover any expenses that resulted from the spill. From that KO, we forged a great relationship. I was touched by the genuine concern he showed, and from that point on, he would always go out of his way to stay in touch. I asked him that night what any normal person would wonder of someone who flattened them for no good reason. What in the world were you thinking?

Over the years, I'm not the only person who has asked that.

I broadcasted the Malice game for ESPN, along with Mike Breen, Bill Walton, and Eddie Feibischoff as the producer in the truck. What stands out most about the contest was the end. The official record shows the Pacers won the first quarter, 34–27, and opened up a big lead before half-time, ballooning their advantage to 59–43. I interviewed an annoyed Artest on camera at the break, and he complained several times about being fouled and not getting calls from the officials. He also promoted an album he had finished that was set to come out a week later. In fact, he had asked the Pacers if he could take a month off during the season to promote the tracks. The team said no, but Artest had appeared to signal his own disinterest in that season before that night. The box score says that 22,076 packed into the stands that night, some with full beer or soda cups in hand, we would find out, a few more dangerous than others. I can't recall the top scorers beyond Artest. I don't know any definitive play.

But the most infamous brawl in NBA history, if not all of sports?

Well, that started when the clock hit 45.9 seconds remaining in the fourth quarter. I was seated near the scorer's table, on the same side as the Pacers' bench. I saw Pistons center Ben Wallace, one of the most rugged players in the league, rise for a layup. The Pacers were well in front, ahead 97–82, so he was padding his statistics at the end of a game his team had already lost. Wallace later told Yahoo Sports! in 2019 that every time the Pistons played the Pacers "it was physical" and "low-scoring, just the way we like it."

So there came Ron Artest, doing what he often seemed to do quite well—agitating a player on the other team. No one infuriated his opponents like Artest, who played defense like a barnacle on a whale. He fouled Wallace and not particularly gently, and Wallace took issue with *that* kind of hack delivered *that* late in a game that had already been decided. So the center known as "Body" and "Big Ben" shoved his antagonist. And when he did, a skirmish broke out between the teams. More like a scuffle, at least at first.

"Totally uncalled for," Bill Walton said of Wallace on the ESPN broadcast.

". . . you can't react that way," added Mike Breen. "You've gotta let it go."

"That's not that hard of a foul," Walton said. And he was right.

Now, history tends to forget this portion of the incident, the skirmish before the war that would rage long enough for nine players to be suspended for 146 games, losing $11 million in salary. But it should not be forgotten. Wallace deserves a good chunk of blame for what took place. Itching for an incident, he started one.

"They need to somehow find a way to get this game over with as quickly as possible," Walton said on ESPN. If only those words had been proven right.

It's also important to note that Artest didn't even fight back once things began to spiral. Strangely, he chose to lie down on the scorer's table mere feet from where I sat, which has to be the only time that ever happened in NBA history. Here was a player who led his team with twenty-four points but incited a shove that started a brawl and then plopped down on the table no one ever lies down on, like he wanted to catch a nap. Only Artest.

I leaned over and told him he would be named the game's star. Asked him to stay on court for the requisite interview. "We're going to talk to you afterward," I said. OK, he responded. I marveled briefly at how Artest tried to control his emotions, how he walked away, intending to remain calm. He tried to diffuse the incident before it started. That did not square with his reputation of never backing down. He behaved, in that moment, more like the guy that I knew, a player who wasn't just a compilation of his worst incidents, a man who added up to more than how strangers had come to perceive him. Even the night of the Malice at the Palace, Artest presented a tangled mass of his contradictions to the world.

Just seconds later, while Artest was still lying on the scorer's table, I watched a full cup of liquid bounce off his chest. The man who threw it would later say he had lobbed a diet soda but that night I thought it was actually beer that sprayed on my arm. Regardless, I couldn't believe my eyes. The drink had been thrown from the stands with precision accuracy, and if the idiot who had tossed the cup intended to incense Artest, then that idiot succeeded. I knew right away what was coming—pandemonium and chaos of the worst kind. As Artest jumped up and charged into the stands, and as his teammates including Stephen Jackson followed him, I didn't see any security guards. Another fan, after scuffling with Artest, was nearly struck by Indiana center Jermaine O'Neal, who wound up his right arm like a menacing heavyweight. I thought, *Oh, my God, this guy is going to get killed*. O'Neal threw a long, looping right as he slipped toward the floor, his fist glancing this guy's face, connecting but lightly. *Whew*, I thought. But the brawl continued.

"I got ready [to fight]," Wallace would later say in that same Yahoo Sports! interview. "And then I saw him veer into the stands and I was like, 'Oh, this isn't good.'"

I wondered the same thing as the thousands who remained in that arena and the millions more who were now watching on TV. *How in the world is this going to end?*

When Artest charged up into the stands that night, I kept hoping that somebody would stop him. He jumped over the barricade that separates the players from the fans. He tripped, but that hardly deterred him, as he continued toward the area where he thought Mr. Beer Flinger might be standing. *Uh-oh* ran through my head. *There he goes.*

It's hard to come up with a comparable moment in my career. One that came close happened at a Julio Caesar Chavez fight in Mexico City, against Miguel Angel Gonzalez in 1998, the one that ended in a controversial draw. The crowd started to riot. They threw beer bottles and even tossed chairs into the ring. At one point, the bombastic promoter Don King grabbed one of those seats and held it over our heads like a metal umbrella, while I conducted an interview in what might fairly be described as a hostile work environment and he protected his famous hair. Then officials let the police dogs loose. They were barking and biting people, but it scattered the crowd, ending the disturbing and scary experience shortly after it started. That same weekend, thieves held King up at gunpoint and robbed him for a diamond-encrusted Rolex reportedly worth $100,000 and cash. But even that failed to rise to the level of what happened that night in the arena outside Detroit. In Mexico City, no fan climbed into the ring and no fighter went into the stands. In Michigan, all boundaries were broken.

Meanwhile, Mike Breen was on the air, coming through my earpiece, saying, "He's in the stands! Artest is in the stands!" His inflection said as much as the words that tumbled from his mouth, the tone falling somewhere between I CAN'T BELIEVE MY EYES and holy shit.

"Oh, this is awful," he continued. "Fans are getting involved. Stephen Jackson's in the stands."

"This," Walton added, "is a disgrace."

"This is a low moment in NBA history," Walton said a few minutes later.

No one could tell where or when this melee might end. Jackson, a critical Pacers forward, went up in the stands after Artest. Punches flew. Beers sailed. Arena-goers grabbed anything within reach and tossed items around like javelins. In ESPN's studios, the late, great John Saunders wondered aloud if he should use the word *fan* on-air to describe the madness in the stands that night. "They're clearly making matters worse," he said. Wallace's brother, David, punched Pacers guard Fred Jones. Another fan threw a plastic bottle at one player's face.

I settled in the middle of the court, guessing that I'd be safer there, close to the brawl but also away from it. I employ the same strategy whenever a melee breaks out after a boxing match. I try and get to the middle of the ring. Or stand next to the officials, because no sane athlete would hit them, or, if they did, they would be banned from their sport for life. Even still, while standing next to the referee, I held my ESPN microphone high to identify myself so no one would mistake me for someone looking for trouble. One man approached Artest, fists raised, like he wanted to box. What was that guy thinking? That he's going to beat up an NBA all-star?

Someone started spraying something, maybe mace, and some of the residue landed in my eyes. I began to cough, eyes watering. Some would later surmise that I was crying, shaken by the events that unfolded right in front of me. But I owed the tears to those chemicals instead.

Pacers assistant Chuck Person and forward Reggie Miller eventually grabbed Artest, and several teammates helped him off the court and back into the locker room. More items rained down from above.

ESPN went crazy. We broadcast from the scene nonstop, and I delivered news hits from the court. The analysts in the studio at first defended Artest. They blamed the fans for breaking the barrier between themselves and the players, which I still consider a fair assessment. Saunders called the folks who had assembled "a bunch of punks." Stephen A. Smith described the Pistons fans as "a disgrace" and said "they should be ashamed of themselves." Tim Legler said it was their fault, "hands down." They were all 100 percent right.

ESPN heard shortly after that from the NBA commissioner, David Stern. *Quit defending Artest and the Pacers players*, he told the executives. All of a sudden, the analysts changed their stance. It didn't matter whether Stern felt like they were right, or whether the fans deserved the blame immediately cast their way (and they did). The commissioner wasn't going to have players running into the stands and beating up people who are now paying to get pummeled. No matter the circumstances, that just can't happen. Stern was right in taking a firm, immediate, and aggressive stance. The hammer came down in real time.

I continued to land interviews. I spoke to the police chief, along with several players on both teams. Pistons officials, including Coach Larry Brown and the late PR director Matt Dobek, told me that Wallace felt bad for igniting the whole thing and had apologized. I reported that on-air. Both the team and player later denied the news, publicly anyway, but Artest confirmed the apology to me—and more than once.

The Pistons organization seemed to feel that by noting his apology, we were tipping the brawl even more over the edge, and that Wallace would have to be held accountable, that he would be blamed, rather than Artest. They determined they didn't want the liability the apology would cause. In that same Yahoo Sports! interview from '19, Wallace said, "We all crossed a line." It was the closest I've seen him come to making an admission of guilt for his part in the brawl.

The reaction that stuck with me came from Brown. I had known Larry since I was a teenager, and I worked as a ball boy for the Denver Nuggets, a franchise for which he played and coached. I went to see him before I left. He was, understandably, badly shaken and upset—with the fans, with Artest, with Wallace. He even threw the PA microphone as he left the court after trying to speak directly to the still-unruly fans. He was upset they would stoop to that. Wondering where the security crew had disappeared to. Brown ached for the institution, the game itself. We all did.


In the middle of this unmitigated disaster one thing became more and more certain. The fallout, the reverberations—all would begin immediately and last long term. It seemed like no one could get enough of the brawl or any coverage that resulted from it. Except, well, the players who were involved and the man who would decide their punishments and anyone who loved the NBA. Everybody else tuned in to watch the analysis of the train wreck. And what a spectacular wreck it was.

Artest retreated to the locker room once he pushed through the barrage of beer cups, programs, and popcorn tubs being lobbed in his direction. He should thank Kevin O'Neill, the Indiana assistant coach, for what happened next. The cops came back to talk to Artest and possibly arrest him, but O'Neill refused to let them in the locker room. He explained, quite calmly, that the Pacers were holding a team meeting and that the NBA would allow no one else inside, amid a volatile and potentially explosive situation, and that only team members and staff would be permitted.

O'Neill kept pointing to the same sign on the door. It read something like, NO ADMITTANCE: NBA PERSONNEL ONLY BY ORDER OF THE COMMISSIONER. He stressed to the police that this was an NBA matter, not a legal affair. He was not confrontational, and yet he was convincing, and he helped defuse an intense situation that could have been much worse. The police had a tough job, let's be clear on that, and they didn't want another incident, so they didn't brandish any weapons, or take out any handcuffs. Mostly, they stood nearby, waiting, while Indiana's staff plotted an exit strategy. Eventually, the entire team left the locker room together. As Artest left, he put his arm around me and told me he didn't want to comment on what had transpired. He did say he had acted in self-defense. No one, police included, would be able to penetrate the fast-moving human barricade. The cops didn't try, standing by as the Pacers went past.

As the team climbed onto its bus, their coach, the same Rick Carlisle from lunch that day, did an on-air interview with me. He said he had tried to settle his players down. The incident had left him in shock, which I could see on his face, like he had seen a ghost. I'm not aware that he ever has spoken about the saga since. He really just wanted to get the Pacers out of Michigan in one piece and was concerned about what might happen in the parking lot. To do that interview, in that moment, struck me as incredibly brave. The police, who might have wanted to make arrests, may have been distracted while waiting to talk to Carlisle as he did the interview. He had to know that what unfolded on the court that night would effectively end the Pacers' promising season and change the course of not only the Indiana franchise but the entire league.

The police chief agreed to an interview right after that. He said both that he wanted and planned to speak with Artest. But we were on the air then, and as he answered all my questions, the rest of the Pacers climbed on board the bus. They would not open the door, or let anyone else on, and then they left the parking lot at the arena and sped straight to the airport. At that point, the police told me the Pacers could leave and there would be no arrest. I believe the officers even escorted them out of town. So Artest was never arrested, never questioned, never arraigned. Never any of that. Everyone helped him avoid a mug shot that would have spread like wildfire and lived forever.

*This is a miracle.* That's all I could think.

*And a mess.* Here were two teams I had previously worked for, two squads coached by men I knew, two teams playing the game I love. I hated what happened for these two franchises. I hated it for basketball. I was upset that the commissioner had to get involved and that ESPN had bowed to him. It was just a sad, horrible, bad night. Nobody came out better than the day before. Even today, nobody looks good. Immediately, the focus trained like a scope on Artest, the explosive athlete who blew his fuse and lost his cool. What about the guy who threw the cup at him? I believe he went to jail.

It wasn't for long enough.


We didn't finish broadcasting for hours and afterward we retreated back to the Townsend Hotel. It was late at night but nobody could sleep, so we began to formulate our broadcast plan for the immediate aftermath. Mostly, we were all still processing what had taken place.

My friend Bill Walton loves basketball. It's his life, along with the Grateful Dead. Pardon the pun, but he would have been grateful to have been dead that night. That's how devastated and despondent he was. All of us sat in silence for stretches, stunned into disbelief.

The producers for *SportsCenter* wanted more coverage for the next morning, correctly anticipating how the melee would continue to dominate the news. We discussed whether I should stay in Detroit, or fly to Indiana, or head to New York to meet with the commissioner.

I ended up staying in Michigan and reporting from the Palace, post Malice, the next day. There wasn't much to update at that point. The teams were of course hesitant to spin through the whole mess again. Artest wasn't talking—not yet, anyway.

I received a ton of radio requests. It felt like the Tyson ear-biting incident all over again. The brawl took place on a Friday night and the next Monday morning I went on the *Today* show. I was interviewed by Larry King. No one had seen anything like this, so they asked me to recap what it felt like to report from the middle of that basketball hurricane. I did more *SportsCenter* hits than I could count. It was inescapable. But there remained a bigger prize out there—the first interview with Artest.

Eventually, I landed that exclusive based on our relationship, after our bond had formed all those years earlier when he introduced his torso to my nose. We wanted to sit down with the suspended swingman right away, and he did speak with me in the aftermath, although not how I had hoped, remaining in contact but off-camera. His lawyers continued to advise him to stay silent, at least in public, declining all sit-downs with reporters. But Herb Simon, the Pacers' owner who is my longtime confidant, ultimately put in a good word. That helped, in a huge way.

Artest's publicist handled the setup for the interview. We sat down in Atlanta, cameras rolling, microphones affixed to our shirt collars. Artest looked me in the eye and answered honestly. He placed no restrictions on the interview, and his publicist complied with his wishes. I found him contrite.

I started by wondering how much harm had been done to both Artest and his reputation. "I take part of the ownership for what happened, so I did a lot of damage to myself that I am going to correct," he said.

That opened a natural segue. "How much damage has been done to the Indiana Pacers?" Artest noted, correctly, that his team cared about winning games and went about that the right way and had never before had its sterling reputation marred by an incident like this one. He noted that his team had still made the playoffs, despite his suspension. But, he added, "Ron Artest not playing with the Indiana Pacers is not a good thing." No, it's not.

How did he plan to correct his actions? When?

"You have to improve yourself," he responded. "You get older, you mature . . . And you should want to improve yourself if things are not going the right way." He would, Artest continued, only play basketball inside arenas from now on. He left the implication hanging but it was obvious. No more fights. No more brawls.

He said he wasn't sure what damage had been done to the league itself. "You can't take it back, because it happened already," he said. "So the best thing to do is move on and forgive everyone that did things toward me. People who kind of got my emotions to run a little bit high. I've forgiven."

His answer didn't sound like lip service, and it would prove true in the years ahead. Artest noted that he had chosen not to react when Wallace shoved him. He said he just "wanted to go home." But that didn't sound quite right, either. Sure, Artest had controlled himself while he lay there on the scorer's table. But why hadn't he done the same after the flying liquid had landed on his lap?

"I didn't expect Ben Wallace to react as he did, and I never had beer thrown in my face before," he said. "Nobody ever threw anything at me, with the exception of a few times . . ." Artest said that sometimes when strangers grilled him about the incident he would ask them how they would react. "I get mixed answers," he continued.

"How certain are you this won't happen again?"

"I'm positive," he said.

Artest told me he hated watching Indiana play without him, especially when the Pacers had fallen to Detroit a few nights earlier. He also said he had not sought out counseling, although he would in later years.

"At the same time, I'm improving myself," he said. "I had a lot of time to think—and reflected on my season. I had a lot of time to find ways to improve myself."

In a mild surprise, Artest said he held no ill will toward Stern, at least not publicly. In the interview he said he loved the commissioner and described him as consistent above all else. "He's like the daddy, the father of the NBA," Artest said. "Sometimes you gotta discipline your kids." Then he added that Stern hugged him when he handed the suspension down. That answer provided great insight into both men. Stern loved his players. He wanted the best for them. And because he was authentic, his style came across as fair.

It went well, for Artest and the broadcast, and yet the second the interview ended, the publicist told us that the forward would be appearing on TNT that same night. We had not finished in time to make any show earlier than the 11 P.M. SportsCenter. I had to call Herb Simon. "We've been working on this for months and now he's going on a tour?" I asked. He called Artest's rep and told her not to submit Artest for any other interviews. They agreed. Our exclusive aired later that same night.

I understood how Stern's viewpoint had informed his actions in the aftermath. He wanted the penalties he handed down to be definitive and harsh in order to send the most crystal clear message possible: that the NBA would not permit something like the Malice at the Palace to happen ever, ever again; no matter the circumstances, the teams, the players, or the rivalry involved, nothing like that would ever transpire, no matter what. He was exactly right.

I saw Simon's side, too. Herbie is like a brother to me. Frann would say he has been like a father since my dad's passing. We confide in each other. We look out for each other. Before that chaotic night in 2004, I thought he had a chance to win the NBA championship. The Pacers had one of the league's best teams. Just look at the roster Indiana had put together for that 2004–05 season. The Pacers not only featured Artest but also an aging-but-still-accurate Reggie Miller, the explosive and versatile Jackson, an all-star in O'Neal, and a full complement of role players around them. That team, even after the brawl and all the ensuing penalties, still won forty-four games and finished third in the Central Division. Larry Bird had performed capably as general manager. Carlisle did an amazing job, somehow holding everything together, finishing the final twenty-nine regular-season games with seventeen wins. The Pacers even upset the Celtics in the first round of the playoffs, before losing to, of all teams, the Pistons in Round 2.

Stern decimated Simon's franchise to the point where Indiana almost didn't recover. The Pacers lost tens of millions of dollars due to the backlash—the season tickets not renewed, the playoff revenue never realized. The franchise's chance to win the NBA title that season vanished as that full cup floated toward the scorer's table, because Artest failed to control himself and nobody even attempted to rein in the fans. Indiana was the best team in the league when that game tipped off. Many who backed the Pacers didn't sign up again for season tickets. It took a decade to recover, and Simon was deeply hurt, distraught, and distressed, especially when San Antonio won that season's title. He had been close with the commissioner, but their relationship suffered a setback, only to be mended a year or so later.

Indiana felt those consequences immediately, when the suspensions went out on November 21. The Pacers lost Artest for the remainder of the season, Jackson for thirty games, O'Neal for twenty-five, and guard Anthony Johnson for five contests. Miller received a single-game penalty for leaving the bench. At a press conference, Stern said, "The penalties issued today deal only with one aspect of this incident—that of player misconduct . . . We must affirm that the NBA will strive to exemplify the best that can be offered by professional sports, and not allow our sport to be debased by what seem to be declining expectations for behavior of fans and athletes alike."

The incident—and the penalties delivered in its wake—altered no less than the course of NBA history and the nature of fan-player interaction.

That's heavy stuff, I know, but it comes back to the way those dealings used to be. There seemed to be a better atmosphere in arenas, at least when there wasn't racism, which should never be tolerated. Overall fan behavior has changed since then. Somehow many forgot a simple truth. That just because you pay for a ticket to the game does not give you the license to act like a fool.

So how did that happen? The games evolved. The tickets cost more, pricing out the average fans and raising their expectations the few nights a season they could attend. The seats inched closer to the action, until a celebrity fan like Drake could lean over in 2019 and massage the shoulders of Toronto's soon-to-be championship coach. Somehow, somewhere, it became acceptable for the seat occupiers to yell whatever they wanted, at whoever they wanted, just because they had used a por-tion of their savings on those tickets. Bigger contracts and bigger ticket prices grew the gulf between players and fans. Frustration and anxiety swirled in that cauldron, especially when the performances didn't match the price. And in eighty-two games over the course of a full regular season, how many times could that possibly happen? Thus the canyon deepened, until a fan in an arena outside Detroit decided he could throw a cup of whatever at an NBA all-star.

Stern's reaction to the incident marked something of a course correc-tion. Now they don't just throw fans out of games. Team officials take their season tickets away. They press charges for the really egregious stuff.

I don't know what happened exactly in 2019, during those same NBA Finals, when Warriors minority owner Mark Stevens reached over his wife to shove Toronto Raptors guard Kyle Lowry, who had jumped into the first row trying to save a ball sailing out of bounds, while Stevens reportedly shouted obscenities at him. That Stevens owned part of the team didn't excuse his abhorrent behavior; in fact, it made it worse. Was liquor being served? Was he too close to the action? Was he worried about his wife? Tough to tell, but I'm certain that all involved would love to take back their worst moments, from Artest to Stevens and all the low points of fan-athlete interaction from 2004 to 2019. That Lowry didn't react and that Stevens was heavily penalized, to the tune of a one-year ban and a $500,000 fine from Stern's protégé, Adam Silver, showed how far the NBA had come. (And, for certain, owed to Lowry's incredible restraint.)

As bad as what happened with Artest was, the players saw the penalties that Stern imposed. The fans saw the charges handed down. That had the intended effect, curtailing anybody who thought they might do something similar, perhaps right up to and including Kyle Lowry. It wouldn't have been Lowry's fault, just like I don't think it was Artest's fault that he had a visceral reaction.

Still, I do wonder. Do fans have large ambitions to attend games anymore? You're chasing rational supporters away because a few unruly types can't behave with the proper decorum. So few ruin so much for so many. Sometimes, when in the stands at one game or another, I can't believe what people yell at these players. I cringe when I hear them. Why can't fans just go to games, root for their teams, enjoy the athletes, and go home? It should be that simple. It's not.

Everybody needs to tone it down. Sports are fun and games, entertainment. How did we get to this point? Where is the voice of reason? This book is not designed to offer a solution; if I knew one, I'd probably be an emperor somewhere, out in the world restoring public decency and common courtesy. Alas, I am not.

But I do know one unlikely place where reason was voiced in the years after the brawl. Starting with the man who started it. None other than Ron Artest.


Artest changed his name in 2011 to Metta World Peace and retired after the 2016–17 season, his sixth with the Los Angeles Lakers. He played for six teams over seventeen NBA seasons, averaging 13.2 points, 4.5 rebounds, and 2.7 assists. Those numbers tell the story of both his versatility and longevity and his high level of skill. But many don't remember that Artest won an NBA title in 2010; he even hit the confetti-clinching three-pointer. Others forget that he earned the NBA Defensive Player of the Year award in 2004, the same year he made the all-star team. Instead, he's remembered most for the brawl. And the name changes.

What's also often lost is the good that Artest has done over the years. He auctioned off his title ring for mental health, lobbied for the Mental Health in Schools Act, thanked his therapist after winning the championship, received the J. Walter Kennedy Citizenship Award from the NBA in 2011, and even befriended the guy who threw the drink at him. Artest had changed. In fact, now it seems Metta is at peace.

# CHAPTER 18

# THE
# DECISION

In the spring of 2010, before LeBron left Cleveland for Miami, I happened to be at a Lakers' home game for the first round of the playoffs. I spied Maverick Carter, James's best friend and business partner, and Ari Emanuel, the CEO of William Morris Endeavor (WME), the talent and media agency. They were sitting in Ari's courtside seats, right next to the home bench. I had an idea that I wanted to share with them both.

"Maverick," I said, as we shook hands, "I'd like to do the first interview with LeBron after he decides where he's going."

"OK," Maverick said. "I'll let him know."

I continued to expand my pitch. "I did one with him in high school, one when he got drafted, his first game in Sacramento," I continued. "I have interviewed him so many times."

Maverick nodded. He already knew how far back that relationship extended. "You don't have to explain all that," he said.

I sensed an opening. "What we should do is a live show," I said. "Announce his decision right there, on the air."

"That's a brilliant idea," Ari chimed in.

"Yeah," Maverick said, "and we could give all the money to charity."

"That's a great idea, too," Ari said.

(ESPN would report in 2020 that a fan had written to a network columnist with a similar idea minus the charitable component in 2009. I had never read that writer's mailbag column or the letter.)

Maverick said he would look into it. I had gained respect for him, LeBron, and their small group of confidants ever since I had been introduced to them years earlier. When LeBron first came into the NBA, I would see Maverick in Las Vegas during the summer league. Sometimes, he would hang out with me and Julius Erving at the Wynn hotel. He struck me as likeable, curious, and smart. I admired how Maverick, James, and the rest of their group had all stayed together, invested in each other, made their business more than just LeBron. They trusted each other. They had been together from the start. And the best part was they had grown together, too.

Anyway, I stayed in touch with Maverick and Ari. We tried to take the idea to NBC at first, as I had a long-term relationship with the network. Eventually, though, Maverick decided it would be best to do the special with one of the NBA's broadcast partners. That eliminated NBC and left us with three options: ESPN, ABC, or TNT. All those choices were fine by me. It ended up going to ESPN.

We had a conference call with executives at the Worldwide Leader. A few minutes in, I'm still not sure why, I blurted out, "It should be called 'The Decision' and nothing else."

"That's great," responded ESPN executive Keith Clinkscales, who was in charge of the show. "'The Decision.'"

By the time mid-May rolled around, I started to feel restless. I continued to check back in with Ari and Maverick. Both men assuaged my greatest fear—that ESPN, a network I had left in 2008, would choose to go with another interviewer. And the network did want to use its own people, but Maverick, LeBron, and Ari remained loyal to me. (If this had not been my idea, why wouldn't ESPN have gone with one of its own stars?)

When Maverick and Ari told ESPN's then president, John Skipper,

that it had to be me doing the interview on the special, he understood
and agreed. All we had to do was make something that had never happened before come to be.


I first became aware of the phenom known as LeBron James through
Rudy Durand, a close friend of Jack Nicholson. "You're not going to
believe this kid," Durand told me. "He's going to change the world."
Now, a lot of people say a lot of things, especially to reporters and especially in the world of sports, but there was something about the way
that Rudy said this, the exuberance in his delivery, that captured my
interest. Plus, Rudy, is one of those guys who knows everyone, so he
introduced me to LeBron's first coach.

I traveled to Akron, Ohio, to meet the kid who would become the
King. James knew me from the NBA interviews I did on television. I
watched him practice and play one game and asked him a few questions.
I found him smart, motivated, and enthusiastic, and he managed to pull
all that off without coming across as arrogant or conceited. His ceiling
seemed as high as Durand had surmised.

I covered the NBA draft lottery that fateful night in May of 2003, back
when it looked like the Denver Nuggets or Toronto Raptors might land
the most coveted number 1 draft pick in years. But the Cleveland Cavaliers also had as good a statistical chance as any team to snag the genera-
tional talent from nearby Akron. And, knowing my relationship with both
LeBron and the franchise, ESPN assigned me to shadow the team's owner,
Gordon Gund, on a night that would prove historic, one way or another.

I had covered Gund previously, for NBC. In a most remarkable life, he
had attended Harvard and served in the navy and then began a career
in banking, when, suddenly, he started to lose his vision. By 1970, he
had gone totally blind and started the Foundation Fighting Blindness.
Losing his eyesight didn't stop or slow Gund. He learned to ski all over
again, and I went up to Aspen to profile him, this blind businessman
who could also navigate mountain slopes with the right kind of equipment and assistance. I started playing in the golf tournament for Gund's

charity every summer. Gordon even hired me to do the television play-by-play for the Cavs in the 1990s.

I had spoken to Gund several times before the lottery, and it quickly became clear how much he loved LeBron and how much it would mean to him, the franchise, and the city of Cleveland for the local superstar to end up there. That night, when one of the most important ping-pong balls in NBA history did bounce his way, Gund was positively euphoric. I could see both the relief on his face and this incredible high he must have felt. The Cavaliers had lived through so much, from the losing seasons to Michael Jordan's famous shot over Craig Ehlo, and by obtaining the first-overall pick they would be able to draft LeBron and compete for the title that Gund most coveted.

The Cavs took LeBron, as expected. I covered his first game in Sacramento, as a sideline reporter for ESPN. We did halftime and postgame interviews. We began to build a relationship, which started on that trip to Akron and was reinforced on draft night and grew from there, as I covered dozens of games and conducted several interviews. He was always accessible and forthcoming. While covering the PGA tournament at Firestone in Akron one summer, I went out to a nightclub with Maverick and his friends, as our bond continued to solidify.

I knew right away how good he'd be. Everybody did. By that point, James had graced the cover of *Sports Illustrated*. He had been featured by ESPN countless times. He had gone straight from high school basketball into the NBA, without any of the usual issues in transition. His friends remained close, all part of his team. Watching LeBron in those early years felt like watching Tiger as he started to win those US amateurs. In both instances, I'm thinking, *Wow, maybe there is greatness here. Maybe we're on the precipice of something special, about to jump off a cliff into something real and without precedent.* The only question at that point was: How many titles is he going to win?

Cleveland needed LeBron. Nothing good had happened to the city's sports fans in forever. Art Modell had moved the football team to

Baltimore, and the NFL had replaced a local treasure with an expansion outfit. The Browns had already twice fallen short of the Super Bowl, losing famously to Denver via The Drive and The Fumble. Jordan had felled the Cavs with his late-game heroics. The Indians mostly lost, and when they did win, they could never get past the Braves, Marlins, or Yankees. All this history—not just losses but calamitous, terrible, cursed losses—swirled as the backdrop to LeBron's arrival. He stepped into a desolate sports landscape brightened by his talent and the obvious potential his future held. He gave his home state the hope that Ohioans had lacked.

It seemed fair to wonder if LeBron *was* the second coming. If he might match Jim Brown, one of the greatest players in Cleveland sports history, in terms of spectacular athletic feats. If he might deliver to the city the hardware those long-suffering fans deserved. Either way, he would chart the future of both a downtrodden franchise and an entire league he would help ascend again.

To that end, I created a show and set up a group interview with

*The first time that NBA legends Magic Johnson and Larry Bird got together with rookie stars Carmelo Anthony and LeBron James in 2004 at Hoosier Gym in Knightstown, Indiana.*

LeBron, Carmelo Anthony, Magic Johnson, and Larry Bird. The conversation would run for an hour on ESPN, under the banner "Two-on-Two," in regard to the two retired legends and two young superstars readying to take their place. It was Old School meets New School.

The interview aired in June of 2004, after James's and Anthony's rookie season. We focused mostly on the league's changing of the guard, filming for an hour and a half. The respect that James and Anthony held for their elders was apparent. A lot of young luminaries might have been more brash, more braggadocios, but they weren't trying to prove that they belonged. Their admiration shone through. They didn't want to be the focus.

What made headlines across the country was Bird's response to whether the NBA lacked white superstars. He had answered in the affirmative, while serving as the Pacers' president of basketball operations. "You know, when I played, you had me and Kevin [McHale] and some others throughout the league," he said. "I think it's good for a fan base because, as we all know, the majority of the fans are white America. And if you just had a couple of white guys in there, you might get them a little excited. But it is a Black man's game, and it will be forever. I mean, the greatest athletes in the world are African American."

"We need some more LBs—Larry Birds. . . . Larry Bird, you see, can go into any neighborhood," Johnson added. "When you say 'Larry Bird,' Black people know who he is, Hispanics, whites, and they give him the respect."

I asked the younger players if race played any issue in the league. Their answers differed from what the legends said. "I don't think so. I think the fans look at the game, [they're] not looking at the race," James said. "[They're] looking who can play basketball. Or who's athletic. . . . When you [were] a kid and you used to go outside, it didn't matter who was the best player in the league. If Bird was my favorite player, I'm out shooting threes. . . . If Magic was my [favorite] player, I'm out there throwing my best passes. It's not the race issue. If you can play the game of basketball, you know fans are gonna love you."

We would soon find out that they wouldn't *always* love you, a notion highlighted by the reaction to "The Decision."

———

There was one other event that led to our moment in sports television history, and that's the original version of "The Decision," which took place on Halloween in 1987 and featured both me and Eric Dickerson. I had known the future Hall of Fame running back for years, covered him fairly, gained his trust. He noticed a number of stories that I had broken and told me he liked my work.

Throughout that '87 summer, Dickerson had been feuding with the Rams' owner, Georgia Frontiere; the team's then vice president of finance, John Shaw; and their head coach, John Robinson. Dickerson had set the NFL's single-season rushing record (2,105) in 1984 and, in 1986, he led the league in rushing yards (1,821) and yards from scrimmage (2,026). He had played three games for the Rams by Halloween, but under the most contentious of circumstances and with a long gap between the first two and the third.

In between, he lashed out at his coaches, often publicly—and most often in interviews he did with me. He had famously said that, "John (Robinson) makes more than all of us. He makes more than me. Let him run the 47 Gap." Dickerson declined the offer from ownership to furnish his new house. He wanted a $1 million contract—which was an astronomical number at that time—and would show, he believed, how much the team respected him. While he sought that new deal, he threatened to continuously hold out. Negotiations eventually became so contentious that Dickerson wouldn't talk to any reporter except me.

So Halloween rolled around. Dickerson invited me to a party in Malibu that he planned to attend, and I called to check in with him while at a gym nearby. He told me he had just hung up with Ron Meyer, his former coach at SMU and current head coach of the Indianapolis Colts. He sounded both happy and stunned.

"I can't go to the Halloween party," he said.

"Why not?"

"Well, I've been traded to the Colts."

I sped straight over to his house. The Rams had not yet announced this transaction. In fact, because this happened before social media or scrolling tickers, the Colts planned to tell the world at a press conference thirty-six hours later, the night before Dickerson would play for *them* in New York.

I asked Dickerson if I could call ESPN. He said yes, and that led to me asking him for an interview, one I suggested we conduct before he left. "Eric, c'mon," I said. "We've got to do this. Let's get into the car, and we'll stop by the studio. (After that,) I'll take you to the airport and bring your car back here." Eventually, he relented and packed his belongings and we sped off but not before he let me borrow a dress shirt and tie from his closet for the interview. The shirt was six sizes too big, but better than the costume I had picked out for the party. I called the network and told them we were on our way to the studio about forty-five minutes away.

There were no satellite trucks on call in those days, so we slogged through traffic from his home in Calabasas to the closest studio in L.A. The delay was so bad on the 101 South that I had to drive on the inside of the shoulder, desperate to make it on time. Finally, we got to the intersection of Sunset and Vine near the studio, and we couldn't find a parking spot. We had to get inside quickly in order to get on the air live for the 11 P.M. *SportsCenter* or we wouldn't be able to get on TV that night at all. In desperation, I double-parked, and we raced to the elevator, went up sixteen stories, and stumbled into the studio with one minute to spare. Dickerson walked viewers through the trade and why he left. He described the Rams move as "stupid" on national TV. The best player in the NFL announcing his own trade live on TV made international news, of course. (By the way, I returned Dickerson's tie, jacket, and car. After breaking every conceivable traffic law to get there on time, I ended up getting a ticket for making a U-turn while taking Dickerson to the airport. And he got stuck paying!)

The late broadcaster Tom Mees, my ESPN colleague and one of the original *SportsCenter* anchors, was on the air with me that night from Bristol. Tom once said that interview helped transform ESPN from a full-time highlight service into a full-blown news-gathering operation.

*The night we grew up*, he sometimes called it. Viewers could come for an inside look at that day's events rather than the replays of yesterday's greatness. Teams could no longer wait for two days to announce something. Players could take more control over their own story. Many stars remained afraid, of course, of the backlash from teams and sponsors that might result from more freedom for the most elite of athletes. But the ceiling that Dickerson cracked in 1987 would be broken by LeBron more than two decades later. The running back would ultimately be viewed as disgruntled, but his actions that season marked a big step toward player empowerment and the night that sports figures in our country began to communicate through ESPN.

Which leads us to "The Decision."

As I waited to hear back from James's reps, I played the usual waiting games in my own head. Would the news of where James planned to play in the 2010–11 season leak out? Would the Cavs, if they knew, release the information? Would they want to celebrate publicly if he planned to stay? Would Maverick and LeBron have a change of heart in regard to who they wanted to conduct the interview? So many questions that could not yet be answered.

Finally, in June of 2010, I received good news: ESPN did want to air our special, and they confirmed I'd be the host. I didn't speak to LeBron in the weeks leading up to the taping of the broadcast; I didn't want to know where he was going, didn't want to unintentionally blurt it out or give anything away. If I didn't have any information, I could honestly tell people I didn't know.

The morning of July 8 arrived. My first stop was the Connecticut home of Mark Dowley, a marketing representative from WME. The network had assigned longtime producer Bob Rauscher, and I brought Eddie Feibischoff, the producer I trusted implicitly and had worked with for years. He was also at that point the lead NBA producer at ESPN. We went over—and over and over—the questions that I planned to ask, which ESPN and Rauscher were in agreement with, in contrast to what

ESPN inaccurately reported in 2020. I mingled with James's team— LeBron, Maverick, then-agent Leon Rose, and then-publicist Keith Estabrook.

LeBron and Maverick met with me in Dowley's library office, just the three of us. We went over the line of questioning I hoped to conduct again; not a blow-by-blow of every sentence but more of a general overview. I told them I wanted to know what everybody wanted to understand. Why did LeBron make this particular decision? What was his thought process? Why did he desire to stay or leave? I didn't hand over a list of questions, but I walked everybody through my plan. No one voiced any concerns. LeBron and Maverick discussed a few of the points among themselves, walking through how they planned to answer certain questions (in contrast to ESPN's reporting that LeBron had not prepared), and then I said I would get to the heart of the matter and ask, "What's *The Decision*?" Everybody nodded in agreement.

After that briefing, I rode over in a white van to the Boys & Girls Clubs of Greenwich (CT) with LeBron, his high school sweetheart, Savannah, who he married in 2013, Carter, and Rose. We would broadcast the special of his decision live on ESPN from there. I still didn't ask him to tell me what he had decided. Instead, on the ride over, I wondered if he was happy.

"I'm really happy," LeBron told me. "I'm at peace."

"Has it been tough?" I asked, meaning the weeks of endless speculation and renewed angst in Ohio over the possible departure of a homegrown superstar.

A quick aside: in 2019, James and his three closest friends—the same guys I met in Akron all those years ago—would put together a special for ESPN+ titled "More Than an Athlete." In one episode, they would address "The Decision" directly. James would look into the camera and tell viewers that in the moments before his announcement he "was nervous as shit." He had wanted to do something outside of normal conventions, he explained, but he also knew that he had spent seven years in Cleveland and much of the rest of his life in Akron. He had never gone to college, never really been away, and yet he had seen all these high school basketballers announce their decisions in similar fashion, grabbing certain hats. In some ways, he wanted to replicate that, nerves and all. "Kind of have my first-ever feeling of choosing where the hell I was going," he says in the special.

At that time, in that car, all he said was, "Yeah. It's been tough."

I asked who he had spoken with that morning and he responded "very few people." He mentioned that he had called his mother, Gloria James. It was a very pensive ride; no one popped champagne, blasted music, or even cracked a smile. What also piqued my interest was the first thing James mentioned upon arrival. Leaning in toward Maverick, he said, "Let them know," in straightforward fashion, without any emotion. That was the strongest hint that he was going to leave Cleveland. If not, who else would they have to call?

I went into a back room for makeup and while I waited, the rapper/entertainer Kanye West showed up. He seemed pleasant, but remained quiet and sat in the corner, eyes glued to his phone. The broadcaster Robin Roberts was there to interview LeBron after our broadcast for another segment with ABC. The vibe at that point felt very understated and low-key. Even Kanye channeled his inner stoic.

"I didn't realize what team LeBron picked would affect the whole country," Maverick says in "More Than an Athlete." He added that LeBron's team looked at it like they were doing another thing that had never been done before—and raising millions for charity in the process, with all the proceeds going to the Boys & Girls Clubs of America. "And doing something that allowed LeBron to decide how he was going to change teams and tell his message the way he wanted to," Maverick says.

As the interview drew closer, I didn't feel nervous. I felt good about the special, and everything that Maverick would later say, I felt inside. This *had* never been done before. We *would* help people. The plan that started at that Lakers game had fallen into place. The part that came natural to me came next. From my viewpoint, sitting in the director's chair across from LeBron on set, I could sense that he seemed both pensive and nervous. The weight of his decision, apparently, had started to take hold.

The interview kicked off that evening. Cameras rolled. The program started at 9 P.M. from ESPN's studios in Bristol, although the executives there did not send the broadcast our way until over twenty-two minutes had passed. Viewers had waited all that time. As the interview began, I tried to loosen up LeBron with a few simple questions. I wondered where the powder was, in reference to how he'd spray powder everywhere during introductions before games, and he joked that he had left it at home. I asked him about his summer, and he noted how he had completed his first free-agent experience. What did he think about how it went?

"This process has been everything I've thought and more," he said. "And that's what I did a few years ago; I put myself in a position to have this process where I can hear teams' pitches and figure out what was the best possible chance for me to ultimately win and to ultimately be happy."

Well, that was interesting. He hadn't gone through the lavish college recruiting experience since he jumped right to the NBA. Had he enjoyed the come-here, come-now process? LeBron said that he had, that he wanted to thank all six teams that pitched him, that he felt humbled by the "unbelievable experience."

I tried to build to a crescendo. I asked him about the billboards some teams or fans paid for to recruit him, the cap space other franchises had cleared, the way that even President Barack Obama had tried several times to lobby LeBron to join the Bulls. The process, he said, "was everything I expected and more."

James hadn't revealed much to this point. But I hoped the payoff would be worth it. How many people knew of his decision? He said he could probably count the number on one hand. So when had he decided? He said earlier that morning, after that "great conversation" with his mom.

"The last time I changed my mind was probably in my dreams," he said. "And when I woke up this morning I knew it was the right decision."

James then told me the team he had chosen had just found out. The rest of the NBA would find out then, like the rest of us.

He told me his family and his agent had been his biggest influences throughout free agency and that the biggest factor in his choice was his desire to win. I wondered how deep he had gone in that study and what criteria he had used to evaluate which franchise was best positioned to collect victories. He gave a longer answer that boiled down to "you never know."

He said he didn't have any doubts, he didn't need to sleep on it; he'd slept enough or had enough sleepless nights, anyway. It was time to answer to the question that everybody wanted to know: LeBron, what's your decision?

"In this fall . . . this is very tough, in this fall I'm going to take my talents to South Beach and join the Miami Heat."

Why? "Like I said before, I feel like it's going to give me the best opportunity to win and to win for multiple years, and not only just to win in the regular season or just to win five games in a row or three games in a row, I want to be able to win championships," he said. "And I feel like I can compete down there."

I asked him if he had always planned to join Dwyane Wade and Chris Bosh to form a superteam. "Well, I mean, I'm looking forward to it," he responded. "To say it was always in my plans, I can't say it was always in my plans because I never thought it was possible."

The interview continued for a few more minutes, live on ESPN. James said he could share the limelight with two other superstars. How, then, would he explain this departure to the fans of Cleveland? He described his decision as "heartfelt" and, addressing directly his fans in Ohio, he said he had given them all he could for seven years. It wasn't about Cleveland, he said, lapsing into breakup speak; it was about him. "And I never wanted to leave Cleveland," he said. "And my heart will always be around that area. But I also felt like this is the greatest challenge for me to move on." In a perfect world, since his mother still lived in Ohio, since he's from there and since he would keep a home there, he said, he would have loved to have stayed.

As the interview wound down, I wondered if he ever wanted to go through something like this again. "This is tough," he said. "This is very tough, because you feel like you've let a lot of people down. You've raised a lot of people's expectations also. But it was a tough decision, because I know how loyal I am."

I had tried throughout to listen to his answers and react to them, to set the stage for a big moment and follow up once he revealed his destination. I tried to make light in some instances. I wanted to break the ice.

As the interview finished, I'm not thinking about any backlash. Only Miami, his choice, and the rings that might await.

LeBron and Maverick shook my hand and thanked me. "Are you happy?"

"Very happy," LeBron responded. They were headed down to Miami to celebrate.

The network executives loved the ratings. A full 13.1 million people were tuned in at the moment LeBron announced his destination. That's an NFL game-type audience. To this day it is the most watched studio show—not a live event or game—in ESPN's history.

I felt good about the special, too, as did the executives I heard from in the immediate aftermath. None of us saw the cascading avalanche of criticism that was to come. It became clear soon after the announcement aired, though, as ESPN began to show the reaction in Cleveland—all the vitriol spewed, the burning jerseys, the fans who screamed expletives at the favorite son who had spurned them live on national TV. I don't think LeBron was prepared for any of the backlash. I certainly was not.

I went with Eddie to grab a sandwich at Carnegie Deli in Manhattan and took a call from a media reporter, Richard Sandomir of the *New York Times*. After he gave me his less-than-positive opinion of the special—he didn't like any aspect of the broadcast—I started to wonder and review the segment in my head, and not from LeBron's viewpoint but from a television one.

From there, critics all over just piled on, and, when I look back now, at least some of the response seemed grounded in the fact that a Black athlete had taken control of his own story. They may not have liked that he chose the Worldwide Leader in Sports, instead of sitting in front of 150 scribes in a normal press conference. Other skeptics either hated the special, or disdained my questions, or found the whole episode too long or too self-involved. Some outlets, like the Associated Press, grouped "The Decision" in with previous Cleveland sports calamities. Cavs owner Dan Gilbert penned an open letter to fans, describing James's choice as a "heartless and callous action" and a "cowardly betrayal"— and that only fanned the flames of a growing controversy.

I went from feeling good about something groundbreaking to seeing how that moment had been received, twisted, and spit back at us. Everyone in Cleveland seemed upset. Everyone in the media seemed perturbed. I'm sure it was a thousand times worse for LeBron than it was for me, because he went from beloved to hated in the span of one very long evening. The avalanche continued to gain strength. The media made LeBron into a villain, which he is not—not then, not now, not in any way, shape, or form.

In "More Than an Athlete," James admits he never expected that kind of reaction, either. His close friend and adviser Randy Mims says he felt guilty because he hadn't attended the live show and wasn't there when the intense backlash kicked off. Rich Paul, another close

friend and James's eventual agent, said it became clear immediately
that they had hurt the feelings of an entire state. "You're like, Oh, my
God," James says in that special. "All these stories are out there about
me being selfish, which is the last thing I am. And I used to read up on
all that dumb shit, too. I'm 25, 26, and I think that stuff matters . . .
it affects you."

In the special, Paul says the flight LeBron's team took to Miami right
after the show ranks among the quietest they've ever taken. Upon landing, he says, they checked in at the W hotel. Then they just looked at
each other. Like, he says, "What the hell just happened?"

Them and me both. It's very difficult to be the one upon whom the
avalanche falls. How do you handle the deluge? How do you deploy dignity and class to admit where you could have done better? How do you
not snap at all the critics who refuse to give you a fair shake? Who don't
really know what happened? Who make up stuff to suit their story? It's
not right. It hurt. Many of the same critics who called my interview
with Rose an interrogation now said I had cut LeBron entirely too much
slack. Well, which is it? With Pete, people wanted me to acknowledge
the celebration at hand and get out of the way. Wasn't that exactly what
I had done with LeBron during our special? And I had taken that tack
on purpose, having learned from the Rose saga.

I felt for LeBron. I felt disheartened by the reporters who floated that
I had been paid a six-figure check by his camp, thereby compromising
my journalistic integrity. I barely received a large enough stipend to
cover my expenses; it was less than $1,000 and all the rest of the money
went directly to charity. Nobody acknowledged James's intentions; nobody mentioned who he had helped or how much he had helped them.

I asked Maverick, "How are you planning on handling this? Are we
handling it together or individually?"

"We're just going to let it go," he responded. "We're not doing anything."

By the time I arrived in Puerto Rico for a boxing match that weekend, James's team had put out a release saying that they didn't pay me.
It got that bad, so much so that we needed a public clarification to set

the record straight. And these ideas, these ridiculous notions, had already set in. "The Decision" had been billed as a bust.

A fair question, with the benefit of hindsight: Was it?

As Rich Paul told me many times in the years since "The Decision," "Nobody had that crystal ball." That's true and yet, with that said, we all could have done better. That's clearer now, all these years later, with the benefit of hindsight.

Let's start with LeBron and his team. I don't know what was said between them and Dan Gilbert before the special. But clearly, there was some acrimony bubbling near the surface there and what the owner screamed, combined with the letter that he wrote and was shared widely, reverberates to this day. Gilbert should have never snapped and released that letter. It was repulsive, a huge mistake. Now, Gilbert later apologized, but only while hoping LeBron would return to Cleveland in 2014, which he did, after the owner noted how many good years they had together to contrast with that one terrible moment. But Gilbert's reaction did leave scars.

Maybe LeBron could have said something other than "I'm taking my talents to South Beach." Was that the best way to state it? We'd have to ask him. Kobe had said the same thing fourteen years earlier when he jumped straight to the NBA from high school. I took LeBron's statement in the moment as real and genuine, although he was nervous, and it showed. I thought he spoke to the heartbreak in Cleveland well. But no explanation would have been sufficient for those long-suffering fans who were very hurt by his decision. I don't think it helped that LeBron went straight to Miami and held a flashy celebration press conference with billowing flames and showy introductions, where he predicted the Heat would win multiple titles. "Not one, not two" and all that. But I don't think LeBron deserves much blame at all, even though I've felt over the years like I've been pushed by outside forces and the volume of harsh reaction to cast fault in his direction. I haven't, and I won't. Mostly, when I think of LeBron and "The Decision," I feel responsible that he suffered for something that I helped create.

We—all of us—could have done a better job of considering the feelings of Cleveland sports fans, who had their hearts ripped out again when their homegrown superstar decided he wanted to leave. He did say that it was tough for him, that he had considered it, but we could have expanded on that notion, the raw hurt and history involved there. For that, LeBron has apologized. He also came back and delivered to Cleveland an elusive pro sports championship. He has paid in full, and then some.

In "More Than an Athlete," Maverick says that he wanted to "be in a hole and not be around or hear anything" about how LeBron's decision had unfolded. Eventually, he says they did discuss "what we fucked up and how we were thinking about it." But Maverick also says that James himself was not angry, not with his team or with anyone involved. In fact, Maverick argues in that special that the criticism of "The Decision" brought their group closer together and helped them separate who was with them and against them. "A lot of people who we thought were very close to us, they thought that was the point that we would all crack" he says. "And it was their opportunity."

"An opportunity to drive a wedge and bring LeBron closer to them and push us further away," Paul says in the same special. Which isn't what happened, of course.

Maverick adds that for a while, in every room he walked into, people stared at him. Strangers, friends, acquaintances—they all looked. Anyone reading the paper as the controversy ballooned might figure LeBron for "the worst human being on earth," Maverick says. And yet, he also points out that in the year after "The Decision" took place, LeBron registered his biggest jump in Nike shoe sales. His jersey was the top seller in the league.

ESPN didn't help us, either, upon review. They teased the show and his decision for hours, over and over, then started the interview portion of the broadcast far later than scheduled, much after they had told us they would begin. I wanted to build his answers toward "the answer," but by coming on late and then prolonging the reveal, we exacerbated viewers who wanted to know right away and didn't want to wait almost thirty minutes to find out. Now, I still don't believe you tell the end of any *Star Wars* movie a minute into the first scene. But I can see why it bothered people to have to wait that long to find out something that had been floated for weeks. I had no control over that. LeBron had no control over that. It set an unfair expectation and set the stage for the surge of criticism that landed on our shoulders.

The network did us even worse in the aftermath. They distanced themselves from me, from LeBron, from the questions I asked, and from the special itself. No one from ESPN ever supported LeBron or me, despite enjoying the huge audience. No one said that we went over the line of inquiry in advance, with top-level executives. ESPN should have better explained why we were broadcasting from the Boys & Girls Clubs and that about $6 million had been raised for charity by the special—counting donated ad revenue—and that meant something to this group and would mean something to thousands of kids. The donation marked the largest single contribution ever received by the Boys & Girls Clubs. But nobody knows that, which is because we—all of us—didn't do a good enough job of telling them. In the years since, on three separate occasions while still the president of ESPN, John Skipper apologized to me for the poor execution and the network's lack of support in the aftermath. "Any problems that the show might have had were my fault, and I take full blame for letting you and LeBron down," he told me. It's a shame he didn't say that—or that the producers didn't use that—in the special ten years later.

I took a lot of criticism for the questions that I asked. I could have asked fewer lead-up questions, given the long lead-in we were presented with. I could have asked LeBron fewer ancillary questions, could have followed up on the pain in Cleveland more and had a keener awareness of the fans' disappointment.

After the fact, I called Costas. I wanted an honest assessment of what had transpired from someone in my profession. He told me he had dreaded receiving that very call, that he had seen our special live but didn't want to be part of the criticism raining down. He did offer the honest opinion I had sought, though. He said my first question should have been, *LeBron, what's your decision?* All the other questions were good, he said, but should have come after that one. I wish I had called Bob beforehand; I saw his point.

All that said, I still believe "The Decision" did more good than harm and by a fairly wide margin. In that moment, LeBron found both his footing and his voice. He found out who he could trust, who he could believe in, and what was important as his upward career trajectory continued. I don't think he owes anybody an apology. I don't think any of us owe anyone that. We all learned from it. That's for sure.

In the 2019 special, looking back so many years later, LeBron says he held mixed emotions throughout his first year in Miami. He says he waffled between whether he should have stayed or not. In that same special, Paul calls "The Decision" "a historical moment in sports." He says it allowed their team to grow, allowed LeBron to mature. Maverick again notes the millions raised for the Boys & Girls Clubs, saying both "that was a huge accomplishment" and "the production was a failure."

In the years since, LeBron, Maverick, and his team never, not once, expressed any anxiety toward me or the idea; their only issues were with ESPN's production.

I didn't speak to LeBron about "The Decision" until the Olympic Games in 2012. I had seen him a few times before that but we never had a conversation about the event and the critical response to it. He was at a gym in London, getting ready to work out, and we bumped into each other.

"So what do you think all these years later?" I asked him.

"Hey, Jim, you know, I'm happy in Miami," he said. "You did your best. We did our best. And everybody is living and learning, and we did a lot of good for a lot of people. I don't really think a whole lot about it."

If I'm being honest, his answer provided some relief. "The show was always done with good intentions," I told him.

"I always thought that," he responded. "I always felt that you had the best of intentions."

"Nothing like that will ever happen again," I said.

He started dribbling, warming up. "No," he said. "We broke the mold and when you do that, things happen."

"How are you dealing with all that now?" I asked.

He continued dribbling. "Well, you get used to it. You grow from the trials and tribulations and everybody has grown. My whole group has grown."

Two years later, James returned to Cleveland. He announced that decision in a first-person essay with *Sports Illustrated*. The title: "I'm Coming Home." This time, he received little criticism. So what was the difference? Well, for one, this wasn't live TV; this was an article that probably went through many edits. The piece was beautifully written by Lee Jenkins, and the narrative was far more positive, just naturally, since he was heading back to his home state, rather than spurning the tortured fans that he grew up with. But to answer my own question, there was no difference, other than a writer did the story rather than a broadcaster and James had chosen a smaller outfit over the largest one. LeBron, Maverick, Rich, and Randy had learned from the past, been stung by the machine, and didn't want to return to the spectacle again. LeBron was a two-time champion with the Heat and his return to Cleveland was a feel-good story.

LeBron won that title for the Cavs in '16. Two seasons later, he left again for the rebuilding Lakers and the bright lights of Los Angeles. He didn't have anything to explain anymore. He had delivered on his promises in Miami and Cleveland. He now could wear three rings. There was no need for any fanfare. This time, he announced his decision in a Twitter post with a simple press release. I thought that was appropriate.

In the 2019 ESPN special, Maverick points out that once LeBron announced his choice that way, then "everybody else started doing what we were doing."

"One-sentence press release, boom," LeBron says.

"So that was something different, too," he continues. "We always, we do things differently. But that's just who we are today."

With some time and distance, the legacy of "The Decision" has become more clear. People ask me about it all the time.

Paul has called the broadcast "monumental." I agree. They took the risks and suffered the repercussions and, ultimately, changed the landscape of pro sports and how athletes deal with the media. They made it that so many athletes, in announcing their respective choices on where they will attend college or what team they will sign with, are now "taking my talents" to somewhere. Everybody has a decision these days.

But the legacy of that special runs deeper than that phrase. For one, LeBron showed his fellow athletes that they could seize control of their own narratives, that they could tell their own stories, that they didn't have to present sanitized versions of their lives favored by PR departments, and that they didn't need to rely on traditional media to get their messages out. He gave athletes back their freedom. Outlets like the *Players Tribune* owe some of their existence to LeBron and "The Decision." Social media channels like Twitter and Instagram owe some of their relevance to the same place. Many stars in sports announce their news there. There's no filter, no fear of repercussions, no waiting two days like with Dickerson to announce a trade. This is a new era, one ushered in by LeBron way back in 2010. James is a media mogul now, with television shows, movies, and a production company committed in part to social advocacy.

Beyond that, LeBron's choice to join Wade and Bosh in Miami helped usher in the NBA's current superteam era. The Celtics had formed a constellation of stars before the Heat did, but LeBron and company won two titles soon after he landed in Miami. Without "The Decision," I'd argue, there's no Golden State dynasty and none of the current superstars-team-together movement that's rampant across the NBA. Everybody looks forward to next year now while this year is going on. Look at LeBron and Anthony Davis on the Lakers. Or Paul George and Kawhi Leonard with the Clippers. Or James Harden and Russell Westbrook with the Rockets. All owe some level of gratitude to James's TV special back in 2010. Same goes for the NBA, which is rising in popularity due to all these groupings of star players.

I'll go one step further: James is in some ways comparable to the rightly revered Curt Flood, who, because of the stance he took, helped usher free agency into Major League Baseball. LeBron figured out how to navigate the league's rules and regulations to team with some of the game's best players and take on other squads with similar, elite talent. We've seen that with some teams in the recent past, like when Tim Duncan and David Robinson shone together for the Spurs. But that was different. San Antonio had drafted both of them. We haven't seen anything like what's happening now. And it's taking place in large part because of LeBron.

The critics can have their say. We can have ours, too. In 2019, *Sports Illustrated* called "The Decision" the biggest NBA story of the decade. Its legacy has ultimately been miscast. It should be regarded as a moment that changed sports for the better, that gave athletes the power they had long sought, and that raised a ton of cash for charity. It should be as much a part of LeBron's legacy as his rings and status as one of the best players to ever star in the NBA. The Chosen One took the risk and was ultimately granted his rewards. He single-handedly revolutionized the system that was in place. He also learned from that moment, coming to better understand the power of his voice and his actions, as he dove deeper into social issues. After all this, "The Decision" altered the course of NBA history in ways that continue to reverberate.

# CHAPTER 19

# MY DAD AND
# THE MASTERS

There's a tournament played at the Augusta National Golf Club every year that ranks among my favorite events in all of sports. Some of my most cherished memories have taken place there. I've seen iconic golfers stage epic moments, watched the legends grow for Tiger and Phil and Arnold and Jack. I've walked the eighteenth green, turned at Amen Corner, entered Butler Cabin. I'm speaking, of course, of the Masters, a tourney that lives up to its lofty billing as *A Tradition Unlike Any Other*, the setting for so many of the best days of my life. And yet, when I think about the Masters now, it also makes me sad.

My father, Gerald "Jerry" Gray, met my mother, Lorna, at Denver East High School back when they were teenagers. My mom asked my dad to accompany her to a friend's Confirmation dance, thus marking their first date.

My mom's father, Isadore Sadie, was from London, and her mother, Anne Clein, hailed from Cork, Ireland. Isadore immigrated to Salt Lake City, along with his wife and daughter. It was there that my mother was born. Unfortunately, my grandmother died when my mom was very young.

She and her two sisters remained close and took care of each other. The rest of the family stayed in England and Ireland, although several were killed by Nazi bombings in London during World War II. Because of these losses at such a young age, the only thing that really ever mattered to my mom was her family. She did everything she could to see to it that we stayed together and took care of one another.

My dad's parents came to the United States from Russia. My grandfather Phillip ran from the Russian Army during World War I. According to family lore, he escaped by foot through Poland, traversing to Finland before boarding a boat to sail to the United States. Phillip had risked his life to find his father, Morris, who abandoned the family when he was young and settled in this faraway placed called Denver.

When Phillip found his dad, Morris still wanted no part of him. But my grandfather elected to stay in Colorado and married Mary Neiman, who had immigrated with her parents from a town on the border of Russia and Poland. He became a traveling salesman and hoped to make enough money to bring his mother to the United States. But she didn't decide to come until it was too late to make it out of her country. She was killed in a gas chamber, by the Nazis, in a concentration camp.


I grew up in Denver, as the youngest of three boys. My dad had served in the Naval Reserve and worked at the dog track known as the Mile High Kennel Club, selling and cashing pari-mutuel bets. He later became a certified public accountant and a partner in his own firm: Stone, Gray and Company. He worked there for twenty-eight years, as the firm grew to become the largest local accounting entity in the state of Colorado. He only left that job to partner with Marvin Davis, the oil baron and American industrialist, in a wide-ranging real-estate venture. My dad served as his chief financial officer.

There was a significant age gap between me and my brothers. The oldest, Gary, was born more than seven years before me; our middle brother, Mike, was five and a half years ahead. If I had a problem, I'd run to Gary. Mike and I were more like friends. We'd play basketball outside and challenge another set of brothers from the neighborhood to Wiffle ball games, the Grays against the Kaufmans. I was still pretty young when Mike left for college.

That was the family dynamic, which left me at home for a large chunk of my childhood with only my parents, who became two of my best friends. In some ways, I was an only child in those years. But that wasn't a bad thing. My dad would leave for work every morning, usually before I rode off to school on my bicycle, pedaling the two miles to class on days when it didn't snow. We'd eat dinner together every night, attend events, play sports, watch Walter Cronkite on the evening news. It was a fairly typical American existence. I'm lucky to have grown up that way.

My mom was our family's backbone. Her main goal was to keep the whole brood happy. She'd watch the Broncos' games with us. She took up tennis later in life, because I played the sport, and my dad sometimes played with me. She just wanted to spend time with us. She was selfless and remains so. She was my caretaker, my driver, and my friend. She instilled in me the value of organization; she always wanted everything to be clean and in order, and she taught me discipline. My dad was more my confidant, the one I talked to about anything, the one I went to with my problems.

Whenever I got home from school, my mom would hand me milk and cookies. To this day, we laugh about how she was always there waiting for me at 3:30. If I needed anything, I could count on her. She watched all my games, went to every event, made our lives infinitely better because of the sacrifices that she made. Since there were only two indoor tennis courts in all of Denver, and I was a decent junior player, it fell to her to drive me to them in the winter so I could practice. She did that without complaint.

My dad liked to tell the story of when I was ten or eleven and I discovered a tape recorder that belonged to Mike. I used to sit there, for hours, emulating Frank Gifford or Howard Cosell. Looking back, you can start to see my career line up, based on what I learned from both my parents and with that tape recorder held in my hands.

My dad didn't make every game or match, but he always tried. Sometimes he'd show up near the end. He was a mathematical and financial genius. He was always busy, a workaholic who tried to earn a living to make sure his family was taken care of. That he loved his job made the hours easier to deal with. He dedicated himself to his partners, his clients, and his family, and he instilled that work ethic in me, showing what it looked like to pour all of yourself into your profession. He always told me to put maximum effort toward whatever I wanted to engage in. He didn't want me to half-ass anything. If I wanted to play basketball, he wanted me to play well. If I wanted to read a book, he wanted me to comprehend the information the author was trying to convey. He didn't have a lot of patience. He had a lot of virtues but patience wasn't one of them.

My father also loved sports. He passed that on to me, too. He played golf, racquetball, handball, and a little tennis. He was also a runner who jogged frequently. He enjoyed boxing and would take me to all the local fights. He followed the NBA, the CU Buffs, and the Broncos, and we watched every Bronco game together. He even would go to see the triple-A Denver Bears.

I'd go down to baseball games via bus, when I was eleven or so and my parents had decided I could traverse wide swaths of the city on my own. I'd take a friend, and we'd sit there and watch baseball. It wasn't my favorite sport, because it was played at the minor-league level. I didn't follow Major League Baseball because we didn't have a team, but we would watch the World Series.

We almost had a team, thanks, in part, to my father. My dad and his business partner Davis tried to buy the Oakland A's from Charlie O. Finley, the team's owner from 1960 to 1980 and the man who moved the franchise once before, from Kansas City to the Bay Area. Finley would often call the house late at night or early in the morning.

"James, this is Charles Finley," he'd say, asking for my dad.

I'd tell him my dad was still at the office and ask for a call-back number. For some reason, Finley always called from a pay phone. "I'm at a phone booth and can't be reached," he'd say. He was a character and remained one until his death in 1996.

Anyway, with Marvin's backing, my father put together a secret agreement. They were going to buy the team and move it, turning the Oakland A's into the Denver B's, then hiring Al Rosen, from the Yankees, to be the general manager in Denver. As the date of the sale approached, word leaked that Al Davis also planned to move the Raiders from Oakland; in fact, Davis wanted to do that at the very same time. Baseball's commissioner, Bowie Kuhn, supported the sale, but officials from the Oakland Coliseum filed suit, citing the ten years left on the team's lease. There would be no Denver B's.

In the 1980s my dad negotiated another major deal for Marvin to buy the Dodgers from Peter O'Malley. They reached an agreement in principle. But just hours before the announcement, O'Malley called and asked out, saying he just couldn't go through with the whole ordeal, that he changed his mind and wasn't ready to part with his beloved team. All these deals stemmed from delicate, complicated negotiations. My father knew that I was interested but refused to divulge details, no matter how many times I asked. That's when I first really started digging.

I learned so many lessons from my father. For one, he was a charitable man who believed he held a greater responsibility to the world beyond his family. He remained grounded in his community, supporting this organization he helped establish called the Bridge Project, which helped aspiring college students "bridge" the gap between what college cost and what they could afford. Say the student needed $1,000 and had $100; the foundation would make up the difference. Thousands of pupils benefited, while my dad also served on myriad charitable boards. He raised money for multiple sclerosis, after my aunt passed away from the disease. He helped build a diabetes center for children in Denver, helped get an aquarium made downtown, helped the Broncos' ownership pass a bond to build the team's new stadium. He served as the president of a community center, pro bono. He involved himself in all those things, and served on a number of boards, but he never wanted credit, never stood at the forefront. Which is funny, considering his youngest son has spent a lifetime *in front of the camera*, on TV.

My dad had come to understand the importance of community involvement from his grandfather, Samuel Neiman, an influential figure in helping immigrants from Russia, and throughout Eastern Europe, settle into their new lives on the west side of Denver. He was respected and admired for helping others to live a better life. He was my father's hero and taught him many valuable lessons. He told my dad that if he earned a dime, he should give away a penny. If he had a dollar, he should give away a dime. And if he had ten dollars, he should give someone much more than one dollar. My father spent his entire adult life helping others. Through his words and example, my father passed those values on to me and my brothers. I use them as my guide.

My father was the most principled man I ever met. I've never seen anything like it in my life, the way he conducted himself at work and at home. He kept secrets like world peace depended on his confidentiality. Private conversations remained just that. He had all kinds of big-time clients, major stakeholders, and he knew how they did their taxes, what they wrote off, and he insisted they stringently comply with applicable law. He followed the exact letter of the code, and he knew it like he knew his children, which is to say quite well. If a client didn't like that approach, he told them to find another accountant. As the CFO at Davis Oil and, later in life, an integral part of Twentieth Century Fox, he became a part owner of Pebble Beach Golf Links, Aspen Ski Corporation, Breckenridge Ski Resort, and the Beverly Hills Hotel as part of a real estate company named Miller-Klutznick-Davis-Gray. But my dad never told me any details about his business. My parents resolved their disputes in private, too.

That doesn't mean my father led a perfect life. He didn't. But he lived with great integrity, and he passed that along to all his sons. Whenever I'd ask too many questions, my dad would say, "Jimmy, you're being too penetrating." Perhaps that ethos inadvertently pushed me toward my career path. He knew right from wrong, and he wouldn't deviate. "Jimmy, I know you want to know, but I'm not going to tell you," he would say. That's why his partners, clients, and friends loved him so much. Nobody could crack him. If you told him something, it went into the vault, never to be unlocked. Watching him behave like that taught me great lessons in confidentiality and trust. When someone tells you not to say something, you don't repeat it.

But I also wasn't satisfied with his nonanswers, either. I could've gotten frustrated and stopped asking questions. I did not do that. Instead, his private nature stoked my natural curiosity. When my dad wouldn't tell me something I wanted to know, I'd often ask my mother, or his friends. Not for business secrets but for the stuff that I was interested in. Those were my first sources, and they taught me that I'd have to work hard for information. But when I got it, that same information would be better, more interesting, closer to the truth.

After he retired, my father told me, "I spent my whole life resolving other people's problems, and I just can't do it anymore." The life he lived had exhausted him by the time he was seventy-two or so. It had worn him out mentally. But talk about service. He had made that kind of difference in people's lives.

By then, he had taught me to trust. Where to place it. Not to misplace it. And, if someone burned me, shame on them but I should learn from that experience. He taught me how to listen. How to contribute to the world. How to volunteer. To be judicious with how I spent my days. To not sacrifice my reputation. Because once that's gone, it's impossible to retrieve. He liked to tell me not to lie because I'd forget what I had fibbed about. He used to say, *Act like your life's on-camera.* And he said that back in the 1960s, long before cell phones, cameras on every doorbell, paparazzi, and social media. He was sixty years ahead of his time.

In those early years, I played a lot of tennis, rising to win some youth tournaments in Denver. I would practice for up to nine hours a day in the summers. In my spare time, I served as a ball boy for a local pro, Irwin Hoffman, at a club called Green Gables. I'd hit, then pick up balls, then hit again, until eventually I was good enough to proffer my own lessons. I began to practice against older kids, and when I started to enter tournaments, I managed to stack numerous trophies on a shelf in my bedroom winning club matches and local tournaments.

From the time I was ten, I was a ball boy every year for the WCT Tour event in Denver, the United Bank Tennis Classic. All the pros played in the event, including Rod Laver, Arthur Ashe, Bjorn Borg, Ken Rosewall, and John Newcombe. This marked my first, real, up-close exposure to professional sports. I most remember the approachable guys, like Ashe and Borg, who were my favorites because they never acted like they were above anybody, along with Tom Okker from the Netherlands. He ranked in the top 10 in singles and reached number one overall in doubles, and he'd often let us rally with him. One day, as the crowd filed in, we stood on court before the matches started. Okker handed me one of his rackets, and we started to volley. Fortunately, I was striking the ball well that day, and before we knew it, Ashe was standing next to me, and another ball boy ran next to Okker. We all rallied for about three minutes, at which point I could say that I had played tennis alongside the great Ashe. What a thrill.

By the time I got to high school, I had come to admire more about Borg than just his kind demeanor. He had this amazing two-handed backhand that was so mesmerizing it became my favorite stroke. I also had a decent serve. I wasn't the best player in the greater-Denver area, but I could hold my own, I always competed, and I usually nabbed a middle seed. At Thomas Jefferson High, my team won city championships.

I never really considered trying to play in college. I wasn't good enough.

Still, my father and I strengthened our bond with rally sessions on the weekends in the spring, the summer, and whenever it was warm enough to head outside. We'd play in father-and-son tournaments. Looking back, I can tell that my dad was becoming my best friend. And, as the years passed, we'd bond over golf the same way we once grew closer over tennis.

I didn't know much about the Masters growing up. Sure, I would always watch golf on television with my father every weekend. Some years he'd take me to tournaments nearby, so we could watch the brilliance of Palmer and Nicklaus up close, like at the PGA Championship in 1967, or the US Open in 1978, because both were played in Colorado. Golf interested me, even though I hadn't taken up the game.

I knew little of all the famous traditions at the Masters—or that one day I would have a tradition there of my own. I just knew that my dad loved golf and watched golf and that was good enough for me, because it allowed me to spend time with him.


My dad liked to take golf lessons at Green Gables, the same club where I played tennis. His instructor was Paul Runyan, a professional golfer from the mid-1930s who had played in the first Masters in 1934 and was paired with founder Bobby Jones for the first 36 holes. Runyan placed in the top 10 at the Masters twice and won the PGA Championship in '34 and '42. He would be inducted into the World Golf Hall of Fame in '90 and instruct numerous Tour pros in the second half of his life. My dad once signed me up for a lesson, and after I'd hit balls for a while, Runyan told my father that I had "the most natural golf swing" he'd ever seen. He probably just wanted to sign me up for lessons, but at that moment, I saw my father beam with pride.

After the Ali interview in '78, I asked the bosses at Channel 9 if I could feature Runyan, based on his history and his work with golfers throughout Denver, like my dad. The station agreed. The segment turned out great, and it went over well and was picked up across the country by ABC affiliates, which led to ESPN wanting to air a different version. Those segments set the stage for my increasing interest in covering golf, and my dad loved that.

My father never pushed me into the family business. Both my brothers pivoted that way, and I knew early on that I didn't want to spend all day in an office, adding up numbers, dealing with meetings, forever on the phone. I saw how my dad often left for work at 7 A.M., sometimes before we even got up, and didn't return home until dinner. He had tremendous discipline. I had to find something I really loved, and when I did, in front of the camera, not behind it, my father supported my decision. He wanted me to do whatever I loved, as long as I approached whatever that was with the passion and dedication he applied to numbers and business deals. That meant the world to me. I hoped those golf segments would show my father what might be possible in the line of work I'd chosen. My mother has always been supportive. It always amazed her that I could actually go to sporting events, do interviews, make TV appearances—and someone would pay me for that.

Later in his life, my father liked to say that he had evolved in sequence. First he was Jerry Gray, accountant. Then: Jerry Gray, Davis's partner. Then: Jerry Gray, father to, well, me.

While interning at the local station, my father introduced me to one of his friends, another oil-and-gas executive named Kenny Jastrow, from Midland, Texas. His son, Terry Jastrow, had worked his way up to become the lead golf producer for ABC Sports. He was in charge of the telecasts that featured journalistic titans such as Jim McKay and Chris Schenkel.

Kenny introduced me to Terry, who helped me to land gigs keeping score for PGA Tour events for McKay and others on the broadcast team, starting in 1978. I would sit up in the tower, tallying up the rounds on these big broad sheets. I'd wear a headset, and I could hear producers screaming in my ear, pointing out the players' scores. There were no computers; I inputted the data by hand. What I most remember is how kind McKay was. He struck me as such a gentle, nice man. Despite the chaos that unfolded all around him, he remained eloquent, calm and cool, even in thunder-and-lightning storms. He taught me to see how the broadcast came together, how all those details added up to a cogent whole. I came to understand that I didn't want to grind away on the production side, that I wanted to report, to be in front of the camera, tell the stories, hoping to become someone like McKay. Had he not been so cordial and gentle, I might be an accountant.

I went to the Masters for the first time in 1989. ESPN had already sent me to report on numerous golf tournaments, including US Opens and PGA Championships. Plus, I had the scoring experience in my back pocket.

Neal Pilson, the president of CBS Sports, invited me. They had rented a house at West Lake Country Club, a few miles away from Augusta National. There, I met Bob Kipperman, the man who ran CBS Radio, and Frank Murphy, the executive producer, and they mentioned offhand that perhaps I might do some interviews for them on radio. "Wow, sure, of course," I stammered back, and once they cleared that with Neal, I had my first Masters reporting gig. They invited me back the next year. Eventually, they put me on Tower 12 and tasked me with calling the action down on Amen Corner, the picturesque, signature location on the course. They would later move me to Towers 15 and 16.

More importantly, three years into my reporting there, I started to tell my dad about what a great experience this was, how I loved Augusta and the tournament and the vibe, how there remained so little commercialism or misbehavior, how it all worked so well. They called the fans patrons. Everyone was respectful. Nobody was drunk, or heckling the golfers.

I told my dad how time stood still at the Masters: about the pimento-and-cheese sandwiches that sold for 50 cents, about Magnolia Lane and the azaleas, how they were the most beautiful things I'd ever seen. "Maybe you should come with me," I said.

Thus began my favorite tradition. The one that involved two people. One was me. The other was my dad.


My father retired in 1997, after many years with Davis at Davis Oil and Twentieth Century Fox, and partnering on the other business entities. My dad would fly out every Tuesday morning on Marvin's plane, then fly home on Thursday to spend the weekends with his family. When he finally stepped away, my father went back to school to study economics and science for *fun*, traveled, read, visited museums, and dove deeper into his philanthropic endeavors. For my dad, retirement was hard work, so he found ways to keep his mind sharp.

I asked Neal if he wouldn't mind securing an ID badge for my father so he could attend the Masters with me. Pilson set me up with Frank Chirkinian, who was basically the godfather of golf on television and who knew my father because he was part of the group that had purchased Pebble Beach. One day during football season, I asked Frank if I could bring my dad.

"Sure," he responded. "He can sit in the truck with us or he can sit in the tower with you. We'll figure it out."

They did, and he started coming, every year. Fred Couples won the first tournament that he attended, in 1992, and my dad came back every spring until the 2013 tournament wrapped up. Mostly, he sat with me, at whatever tower I had been assigned to. He'd keep score, much like I had for McKay all those years earlier. I'd be calling the action on, say, the fifteenth hole, and my dad would turn to me and say, "Nick Faldo's third shot, he laid up there." Then we'd go have lunch in the clubhouse, or dinner at one of the local restaurants. We'd stay in the same house together, eat every meal together, attend the same parties every year together, like the one that the broadcaster Jim Nantz, and his producers, Chirkinian and Lance Barrow, held on Tuesday night before the tournament started. These became priceless experiences, some of the best weeks of my life. Every year Nantz would go out of his way to be with my dad and spend time with him. He said quite often that, "seeing the Grays together every year is a tradition unlike any other." Jim had been very close to his dad, so he knew just how special our time together was.

Over the decades, Dad and I established our own traditions within the larger one. Sometimes we would eat lunch with Runyan. We would spend a lot of time with Buzz Davis, a beloved and well-respected club member. His wife, Florence, would invite us to his house every Saturday during the tournament for a grand party. We attended for twenty years. One year the great Cronkite came as his guest. Another year it was Armstrong, the astronaut. In later years, Buzz would invite us to dinners at the clubhouse on Saturday nights, and we'd don coats and ties, eat, then tour the famous wine cellar; or head up to the crow's nest; or visit the Eisenhower Cabin, where he stayed during the tournament, next door to the Nicklaus family. We also befriended the Bessers, Charlie and Rebecca, who owned the Double Eagle Club across the street from Augusta National. My father would visit the club at the end of the day, while I finished up my interviews, and I'd find him over there, drink in hand, deep in conversation about one golfer or another. The Bessers watched over my dad and treated him like royalty.

In the mornings, we'd go early and walk the course, or sit at the driving range and watch the pros warm up, sending towering missives sailing over the pristine grass. My dad watched me interview Woods inside Butler Cabin when he won his first Masters in 1997. He became part of Arnie's Army, another devoted fan of the great Palmer. We saw pros register holes in one. We saw a famous Couples shot roll down the hill on hole number 12 the year he won the tournament, knew that the ball should have dribbled right into Rae's Creek but somehow stayed dry, held up by a wayward blade of grass. We saw Tiger drain an impossible chip shot from an embankment on the sixteenth hole in 2005. We saw Palmer's last round at the Masters. We watched Nicklaus's last round, too.

Some years, after the tournament concluded, my dad and I got to play the course on Monday mornings. That marked another thrill. The radio network was allowed one foursome per year back then, and one year they let me bring my dad and Julius Erving. My father was a 29 handicap. He loved to play and loved the game. He knew the history, all the stories, where all the great shots had been played. He understood every nook and cranny on the course, and trust me, during this round, he actually visited each of those spots.

On another occasion, during lunch one day upstairs in the clubhouse, Arnie walked in. He wore his green jacket, and I noticed his group had not yet joined him. He sat down with us for twenty minutes

that turned into one of the most memorable conversations I can remember my dad having in my presence. Many years after my dad and
his partners had sold Pebble Beach to Ben Hogan Properties, a group
led by Palmer, Clint Eastwood, Dick Ferris, and Peter Ueberroth purchased the historic venue. Arnold thanked my dad for helping to take
such great care of this national treasure, for preserving the course, and
for building Spanish Bay. Here was one of the most popular players
in the history of golf, a sporting hero to my dad, thanking him for
*his* contribution to the game. My dad had accomplished so much in
his life, always avoiding the spotlight and attention, and now in his
eighties, here was Arnold Palmer recognizing him. Every time I think
about that exchange, it brings a tear to my eye.

The Masters experience was like that. It came to signify more than
just those moments, or those parties. It brought my father and me
closer in ways we never could have imagined. Wherever I went, he
went, and vice versa. Some of my favorite memories are just the two of
us, stuck in a rainstorm; or eating candy bars because we didn't have
time for a meal; or out there, in the middle of the course, just taking
it all in; or saying hello to Bernie, our favorite security guard. As my
dad got older, he would always say he wasn't sure if he could make the
tournament. But he did, year after year, and he would say it wasn't
so much about the golf anymore. It was the time he spent with me he
treasured most.

These are the things that I'll never forget.


At the 2013 tournament, I noticed my father was slowing down. That
was a hard year for him. His health was declining, the weather was
hotter, and I was working longer hours, because the changes in how we
broadcast the Masters meant we were on the air for much longer than
before. He had turned eighty-four that year and couldn't move as well.
He didn't want to walk the course as much, but we'd still go out every
morning to check the pin placements. He'd wait for me at the bottom
of the stairs to the press room, rather than ascending them to see the

interviews. He didn't climb up the tower above the eighteenth green like he had for previous finishes; instead, he stood behind the ropes. Even then, in a steady rain, he witnessed a thrilling finish, when Adam Scott seized a green jacket on the second hole of a sudden-death play-off against Ángel Cabrera. That year, I did not interview the winner. I wanted to stand with my dad instead.

It never came up in conversation, but I assumed this would be the last time my father went to the tournament, which only reinforced that all traditions, even the best ones, come to an end. Unfortunately, I was right. I noticed him slowing down even more when we visited him in Denver on the Fourth of July that summer. He spent more time than ever on the couch. By the time Thanksgiving rolled around, he struck me as tired. When we went to a movie, he used a walker because his knee was bothering him. His strength was dwindling.

A day or two later, after Frann and I returned home to L.A., my father couldn't change the channel while watching a random football game. So he called his cable provider, and they told him to swap the batteries on the remote. My father climbed atop a step stool, reached for the batteries, and fell backward, hitting his head. He couldn't get up, and my mother could not help him back to his feet, so they called for help and took him to the hospital. He never really walked again, and he didn't want to live like that, without control and bedridden. He saw no way out and he had had enough. He died right before the holidays, leaving behind an adoring family and numerous close friends.

I found out while in San Antonio, working a Showtime fight in December of 2013. I answered my mom's call.

"Your dad's going to die," she said. "He doesn't want to live anymore. We're taking him to hospice."

She handed the phone over to my dad. "What's going on?" I asked him.

"This is no way to live," he said. "Whatever I have, it's not getting better."

I told my boss, Showtime's sports president Stephen Espinoza, about the situation, and he graciously told me to go home immediately. I did.

I was able to speak to my father for an hour, and we talked about the things we'd done together, the life he'd built. Memories from the Masters were prominent during that conversation. They meant that much, because for those past two-plus decades, that was the one week of the year that we spent together, just the two of us. He lived for another two weeks or so, then passed.

His life meant so much to so many that hundreds of people packed into his funeral, which struck me as unusual for an eighty-four-year-old, since so many people close to him had already died. Many spoke about his extraordinary contributions to the community, the memories plentiful, his life properly honored at the end. I gave the final eulogy, ending it with a quote by Ralph Waldo Emerson. "When nature removes a great man, people explore the horizon for a successor; but none comes and none will. For his class is extinguished with him." I concluded with, "My father, Jerry Gray, was in a class all his own. May God rest his soul. I love you, Dad, you were a great man and a great father." It was by far the most difficult day of my life.

At the cemetery, my mom gathered my brothers and said she had just one wish going forward. My dad had given us a much better life than any of us had ever imagined, and now that he was gone, her hope was that no matter what happened, we would honor him by always sticking together. We have.

The final conversation I had with my dad right before he died started when he asked Frann a question. Since I wasn't with them, they decided to call me, and he asked, "Jimmy, did you ever work with Michael Strahan?" He was the fearsome Giants defensive end who has embarked on a decorated media career after retiring from football. I had no idea why this would cross his mind, other than he watched Strahan on TV in the mornings with my mom. "No, Dad, but I know him." My father then asked, "Do you like him?" I said yes, I do. He said, "So do I."

"Good night, I'll see you soon," I said.

Those were the last words we ever spoke to each other. A couple of months later, I ran into Strahan at a Super Bowl. We were acquainted and friendly but not close. I asked if I could speak to him and told him the story and, by the end, tears ran down both our cheeks. I will always have a soft spot in my heart for Michael, and every time I see him on TV, I think of my dad.

I didn't go back to the tournament right away. Not until 2016, as a guest of the Bessers, after some time had passed. That was because the company I work for, Westwood One, had changed owners. The new group was based in Georgia, and the executives wanted to give my credential to someone who was closer to their headquarters. But it was just as well, because I couldn't bear to go without my dad.

When I did go back, I placed a wreath of flowers on our favorite tower at the fifteenth green. Billy Payne, the chairman of Augusta National had written me a beautiful note when my dad passed, and the Bessers poured a shot of my dad's drink, vodka, in his memory, and placed it next to a chair that sat empty. I went back again in 2018 and 2019 and all the memories resurfaced. Every year, I placed a flower on the chair he would have sat in.

Mostly, I felt sad. I *feel* sad. It wasn't the same experience. There was a void there, because my dad was gone and I wasn't doing the same work. Now with Fox, I'd be conducting an interview, or passing the press room, or eating lunch in the clubhouse, and I'd think of him and the times we shared together and the life my father gave me, the lessons he imparted, the impact he imprinted on my life. I wouldn't be where I am today without him.

I carry all that with me now. My dad taught me to try and be better, to help others, to live for more than just myself. He taught me to be honest, to not screw anybody over, to traffic in decency and trust.

My dad knew stars and lived in celebrity orbits, but he always remained true to himself. He came from a different time. He went out of his way to make other people's lives better, easier. He used all his energy to make a difference in the world. Based on the example he set, I try my best to improve the lives of others. He showed me a better way. He had quirks, he had flaws, he had gaffes, he made mistakes, and he didn't live a perfect life. But he was as close to perfect as anyone I've ever met, and I'll always be grateful for the time we spent together at the Masters and the tradition unlike any other that *we* created, that sustains me now, years after his death.

# CHAPTER 20

# I'M NOT WRITING

# ANOTHER BOOK

## Bored Games with *I Love Lucy*

In the summer of 1984, before the Olympics took place in Los Angeles, my dad's partner, Marvin Davis, and his wife, Barbara, held a party at their home in Beverly Hills. I was regularly invited to events that took place there, and because Marvin owned Twentieth Century Fox, the rich and famous would regularly be in attendance, people like Sidney Poitier and Sammy Davis Jr. and Don Rickles.

On this evening, when several people waited to use the mansion's downstairs restroom, my buddy, Marvin's son, Gregg, told me I could go upstairs instead. As I arrived in the bedroom on that higher level, there sat the queen of television, Lucille Ball, all by herself. "Excuse me," I managed to spit out, as I turned and exited the room.

"No problem," she said, in her gravelly voice. "Go ahead and use the bathroom."

Upon exiting, I knew this was my chance. I *had* to say something.

"You feeling OK?" I wondered.

"I'm tired of them all pawing at me," she said in a matter-of-fact tone. "I'm exhausted by it."

Here was Lucy, as in *I Love Lucy*, someone who I had watched with my parents my whole life. Show after show, rerun after rerun. She was the gold standard. Why would anything cause her to want to escape? Yet I could also feel her despair; she didn't give off an anxious vibe, but she seemed withdrawn and resigned.

As I went to leave the room, though, she invited me to sit down and play backgammon. I had played before, but not often or particularly well, and I didn't really remember all the rules, which of course I didn't mention.

The game started. Lucy opened up. She said her husband, Gary Morton, loved going to all these parties, but that she preferred to stay in, noting that "It's difficult for me at this point being out for show and tell." In her seventies she was still trying to cope with what would never be a normal life. What was that like? I wondered. "Everyone is very nice," she said. "But they all think they know you, and you don't know any of them." She told me she felt that she could never have a real conversation with anyone when it wasn't in a controlled environment, and that it was always hard to shop or eat dinner at a restaurant.

As the game went on, she grew warmer and warmer, even asking me about my life. The edge of the party had worn off. She won that game and the rematch. The scoreboard read: I Love Lucy 2, Gray 0. That made her smile. Imagine me bringing a moment of joy to the First Lady of Television.

## Da Generous Coach

Mike Ditka—Chicago Bears legend, Super Bowl champion player and coach, SNL character, cigar-chomping, hair-slicked-back broadcast partner—who helped teach me a lesson about generosity.

We were partners for the radio broadcast of *Monday Night Football* for years. We also paired up some for NBC. Before we met, I knew Ditka the way most of America knew him, as a gruff guy who wasn't the easiest to deal with and the renowned coach who won a Super Bowl with one of the league's best-ever defenses, the '85 Bears. He never has been, nor will be, concerned with what people think about him. "Just remember, Jimmy, if you have no successes, you have no critics."

Ditka liked to walk around with as much cash as Mayweather. He would carry around wads of hundred-dollar bills an inch thick, and for so many of the people he ran into, he would peel off a Benjamin and hand it over. One for the bellman, one for the doorman, one for the maid, one for the cabdriver, and so on and so forth. It probably cost him $3,500 a day just to be Mike Ditka. One year, I saw him handing out fifties and asked why. "Tough year, Jimmy," he said in that crusty Coach Ditka voice.

When I was in New York, we used to ride together from the hotel we stayed at in Midtown Manhattan to the NBC studio at 30 Rockefeller Plaza. One morning, we walked over, because a snowstorm had all but halted the typical chaos found on Manhattan's busiest streets. Now, Ditka always gave the same homeless man money as we went inside the studio; $100 going in and $100 going out. That same ritual had happened for years. But as we fought our way through the wind and snowflakes, I told Ditka we probably wouldn't see the man. We hoped he had found a shelter. But we *did* see him all right. We saw him get out of a black sedan and jog over to the entrance. He didn't see us, but he had telegraphed the whole charade. He had his own driver!

"Coach, look at that," I said.

"I see it, Jimmy," he responded. "I see everything."

At the door the man stammered out, "He-he-hey, Coach, ha-ha-ha-happy Thanksgiving." I could see Ditka's internal fire roaring at that moment, as if one of his players had missed a block or dropped a sure TD pass. I wondered if he might confront the guy, or if I might have to prevent a physical altercation. Coach turned bright red. You know that color. I'm-going-to-kill-McMahon-or-Harbaugh sideline red. I expected a choke hold to be delivered in response. Instead, Ditka just stared at him for thirty seconds, took out the wad, peeled off a $100 bill, and handed it over. He never said a word. As we stepped in the elevator, it remained clear that he was still steaming. You could see it coming off his ears.

"Why did you give him the money?" I asked.

"Jimmy, he obviously needs it more than I do," Ditka responded.


## At a Loss for Words


I've only really been tongue-tied once in my life. I've met presidents, kings, queens, and even been blessed by the pope, but I've only one time become speechless. I was eating at Toscana, an Italian restaurant in Brentwood, California, with Frann and comedian Garry Shandling. Carol Burnett was already seated in the restaurant, right next to our table. We said hello.

Growing up, when my parents would go out on Saturday nights, they would leave me with the babysitter, and I never missed an episode of *The Carol Burnett Show*. She was so funny and her skits with Tim Conway were so silly and genuine that I spent all week looking forward to them. At the end of each episode, she would look in the camera and softly sing:

> *I'm so glad we had this time together*
> *Just to have a laugh, or sing a song.*
> *Seems we just get started*
> *and before you know it*
> *Comes the time we have*
> *to say, "So long."*

Then she would pull on her left ear and wink at the camera.

Those memories flashed before my eyes in that instant. Once the goose bumps on my arms went down, I stammered out, "You know . . . I see my whole childhood when I see you . . . I've never been in awe . . . but . . . I'm in awe. That's because . . . that's just . . . how great . . . you are."

I could see her reaction; she seemed touched and moved. I was speechless. After all the interviews, all the questions, all the scratching, all the digging, all the Games, all the Super Bowls, all the travel, all the fun—just like Carol Burnett, I'm so glad we had this time together, I have nothing left say.

# AFTERWORD

*Talking to GOATs* went to print in 2020. Between publication and this update, penned in April of 2021, much has happened—both in the world and with the GOATs themselves.

So this afterword begins in the same place as the foreword started, with Tom Brady—the ageless, peerless, unrivaled owner of seven Super Bowl rings. Yes, Brady won again. This time in Tampa Bay, in Super Bowl LV, after the forty-three-year-old quarterback left a two-decade dynasty and elevated the Buccaneers to championship glory.

The exuberance Brady showed during the season and in its aftermath stood out. He exhibited unbridled joy in the victory celebrations, like when he tossed the Vince Lombardi Trophy from a boat for the most unusual throw of his career. This emotion was about a team that stumbled to 7–5, could have missed the playoffs but fought back. Brady repeatedly told me on our radio show that the run was about everyone but him. Still, his teammates and coaches credited Brady for his work ethic, leadership, and changing the culture of the Buccaneers. When I saw Tom hold that trophy, I saw freedom, pure happiness, and excellence. We needed all of that in 2020, more than ever.

As for Mike Tyson, who could have guessed? Not only would

he fight again in 2020, but he would compete in an exhibition bout against Roy Jones, which millions paid to watch and only thirty-five got to attend in person due to COVID-19 protocols. The match ended in a draw. I interviewed the fifty-four-year-old boxer who had again ascended to the most-popular-fighter-on-the-planet status. Tyson took the bout seriously, losing one hundred pounds in the lead-up. Perhaps Jones noticed, because just a few minutes before the fighters were scheduled for ring walks, he didn't want to leave his dressing room. That's understandable. Who in their right mind wants to fight Mike Tyson? Jones, it should be noted, put on a capable performance. Tyson clearly won, but so did everyone involved. All signs point to more exhibition bouts for Iron Mike.

I interviewed Pete Rose again in 2020, more than two decades after our dustup. Rose acknowledged that he had lied in our infamous interview, stating he believed he had to because he didn't want his banishment from Major League Baseball to become permanent. Rose said he mishandled that moment. He also admitted, incredibly, to continuing to bet on baseball, although now by legal means. At the end of the FOX interview, we shook hands, and he took my book and held it high, joking that he planned to rip out the chapter about himself and also hoped that GOATs would sell "a million copies."

Not all news was positive on the update front. Mr. Decency, Hank Aaron, died unexpectedly in January of 2021. This was a man who broke barriers and records and slugged so many home runs that he'll never be forgotten. It's sad for our country to lose that kind of legend, an icon in baseball and the Civil Rights movement.

Like Hank, we lost another great number 44. I gave one of the eulogies for my childhood sports hero, Broncos Hall of Fame running back Floyd Little. Talk about full circle. I told the audience how I used to watch Little religiously in Denver, and that one of the greatest joys in life is when the person you idolize turns out to be an even better human being than the hero you imagined in your dreams.

My dear friend Larry King passed away that same month. I never knew someone who was that accomplished and at the same time so genuinely happy for the success of others. King was also very generous, like when he connected me to Nelson Mandela and Mikhail Gorbachev.

Speaking of world leaders, I questioned Joe Biden this year, marking the tenth time I have interviewed a U.S. president. His answer on how to bridge a divided America stuck with me. He said, "America doesn't give up, it gets up. We've never, never, never failed to do anything once we set our mind to it as a people."

Also in 2021, Tiger Woods suffered serious injuries in a car crash in February. The initial pictures were so scary that I wondered at first if this was another Kobe Bryant–like tragedy. Fortunately, the injuries were not life-threatening, but they raised many questions. Not only about the accident, but about the future of Tiger's career. Would he ever play golf again? Did that even matter? The accident reminded us of his greatness, how truly rare and special the golfer known as Tiger was and we can only hope will be again.

Meanwhile, LeBron James's "decision" continued to reverberate. He won another NBA title in 2020, marking his fourth championship for a third franchise, this time with the iconic Los Angeles Lakers. Players across the league, like James Harden, who forced his way to Brooklyn, continued to retain the kind of say and control over their careers that James first exercised in our TV special.

In the months after publication of *Talking to GOATs*, the names on its front cover—Ali, Jordan, Tiger, Kobe, Phelps, Tyson, LeBron, Brady—continue to resonate. Because just like their accomplishments, GOAT status is forever.

# ACKNOWLEDGMENTS

I've made an exhaustive effort to confirm, verify, track down, and ensure that the stories you read in this book are as accurate as humanly possible. I've called old friends and sources. I've reviewed tapes and transcripts. I've dug deep into my own memory and cross-checked my recollections with those of others. And many of those listed below have provided much of that help—or played a substantial role in my life.

The people who have had the biggest impact are my parents. I got lucky and was blessed with a great mom and dad, Lorna and Jerry Gray. I love them both dearly. Thank you to my mom for her unconditional love and unwavering support and to my dad who I think about every day.

I hit the lottery when Frann Vettor said yes and married me. For the past three decades, she has made many sacrifices while I pursued my career in broadcasting. She always encourages me and takes care of me. She makes my life so much easier. I am extremely grateful for her. She also made significant contributions to this book. I love Riza and Phil Vettor and thank them for raising such a wonderful daughter.

This book would not have been written had it not been for Stedman Graham, who has insisted that I tell these stories. I appreciate all that he has contributed to my life, and I am grateful to Oprah for sharing this incredible human being with Frann and me.

Greg Bishop wrote this book with me. I have so much admiration and deep respect for him. Greg is an amazing writer, with incredible intellect, who has brilliantly organized my more than forty years of broadcasting and tens of thousands of interviews and stories. I will always be indebted for his enthusiasm and diligence on this project. Thank you is insufficient.

Cal Fussman, a dear friend and fabulous writer, also has my enduring gratitude, and his contributions were invaluable. My appreciation goes as well to Ben Baskin for all his efforts.

Thanks to Jan Miller, for guiding me and stewarding this collaboration, as well as to Mauro DiPreta of HarperCollins for his valuable insight, input, and assistance on this book and to Vedika Khanna for her contribution.

My childhood sports hero was running back Floyd Little. Thank you, to the man known as *The Franchise*, Mr. Denver Bronco.

No one in television does anything alone. It takes an ensemble of uniquely talented people working in unison to be successful. So many of my co-workers have contributed to making me look better than I am.

Being able to work on broadcasts and become friends with so many incredible journalists and analysts has been an awesome experience. Thank you Bob Costas, Bill Walton, John Madden, Marv Albert, Terry Bradshaw, Jim Nantz, Phil Simms, Paul Maguire, James Brown, Tim McCarver, Bob Uecker, Joe Morgan, Mike Breen, Chris Berman, Dan Patrick, and Mike Tirico. I have enjoyed every moment and learned a great deal from each and every one of you.

I have had the best producers guide me throughout my career. Off the air, they shared with me their wisdom and knowledge. On the air, they gave me guidance and constant support. My sincerest thanks to Michael Weisman, Dick Ebersol, Eric Mann, Eddie Feibischoff, Tommy Roy, Ricky Diamond, Matthew Hegarty, Rob Silverstein, Bob Stenner, Kevin Smollon, and John Filippelli.

To those who have given me an opportunity along the way—KBTV in Denver, PRISM, Twentieth Century Fox, ESPN/ABC, Showtime, NBC, CBS, Fox, Golf Channel, and Westwood One—it has been a true blessing to be a part of your organizations.

I have been with CBS Radio Sports and Westwood One since 1989. I am grateful to my partners on the air, including Tom Brady, Larry Fitzgerald, Mike Ditka, Don Shula, Larry King, Bill Raftery, John Thompson, Boomer Esiason, Kevin Harlan, Kurt Warner, and Kevin Kugler. Producers Dave Hagen, Larry Costigan, and Brian Finkelstein, along with editorial consultants John Kollmansperger and Harris Feibischoff, have helped me a great deal. Howard Deneroff has been great and I thank him so much.

My boxing family is near and dear to me. I have been at Showtime forever. I will always be grateful to Don King for insisting that Jay Larkin hire me. Matt Blank, Gordon Hall, David Dinkins Jr., David Nevins, and Stephen Espinoza, you all have my everlasting gratitude. My colleagues Al Bernstein, Mauro Ranallo, Brian Custer, Paulie Malignaggi, Steve Farhood, Jimmy Lennon Jr., Bob Dunphy, Gus Johnson, and Steve Albert are and have been a joy to broadcast with.

Buddy Monasch helped me with my first contract at ESPN. Since then I have had two agents, Arthur Kaminsky and Sandy Montag. I will forever be grateful to them.

The School of Journalism at the University of Colorado gave me the opportunity to earn college credit while interning at KBTV. Mike Nolan, the sports director and Corey McPherrin, the weekend anchor, along with Roger Ogden, the news director, and Cecil Walker, were instrumental in my growth, by mentoring me. They put me on the path to being able to work in broadcasting. I will forever be indebted to them.

Relationships are the foundation of my life. Over the years I have been so lucky to have been adopted by Mark and Debbie Attanasio, Mike Meldman, and Joe, Gavin, and the entire Maloof family. I call Attanasio by Uncle Mark because he takes care of everything for us. We are so blessed to have this group in our lives, as no one on the planet could have better or kinder friends.

I was so fortunate to have Julius Erving and his first wife, Turquoise, treat me like part of their family early in my career. The way they looked out for me, I look out for my close and treasured friend, Larry Fitzgerald.

Herb Simon is as dear a friend as I can have. Not a day goes by without us talking. He will always hold a special place with me.

Tilman Fertitta has been incredibly supportive and a great friend. I cannot thank him enough for all he has done for me.

The same applies to Jim and Julia Davidson, Jerry and Rosalind Richardson, Mark Davis, Dean and Susie Spanos, Tom and Galynn Brady, Mike Milken, Frank Luntz, Jack Nicholson, Sam Reeves, Jimmy Dunne, Charles Barkley, Jerry and Gene Jones, Adam Silver, Jeffrey and Sheri Osborne, Lonnie Ali, John Shaw, Steve Wynn, Gregg Davis, Greg Cappelli, John Elway, Terry and Tina Lundgren, Charlie and Rebecca Besser, Ron Burkle, Brad Martin, Courtney Holt, Bobby Freedman, Scott Friedman, Gary Romero, Suzanne Scott, Steve Spira, Jay Wallace, JJ Dudum, Wayne Gretzky, Mike Fisher, John Black, Bruce Ghani, Kiki Tyson, Wendell Driver, Rudy Durand, Freddy Ford, Howard Sacks, Mary Anne Shula, Lori Walton, Jerry Solomon, Bill Perocchi, Dave

Mason, Michael Yamaki, Rick Reilly, Alex Guerrero, Andy Bernstein, Steve Dubin, the Blank family, Fritz Wolff, Sam Watson, David Plati, Richard Schaefer, Mark Shapiro, Ed White, Troy Schmidt, Chris Gilmore, the Richards family, Chris DeBlasio, Dr. Neal Elattrache, Dr. Eric Esrailian, Dr. Gary Gitnick, Dr. Michael Lee, and Dr. John Belperio. These doctors are incredible and always there for us.

I'd also like to honor the memory of people I've lost along the way: Garry Shandling, David Stern, Gary Papa, Marvin Davis, Dick Enberg, Snapper Jones, LeRoy Neiman, RJ Harper, Mike Heisley, and Alex Spanos.

All my good fortune has led to two amazing honors and recognition that I'm grateful for. First, my induction into the International Boxing Hall of Fame, class of 2018. Thanks to executive director Ed Brophy and the voters. And for being honored by the Naismith Basketball Hall of Fame, class of 2020, with the Curt Gowdy Media Insight Award. I'm so appreciative of chairman Jerry Colangelo and president John Doleva and the voters.

Finally, thank you to my family, my brothers Mike, Gary (Sheri), my brother-in-law Michael (TJ), my nieces and nephews: "Main Man" Phillip, Caroline (Alex), Natalie, Connor, Rebecca, Hart, and William. What Al Davis said to me, I now say to you. You all represent the link to my past. But, more importantly, and from here on, you carry the torch forward, as you all will represent us in the future. Frann and I love you all.

Life changes so quickly, and, in 2020, it shifted faster and more dramatically than at any other point in recent history. The devastation of COVID-19, along with continued racial injustice and discrimination, has impacted all of us here and people across the world. I grieve the loss of life, the millions who suffered, and the economic impact, and I honor the memory of those who are no longer with us.

During this unprecedented time, the sports world took a long and necessary pause. But as the games return, there will be more stories, more moments, and more GOATs.

# PHOTO CREDITS

# INDEX